THE FIELD ARTILLERY CANNON BATTERY

Army Techniques Publication
No. 3-09.50

*ATP 3-09.50

Headquarters,
Department of the Army
Washington, DC, 4 May 2016

The Field Artillery Cannon Battery

Contents

		Page
	PREFACE	vii
	INTRODUCTION	viii
Chapter 1	ORGANIZATION AND KEY PERSONNEL	1-1
	Section I – Cannon Battalion Overview	1-1
	Army Cannon Battalion	1-1
	Marine Corps Cannon Battalion	1-1
	Cannon Battalion Limitations	1-1
	Section II – Cannon Battery Overview	1-2
	Army Firing Battery	1-2
	Marine Corps Firing Battery	1-2
	Tactical Duties of Key Personnel	1-2
	Howitzer Capabilities	1-6
Chapter 2	KEY CONSIDERATIONS	2-1
	Section I – Employment	2-1
	Introduction	2-1
	Employment Techniques	2-1
	Section II – Survivability Movement Control	2-2
	Survivability Movement Control Techniques	2-2
	Survivability Movement Tracking Techniques	2-3
	Section III – Tactical and Technical Fire Direction	2-4
	Direct Control By the Fire Direction Center	2-5
	Platoon Operations Center Control of All Battery Howitzers	2-5
	Section IV – Climate and Terrain	2-6
	Mountains	2-6
	Jungle	2-6
	Cold Regions	2-6
	Urban	2-7
	Desert	2-7
Chapter 3	RECONNAISSANCE, SELECTION, AND OCCUPATION OF A POSITION	3-1
	Section I – Reconnaissance	3-1

Distribution Restriction: Approved for public release; distribution is unlimited.

*This publication supersedes ATP 3-09.50/MCWP 3-1.6.23, dated 07 July 2015.

Contents

	Considerations	3-1
	Reconnaissance Techniques	3-2
	Planning the Reconnaissance	3-2
	The Reconnaissance Party	3-3
	Movement Briefing	3-4
	Route Reconnaissance	3-4
	Section II – Selection	**3-5**
	Considerations	3-5
	Positioning Techniques	3-5
	Dispersion Techniques	3-5
	Section III – Occupation	**3-8**
	Considerations	3-8
	Occupation Techniques	3-8
	Preparation Techniques	3-9
Chapter 4	**LAYING, MEASURING, AND REPORTING**	**4-1**
	Section I – Orienting Equipment	**4-1**
	Aiming Circle	4-1
	Gun Laying and Positioning System	4-1
	M2 Compass	4-2
	Section II – Laying For Direction	**4-2**
	Reciprocal Laying	4-2
	Techniques for Laying	4-4
	Section III – Measuring and Reporting Data	**4-13**
	Backward Azimuth Rule	4-13
	Reporting the Correct Deflection	4-13
	Measuring the Azimuth of the Line of Fire	4-14
	Boresight Verification	4-18
	Section IV – FDC-Howitzer Communications	**4-18**
	Types of Communications	4-18
	Record of Missions Fired	4-20
Chapter 5	**BATTERY DEFENSE**	**5-1**
	Section I – Considerations	**5-1**
	Threat Capabilities	5-1
	Battery Responsibilities	5-1
	Section II – Defense	**5-1**
	Techniques for the Defense	5-2
	Defense Diagram	5-3
	Section III – Threat	**5-7**
	Defense Against Armored or Mechanized Forces	5-8
	Defense Against Air Attack	5-8
	Defense Against Dismounted Attack	5-8
	Defense Against Indirect Fire	5-8
	Defense Against Chemical, Biological, Radiological, and Nuclear Attack	5-8
Chapter 6	**HASTY SURVEY TECHNIQUES**	**6-1**
	Section I – Survey Control	**6-1**

	Section II – Direction 6-1
	Simultaneous Observation 6-1
	Directional Traverse 6-3
	Section III – Location.. 6-3
	Techniques for Location 6-3
	Techniques for Distance 6-3
	Techniques for Altitude 6-10
Chapter 7	**FIRE COMMANDS** 7-1
	Means of Transmitting Fire Commands 7-1
	Elements of Fire Commands 7-1
	Sequence of Fire Commands 7-5
	Fire Commands For Direct Fire 7-6
	Special Methods of Fire 7-6
	Check Firing 7-7
	Cease Loading 7-7
	End of Mission 7-7
	Planned Targets 7-7
	Repetition and Correction of Fire Commands 7-7
	Firing Reports 7-7
	Record of Missions Fired 7-8
Chapter 8	**MINIMUM QUADRANT ELEVATION** 8-1
	Responsibilities 8-1
	Elements of Computation 8-1
	Measuring Angle of Site to Crest.. 8-2
	Measuring Piece to Crest Range 8-2
	Computation for Fuzes other than Armed Variable Time 8-3
	Computing for Armed Variable Time Fuzes (Low-Angle Fire) 8-4
	Mark 399-1 Fuze 8-6
Chapter 9	**COMPOSITE UNITS** 9-1
	Overview... 9-1
	Unit Composition (Light and Medium Howitzer Mix) 9-2
	Manning Levels 9-2
Chapter 10	**DISTRIBUTED UNITS**.. 10-1
	Overview... 10-1
	Personnel.. 10-1
	Communications 10-3
Chapter 11	**OTHER CONSIDERATIONS FOR COMPOSITE OR DISTRIBUTED UNITS** 11-1
	Section I – Training 11-1
	Planning Considerations... 11-1
	Techniques 11-1
	Section II – Battery Tasks 11-3
	Planning Considerations... 11-3
	Techniques 11-3
	Section III – Sustainment 11-8
	Planning Considerations... 11-8

	Techniques	11-8
	Section IV – Communications	**11-10**
	Planning Considerations	11-10
	Techniques	11-10
	Section V – Fire Support	**11-13**
	Planning Considerations	11-13
	Techniques	11-13
	Section VI – Meteorology and Survey	**11-17**
	Meteorological Data	11-17
	Survey	11-18
Chapter 12	**DEPLOYMENT**	**12-1**
	Overview	12-1
	Planning Considerations	12-1
	Techniques	12-1
	Home Station Training Prior to Deployment	12-2
Appendix A	**PRECISION MUNITIONS AND AMMUNITION MANAGEMENT**	**A-1**
Appendix B	**SAMPLE MISSION CHECKLISTS**	**B-1**
Appendix C	**COMMON MISTAKES AND MALPRACTICES**	**C-1**
Appendix D	**FORMS**	**D-1**
Appendix E	**DECLINATING THE AIMING CIRCLE AND THE M2 COMPASS**	**E-1**
Appendix F	**KILLER JUNIOR**	**F-1**
	GLOSSARY	**Glossary-1**
	REFERENCES	**References-1**
	INDEX	**Index-1**

Figures

Figure 2-1. Howitzer tracking chart example	2-4
Figure 3-1. Example terrain gun positioning	3-6
Figure 3-2. Platoon in wedge and battery in star formation example	3-7
Figure 3-3. Battery in line or in lazy-w formation example	3-7
Figure 4-1. Example reciprocal laying	4-3
Figure 4-2. Computation of the orienting angle example	4-6
Figure 4-3. Computation of the grid azimuth example	4-7
Figure 4-4. Reciprocal laying from another howitzer (M100-series sight)	4-11
Figure 5-1. Defense diagram matrix example	5-4
Figure 5-2. Constructing the matrix example	5-5
Figure 5-3. Defense diagram with sectors of fire for a platoon example	5-6
Figure 8-1. Angles of minimum quadrant elevation	8-1
Figure A-1. Field artillery munitions precision capabilities	A-1
Figure C-1. Aiming circle sight picture at 100 meters example	C-3

Figure C-2. Aiming circle sight picture at 50 meters example C-3
Figure D-1. DA Form 4513 example D-1
Figure D-2. DA Form 5212 example D-5
Figure D-3. DA Form 5698 example D-7
Figure D-4. DA Form 5969 front example D-9
Figure D-5. Reverse of DA Form 5969 .... D-10
Figure D-6. DA Form 5699 example D-12
Figure E-1. Proper sight picture E-2
Figure E-2. Centering the magnetic needle E-2
Figure E-3. M2 Compass E-4
Figure F-1. DA Form 5699 Killer Junior data example F-3

Tables

Table 1-1. Howitzer ammunition and range capabilities 1-7
Table 3-1. Reconnaissance Movement Order Briefing 3-4
Table 4-1. Laying by orienting angle (aiming circle) 4-6
Table 4-2. Laying by grid azimuth (aiming circle) 4-7
Table 4-3. Laying by M2 compass 4-9
Table 4-4. Laying by aiming point deflection method 4-10
Table 4-5. Laying by howitzer back-lay method 4-10
Table 4-6. Verifying the lay (aiming circle) 4-12
Table 4-7. Reporting the correct deflection 4-14
Table 4-8. Measuring the azimuth with a gun laying and positioning system 4-17
Table 4-9. Measuring the azimuth with an aiming circle 4-17
Table 4-10. Measuring deflection with the panoramic telescope 4-18
Table 4-11. Howitzer parameter card example. 4-19
Table 5-1. Example related information 5-7
Table 6-1. Example simultaneous observation 6-2
Table 6-2. Subtense using a 2-meter base (bar) 6-4
Table 6-3. Subtense using rifle or carbine as base 6-5
Table 6-4. Subtense using a 60-meter base 6-6
Table 7-1. Fire command sequence 7-6
Table 7-2. Fire commands for direct fire example 7-6
Table 8-1. Computing minimum quadrant elevation 8-3
Table B-1. Mission checklist example B-1
Table B-2. Precombat checklist for ground threat (mounted) example B-2
Table B-3. Precombat checklist for ground threat (dismounted) example B-3
Table B-4. Precombat checklist for air threat example B-3
Table B-5. Precombat checklist for counterfire example B-4

Contents

Table B-6. Precombat checklist for chemical, biological, radiological, and nuclear (CBRN) threat example B-4
Table B-7. Precombat checklist for medical evacuation example B-5
Table B-8. Precombat checklist for artillery raid example B-6
Table B-9. Precombat checklist for scatterable mines example B-6
Table B-10. Precombat checklist for massing fire example B-7
Table B-11. Sample inventory of assets B-8
Table B-12. Sample critical events time line B-8
Table B-13. Unit defense checklist example B-9
Table D-1. Instructions for DA Form 4513 .... D-2
Table D-2. Instructions for DA Form 5212 .... D-6
Table D-3. Instructions for DA Form 5698 .... D-8
Table D-4. Instructions for DA Form 5969 .... D-11
Table D-5. Instructions for DA Form 5699 .... D-12
Table F-1. Completing the DA Form 5699 for Killer Junior F-4

Preface

Army Techniques Publication (ATP) 3-09.50 contains *techniques* — non-prescriptive ways or methods used to perform missions, functions, or tasks (Chairman of the Joint Chiefs of Staff Manual (CJCSM) 5120.01A). These techniques and associated considerations for cannon batteries include those units operating as composite or distributed units.

The principal audience for this publication is all members of the profession of arms. Trainers and educators throughout the Army will also use this publication.

Commanders, staffs, and subordinates ensure their decisions and actions comply with applicable United States, international, and, in some cases, host-nation laws and regulations. Commanders at all levels ensure their Soldiers operate in accordance with the law of war and the rules of engagement. See field manual (FM) 27-10.

ATP 3-09.50 implements Standardization Agreement (STANAG) 2484 and STANAG 2934.

ATP 3-09.50 uses joint terms where applicable. Selected joint and Army terms and definitions appear in both the glossary and the text. Terms for which ATP 3-09.50 is the proponent publication (the authority) are italicized in the text and are marked with an asterisk (*) in the glossary. Terms and definitions for which ATP 3-09.50 is the proponent publication are boldfaced in the text. For other definitions shown in the text, the term is italicized and the number of the proponent publication follows the definition.

ATP 3-09.50 applies to the Active Army, Army National Guard, Army National Guard of the United States, and United States Army Reserve unless otherwise stated.

The proponent of ATP 3-09.50 is the United States Army Fires Center of Excellence. The preparing agency is the Directorate of Training and Doctrine, United States Army Fires Center of Excellence. Send comments and recommendations on a Department of the Army (DA) Form 2028 (*Recommended Changes to Publications and Blank Forms*) to Directorate of Training and Doctrine, 700 McNair Avenue, Suite 128 ATTN: ATSF-DD, Fort Sill, OK 73503; by email to usarmy.sill.fcoe.mbx.dotd-doctrine-inbox@mail.mil; or submit an electronic DA Form 2028.

Introduction

Army Techniques Publication (ATP) 3-09.50 provides doctrinal guidance for commanders and subordinate leaders who are responsible for conducting cannon battery functions or tasks. It serves as an authoritative reference for personnel responsible for developing:

- Doctrine (fundamental principles; tactics, techniques, and procedures) material and force structure.
- Institution and unit training.
- Tactical standard operating procedures for cannon battery units.

ATP 3-09.50 reflects and supports unified land operations doctrine contained in Army Doctrine Publication 3-0 and Army Doctrine Reference Publication (ADRP) 3-0.

ATP 3-09.50 contains 12 chapters and 4 appendices:

- **Chapter 1** provides an overview and discussion of Army and Marine Corps cannon unit organizations and the tactical duties of key personnel. The chapter discusses the Army transition from 2 firing batteries of 8 howitzers each to 3 firing batteries of 6 howitzers each in brigade combat teams and the introduction of composite (mixed-caliber) battalions in Infantry brigade combat teams.
- **Chapter 2** discusses considerations for employing a cannon battery in various climates and terrain.
- **Chapter 3** provides an overview and discussion of techniques and associated considerations for reconnaissance, selection, and occupation of a firing position.
- **Chapter 4** considers techniques for laying the platoon or battery, and measuring and reporting data associated with the gunnery solution. The chapter covers use of the gun laying and positioning system, M2A2 aiming circle, M2 compass, and reciprocal laying by other howitzers.
- **Chapter 5** provides an overview and discussion of techniques and associated considerations for battery defense against armored or mechanized forces, air attack, dismounted attack, indirect fire, and chemical, biological, radiological, and nuclear attack.
- **Chapter 6** identifies the techniques and associated considerations for hasty survey.
- **Chapter 7** discusses the types, elements, and sequence of fire commands.
- **Chapter 8** provides a summary of the steps for computing minimum quadrant elevation.
- **Chapter 9** provides an overview and discussion of other considerations unique to composite units.
- **Chapter 10** provides a brief overview and discussion of techniques and associated considerations unique to cannon batteries operating as distributed units.
- **Chapter 11** discusses other considerations for cannon batteries operating as composite or distributed units – training, battery tasks, sustainment, communications, fire support, survey, and meteorological tasks.
- **Chapter 12** Identifies planning considerations associated with deployment as early as possible in the military decisionmaking process.
- **Appendix A** provides techniques and associated considerations for precision munitions and ammunition management.
- **Appendix B** identifies sample mission checklists.
- **Appendix C** addresses techniques and associated considerations for overcoming common mistakes and malpractices.
- **Appendix D** provides examples and discussion of required forms.
- **Appendix E** discusses the declination of the aiming circle and the M2 compass.
- **Appendix F** describes the employment of Killer Junior – the use of high explosive direct fire against dismounted attacks.

Introduction

ATP 3-09.50 is a reference intended to provide general guidance to commanders and their principal subordinates. This publication provides a starting point from which commanders can adjust their battery tasks and training based on local training scenarios and mission variables. The publication is an aid to develop or refine unit standard operating procedures. Use this publication in conjunction with the digital training management system, equipment technical manuals, training circulars, Soldier's training publications, and trainer's guides.

The techniques described herein are guidelines that remain flexible. Each situation in combat must be resolved by intelligent interpretation and application of the techniques in this publication.

ATP 3-09.50 is not intended as the sole reference for cannon batteries; rather it is used in conjunction with existing doctrine. This publication supplements doctrine and tactics and techniques addressed in Army Techniques Publication (ATP) 3-09.23 and FM 3-09. As applicable, those techniques that do not differ significantly from those described in the mentioned publications are not repeated in this publication.

As used throughout this publication, the terms cannon battery, firing battery, and battery are synonymous.

Chapter 1
Organization and Key Personnel

As Army operations and organizations continue to change, the tactics, techniques, and procedures for future cannon batteries will continue to reflect technological advancements in weapons, munitions, and communications as well. The following chapters provide techniques and associated considerations for cannon batteries. This chapter provides a brief overview of the organizational framework for the cannon battery. Section I begins with a brief description of the cannon field artillery battalion and general organization. Section II closes with a brief discussion on cannon battery organization and tactical duties of key personnel.

SECTION I – CANNON BATTALION OVERVIEW

1-1. The Army cannon battalion has a command relationship or support relationship with a brigade combat team or a field artillery brigade. The Marine Corps cannon battalion supports a Marine Corps infantry regiment.

ARMY CANNON BATTALION

1-2. In the armored brigade combat team, the cannon battalion has three batteries of M109-series self-propelled 155 millimeter (mm) howitzers. In the infantry brigade combat team, the battalion typically has two batteries of M119-series towed 105-mm howitzers and one battery of M777-series towed 155-mm howitzers. The exception is selected airborne units that have only either one battery of M119-series howitzers and one battery of M777-series towed 155-mm howitzers or a single battery of M119-series howitzers. In the Stryker brigade combat team, the cannon battalion has three batteries of M777-series howitzers. Cannon battalions assigned to an Army National Guard field artillery brigade are typically organized with three 4-gun firing batteries rather than the three 6-gun firing batteries found in brigade combat teams.

Note. For more information on the Army cannon battalion, see Field Manual (FM) 3-09 and ATP 3-09.23. For further information on the M109A6 Paladin howitzer, see ATP 3-09.70.

MARINE CORPS CANNON BATTALION

1-3. The Marine Corps artillery cannon battalion has three firing batteries. Each battery always has six M777-series towed 155-mm howitzers. This totals 18 howitzers in the battalion. The artillery battalion also has one headquarters battery that contains the supporting elements for the firing batteries.

CANNON BATTALION LIMITATIONS

1-4. All cannon battalions have several limitations. The firing signature of howitzers makes the unit vulnerable to detection by threat target acquisition assets. The battalion has limited self-defense capabilities against ground and air attacks. The battalion also has a limited ability to destroy armored moving targets.

SECTION II – CANNON BATTERY OVERVIEW

ARMY FIRING BATTERY

1-5. The Army cannon battery table of organization and equipment typically provides of a battery headquarters, two firing platoons, a supply section, and two ammunition sections (does not apply to Stryker brigade combat team units). Each firing platoon consists of howitzer sections, a platoon headquarters, and a fire direction center (FDC). The battery headquarters has personnel and equipment to perform administration, sustainment, and limited chemical, biological, radiological, and nuclear (CBRN) tasks. Each firing platoon has personnel and equipment to determine firing data and conduct fire missions. The supply section provides limited sustainment support. Each ammunition section has personnel and equipment to provide limited ammunition support. Some units may consolidate ammunition sections at battalion level.

1-6. The capability of the cannon battery is enhanced through the flexibility and survivability of the platoon-based organization. The platoon FDCs are equipped with the Advanced Field Artillery Tactical Data System (AFATDS) computer as the primary digital interface between the battalion command post and the howitzers.

Note. The use of FDCs, platoon operations centers (POC), or battery operations centers (BOC) is dependent upon the organizational structure and positioning options. Unless specified, FDC, POC, and BOC are used interchangeably in this document.

MARINE CORPS FIRING BATTERY

1-7. One Marine artillery firing battery will normally support one infantry battalion. The artillery firing battery consists of two platoons – the headquarters platoon and the firing platoon. The headquarters platoon consists of an FDC section, ammunition section, communications section, motor transport section, and liaison section. The firing platoon consists of a platoon headquarters section and six howitzer sections. A howitzer section consists of a section chief and nine cannoneers.

TACTICAL DUTIES OF KEY PERSONNEL

1-8. Unit tables of organization and equipment, commander's preference, personnel strength, and individual capabilities may require the commander to modify or reassign duties based on factors of mission variables mission, enemy, terrain and weather, troops and support available, time available, and civil considerations (METT-TC), and unit tactical standard operating procedures. For more information on standard operating procedures development, see Army Techniques Publication (ATP) 3-90.90.

BATTERY COMMANDER (MARINE CORPS – COMMANDING OFFICER)

1-9. The battery commander is responsible for all aspects of battery operations. The battery commander locates himself in a position to best command the battery, considering mission variables and the level of unit training. The commander has specific responsibilities, which include:
- Conduct troop leading procedures.
- Supervise the operation of the platoons.
- Conduct general reconnaissance of future positions.
- Determine the azimuth of fire, if not provided by higher headquarters.
- Plan unit marches and movements according to tactical plans established by higher headquarters.
- Determine operational employment (for example, centralized or decentralized and consolidated or dispersed) and survivability movement criteria for his battery with the field artillery battalion commander and the battalion or brigade operations staff officer (S-3).
- Coordinate survey support.
- Develop the overall battery defense plan.

Organization and Key Personnel

- Coordinate with adjacent units for mutual support.
- Verify platoons maintain an effective defensive posture.
- Enforce communications and electronics security.
- Coordinate ammunition resupply.
- Determine requirements for resupply of food service, supply, and maintenance items.
- Inform the battalion command post and battery personnel of changes in the situation.
- Supervise safety during battery operations.
- Perform risk management.
- Develop the battery tactical standard operating procedures.

FIRST SERGEANT

1-10. The first sergeant is the principal enlisted advisor to the battery commander. The first sergeant has specific responsibilities, which include:
- Verify communication of the battery commander's directions and intent to the Soldier and that their feedback and concerns are reaching the commander.
- Advise the battery commander on matters pertaining to enlisted Soldiers.
- Supervise the platoon sergeants, gunnery sergeants, and section chiefs, whenever possible by maintaining a presence on the gun line.
- Assist the battery commander during reconnaissance.
- Assist the battery commander in the execution of the battery defense plan.
- Coordinate administrative and sustainment support (less ammunition), to include::
  - Water and food service.
  - Mail.
  - Laundry.
  - Showers.
  - Maintenance.
  - Personnel and equipment evacuation.
- Monitor battery personnel's morale, welfare, and hygiene.
- Direct evacuation of casualties to the battalion aid station, or other locations, as directed by higher headquarters.

EXECUTIVE OFFICER (MARINE CORPS)

1-11. The executive officer is normally the next most experienced artillery officer in the battery and is in charge of the battery position. The executive officer is prepared to assume command in the absence of the battery commander.

PLATOON LEADER

1-12. The platoon leader is responsible for all aspects of platoon operations. The platoon leader will locate in a position to best lead the platoon, considering mission variables and the level of unit training. The platoon leader will rely heavily on the platoon sergeant to supervise the firing platoon and the gunnery sergeant to supervise the detailed platoon reconnaissance, selection, and occupation of a position (RSOP). The platoon leader has specific responsibilities, which include:
- Establish the platoon's firing capability.
- Supervise the platoon's displacement, movement, and occupation of a position.
- Be prepared to perform the fire direction officer's duties to facilitate 24-hour operations.
- Supervise the use of the muzzle velocity sensor.
- Supervise the maintenance of platoon equipment.
- Verify the platoon maintains continuous security, with emphasis during position displacement and occupation.

Chapter 1

- Verify minimum quadrant elevation for each howitzer.
- Confirm submission of weapon location data to the FDC.
- Supervise hasty survey procedures.
- Supervise ammunition management within the platoon.
- Supervise safety during platoon operations.
- Confirm submission of reports to the battery commander and battalion command post.
- Verify the lay of the platoon.
- Conducting dual independent checks of firing safety data, AFATDS database and howitzer locations.

ASSISTANT EXECUTIVE OFFICER (MARINE CORPS)

1-13. The assistant executive officer assists the executive officer and the fire direction officer in the execution of their duties. The assistant executive officer assists on the advance party upon battery movement and works closely with the local security chief. The assistant executive officer may serve as the platoon commander to the firing platoon.

FIRE DIRECTION OFFICER

1-14. The fire direction officer is responsible for all aspects of fire direction operations. The fire direction officer should be familiar with the duties of the platoon leader or battery executive officer. The fire direction officer can perform duties as platoon leader. The fire direction officer has specific responsibilities, which include:

- Verify the AFATDS database.
- Verify targets meet target selection standards and attack guidance.
- Issuing a fire order.
- Determine accurate and timely firing data.
- Verify maintenance checks on the section vehicle, radios, computer, and generators in strict compliance with applicable technical manuals.
- Verify that the tactical situation map is current.
- Verify accuracy of records of missions fired.
- Verify dissemination and understanding of data for prearranged fires.
- Verify that data from the other platoon is recorded and accessible.
- Supervise assumption of control of the fires from the other platoon.
- Perform independent safety computations.
- Maintain muzzle velocity variance information for all howitzers.
- Control howitzer movement and positioning.
- Issue movement orders based on commander, platoon leader, and advance party guidance.

PLATOON SERGEANT (ARMY)

1-15. The platoon sergeant is the primary enlisted assistant to the platoon leader. The platoon sergeant should be prepared to assume duties as platoon leader. The platoon sergeant has specific responsibilities, which include:

- Supervise firing platoon operations.
- Ensure howitzers maintain firing capability.
- Supervise platoon occupations and displacements.
- Supervise maintenance.
- Direct the platoon defense plan.
- Provide the first sergeant with the platoon defense diagram for integration into the overall battery defense plan.

- Confirm each section chief knows the location and route to alternate and supplementary positions.
- Verify completion of Department of the Army (DA) Form 2408-4, *Weapon Record Data,* after each day of firing.
- Verify ammunition handling procedures.
- Verify safety procedures during firing.
- Supervising the use and maintenance of the muzzle velocity sensor.
- Determine minimum quadrant elevation for the position.

GUNNERY SERGEANT (BATTERY GUNNERY SERGEANT – MARINE CORPS)

1-16. The gunnery sergeant supervises platoon or battery advance party operations. The gunnery sergeant should be prepared to assume duties as platoon sergeant. The gunnery sergeant has specific responsibilities, which include:

- Perform in depth reconnaissance of route and battery and platoon positions.
- Select howitzer locations based on commander's employment criteria.
- Select a tentative location for the FDC, complete with radio check to battalion tactical operations center to confirm radio communications capability.
- Verify howitzer locations for radio communications with the FDC.
- Reconnoiter possible logistic resupply points along the route of march and report them to the battery commander.
- Coordinate with the battery commander and survey elements for emplacement of survey control points.
- Assist the platoon sergeant in verifying howitzer section chiefs input correct information when initializing or reinitializing the fire control system.
- Lay the platoon or battery, as required.
- Perform hasty survey, as required.
- Initiate development of the platoon or battery defense plan.
- Reconnoiter alternate and supplementary positions.
- Supervising the use and maintenance of the muzzle velocity sensor.
- Supervises the local security chief (Marine Corps).

Note. The gunnery sergeant is the battery's primary reconnaissance expert and spends a great deal of time away from the platoon. The gunnery sergeant selects howitzer locations based on employment criteria from the battery commander, which may range from very precise locations to simply the center of a firing area and a radius. The FDC uses this data to formulate movement orders for the howitzers.

LOCAL SECURITY CHIEF (MARINE CORPS)

1-17. The local security chief is the next senior enlisted Marine cannon crewman in the battery and assists the battery gunnery sergeant as the platoon sergeant to the firing platoon. As the senior enlisted artilleryman on the advance party, the local security chief works closely with the assistant executive officer. The local security chief advises the commanding officer on all matters concerning battery defense and local security, and plans, executes and trains the battery in defensive operations.

HOWITZER SECTION CHIEF

1-18. The howitzer section chief is responsible for all aspects of howitzer section operations. The howitzer section chief has specific responsibilities, which include:
- Supervise emplacement of the howitzer using the memory aid **TLABSPAP** steps as a guide:
    - **T**-trails, spades or firing platform properly emplaced.

- **L**-lay the howitzer.
- **A**-aiming point emplaced.
- **B**-boresight verified.
- **S**-second means to verify lay.
- **P**-prefire checks performed.
- **A**-ammunition prepared.
- **P**-position improvement (for example, determine site to crest, establish alternate aiming points, camouflage and harden position).

Note. Unit tactical standard operating procedures and the applicable howitzer technical manual will dictate when to dig in spades.

- Verify digital and voice communications with the FDC.
- Transmit emplacement data to the FDC.
- Verify segregation of ammunition by type, lot, and weight.
- Verify safety during firing (for example, firing data, ammunition, and sight picture).
- Verify the DA Form 4513, *Record of Missions Fired*, is current, legible, and accurate.
- Maintain DA Form 2408-4 information for computing and recording equivalent full charge data.
- Verify data on the DA Form 5212, *Gunner's Reference Card*.
- Verify range cards for the howitzer and crew served weapons.
- Supervise preventative maintenance checks and services on vehicles and equipment.
- Operate and maintain the muzzle velocity sensor.

FIRE CONTROL SERGEANT (OPERATIONS CHIEF – MARINE CORPS)

1-19. The fire control sergeant is the technical expert and trainer in the FDC. The fire control sergeant ensures smooth performance of the FDC in 24-hour operations and functions as the fire direction officer in the fire direction officer's absence. The fire control sergeant has specific responsibilities, which include:

- Supervise creation and updates applied to the AFATDS database.
- Supervise safe, accurate, and timely computation of firing data.
- Ensure section crew drills are adhered to in accordance with appropriate FMs, standard operating procedures, and regulations.
- Ensure appropriate records are maintained.
- Verify preventive maintenance checks and services on section vehicles and equipment.
- Ensure required reports are accurate, and submitted in accordance with standard operating procedures.

HOWITZER CAPABILITIES

1-20. A summary of howitzer ammunition and range capabilities is at table 1-1 on page 1-7. For greater detail, see the appropriate weapon technical manual.

Table 1-1. Howitzer ammunition and range capabilities

Artillery	Ammunition		Range (meters)		Rates of Fire (rounds per minute)	
	Projectile	Fuze	Maximum	RAP	Sustained	Maximum
105-mm M119-series[1]	HE, HC, WP, ILLUM APICM, DPICM, M825 Smoke SCATMINE Excalibur[2]	PD VT, MT, ET, MTSQ, Delay PGK (Only M109A6 and A7; M777-series with shell M795 or M549A1)	11,500 (Charge 7) 14,000 (Charge 8)	19,500	3 for 30 minutes	8 for 3 minutes
155-mm M109A5[2,3]			18,000 (Zone 7) 22,000 (Zone 8 or MACS Zone 5)	30,000 (M203 Zone 8 or MACS Zone 5)	(Zones 1-7) 1 rd/min (Zone 8) 1 rd/min for 60 min. 1 rd every 3 min thereafter.	4 every 2 minutes
155-mm M109A6[4,5]			18,000 (Zone 7) 22,000 (Zone 8 or Zone 5 MACS) 25,300 with XM982 Excalibur (Zone 4 MACS) 37,500 with M982 and M982A1 Excalibur (Zone 5 MACS) 22,000 (M795 with PGK and Zones 7, 8 or MACS Zone 5).	30,000 (M203 Zone 8 or MACS Zone 5) 27,000 (PGK M549A1 and Zones 7, 8 or MACS Zone 5).	Zones 3-7: 1 round per minute. Zone 8: 1 round per minute until limited by tube temperature sensor.	
155-mm M777-series[5,6]			14,800 (M4 Charge 7 White) 24,000 (M119-series) 30,000 (Zone 5 MACS) 25,400 with XM982 Excalibur (MACS Zone 4) [5] 37,700 with M982 and M982A1 Excalibur (MACS Zone 5)[5]	30,000 (M203 Zone 8 or MACS Zone 5) 27,000 (PGK M549A1 and Zones 7, 8 or MACS Zone 5).	2 in accordance with thermal warning device	

Notes:
1. TM 9-1015-260-10 technical data.   2. Excalibur not authorized for M109A5   3. TM 9-2350-311-10 technical data.
4. TM 9-2350-314-10-1 technical data.   5. TM 9-1320-202-13 technical data.   6. TM 9-1025-215-10 technical data

APICM antipersonnel improved conventional munitions	PD point detonating
DPICM dual purpose improved conventional munitions	PGK precision guidance kit
ET electronic time	RAP rocket assisted projectile
HC hexachloroethane smoke	rd/min round(s) per minute
HE high explosive	SCATMINE scatterable mines
MACS modular artillery charge system	TM technical manual
MTSQ mechanical time and superquick	VT variable time (proximity)

Chapter 2

Key Considerations

This chapter discusses techniques and key considerations for cannon battery operation. Section I discusses employment techniques and associated considerations. Section II discusses movement control techniques and associated considerations. Section III discusses techniques and associated considerations for climate and terrain.

SECTION I – EMPLOYMENT

2-1. The cannon battalion is a principal means of fire support to the maneuver commander. The agility, flexibility, and employability of cannon batteries enhance the cannon battalion's ability to deliver responsive and accurate fires throughout the depth of threat formations.

INTRODUCTION

2-2. The primary control node for the cannon battery is the fire direction center (FDC). Methods of employment available to the firing battery affect the delivery of fires. Choosing the correct method of employment based on mission variables allows well-trained units able to deliver fires in support of the mission. The battery commander and platoon leaders disperse in the battery or platoon position to increase redundancy and enhance control of the battery.

2-3. The FDC should be positioned outside of the firing area to reduce detection. Position the FDC to effectively communicate with higher headquarters and howitzers. Once positioned, the FDC does not routinely move within the battery or platoon position, but instead relies on cover and concealment for survivability.

EMPLOYMENT TECHNIQUES

2-4. Cannon batteries are employed using battery, platoon, paired or grouped, and single howitzer methods. The FDC can control the howitzers as a battery element, two platoons, in three pairs, or as single howitzers. The battery commander's guidance and mission variables dictate the method of employment. Under normal conditions, the smallest unit of employment is the firing platoon. This facilitates command, control, and sustainment, as the platoons operate as individual units. As the distance between elements increases, so does the difficulty of control and sustainment.

BATTERY

2-5. In a battery-based unit, the unit operates from one centralized location. This provides for maximum defensibility of the position. The battery commander may designate one of the platoon operations centers (POC) as the battery operations center (BOC) when both platoons are collocated in a single battery position. One of the POCs acts as the battery FDC that controls the firing of the battery. That FDC is required to maintain the current tactical situation and respond to the supported unit and higher headquarters. The other POC acts as the BOC. The battery commander and BOC facilitate control of the firing battery. The BOC serves as a focal point for internal battery operation including battery defense, coordinating sustainment, and all other operational functions normally performed by a headquarters. It also serves as the alternate FDC by providing backup fire direction capability with a tactical automated fire control system.

Platoon

2-6. In a platoon-based unit, firing platoons operate independently in separate platoon locations with a FDC controlling the howitzers. The numbers of howitzers in each platoon and employment method vary based on the unit table of organization and equipment, the tactical situation or mission requirements. Howitzers normally position individually and work together under the lead of the senior section chief. If the platoon divides into pairs or groups, a designated senior section chief acts as team leader.

2-7. In a platoon-based unit, the requirement for control exists at both platoon and battery levels. The POC achieves this requirement in the platoon. The POC is an FDC with added operational responsibilities. The POC is not a separate element and does not require a separate vehicle. The functions of the POC include technical and tactical fire direction, the traditional functions of the FDC. Additional functions of the POC are executing orders from higher headquarters, coordinating sustainment, and all the other operational functions normally performed by a headquarters based on guidance from the battery commander and platoon leader.

Pairs or Groups

2-8. Consider employment of pairs or groups when the counterfire threat is high and the threat from a dismounted ground attack is low. Control is critical to maintaining responsiveness and survivability of platoons. Platoon leaders must understand and use troop leading procedures that reinforce and expedite dissemination of information to the platoon.

Section

2-9. Section operation is the least preferred, because the section is isolated and must provide for its own defense. Consider employment of single howitzers for special missions, as this the most difficult method to command. This method requires the highest degree of crew training and does not provide for mutual support against air or ground threats. A howitzer section consists of a howitzer, prime mover (if a towed system), ammunition vehicle, and cannoneers. The howitzer section chief is responsible for the howitzer and prime mover, except in special cases (for example, airmobile missions) when control of the prime mover will go to other battery or platoon personnel.

2-10. There are three positioning options for section operation. The mated option (howitzer close to prime mover) is the standard method used since it allows the section to displace rapidly. The separated option (howitzer at a distance from the prime mover) is used only in special circumstances, which forces the howitzer to rely on the on board power supply or other power source for electrical power. The overwatch option combines both the strengths and weaknesses of the mated and separated modes. In the overwatch option, the prime mover is stationed a short distance away from the howitzer to provide early warning and covering fires, particularly during firing. All three options have their advantages and disadvantages.

SECTION II – SURVIVABILITY MOVEMENT CONTROL

2-11. One of the key responsibilities of the FDC or POC is to control movement of the battery, platoon, pairs, groups, or individual howitzers. Uncontrolled movement within the position area may result in howitzers occupying positions recently vacated by other howitzers. Survivability moves of 300-500 meters remove the platoon or howitzers from the target footprint of most threat artillery systems. Tracking the movement of three, four, or six howitzers is a major addition to the FDC tasks.

SURVIVABILITY MOVEMENT CONTROL TECHNIQUES

2-12. The FDC manages the movement of the howitzers based on the battery commander's movement criteria. The two methods of control available to manage this movement are centralized and decentralized.

Centralized

2-13. Under the centralized control method, the FDC directly controls the howitzers. The howitzers move to new locations only when directed by the FDC. The centralized method of control is best suited for positions with limited terrain. The battery commander may also choose the centralized method to exercise maximum control, when one or more howitzers experience system failures, or to train inexperienced crews. For example in a platoon operating under centralized control, the POC directly controls all howitzer movement. The POC designates the new location as a grid location, direction and distance, or quadrant. In the quadrant method a radius is drawn oriented to the azimuth of fire to facilitate the layout of quadrants (upper left-quadrant 1, lower left-quadrant 2, upper right-quadrant 3, and lower right-quadrant 4). The howitzers move on the specific order of the POC. This method of control increases allows the platoon leader or fire direction officer to position assets based on the other friendly elements collocated in the platoon position area.

DECENTRALIZED

2-14. The decentralized method of control takes full advantage of the modern howitzers capabilities. These howitzers deploy within their own assigned firing areas. Howitzers move at the discretion of the senior section chief. Battery commander's guidance, tactical standard operating procedures, or the threat (for example, counterfire, or ground attack) will dictate movement of the howitzers.

2-15. There are disadvantages to the decentralized method of control. Tracking the location and status of the howitzers is difficult, as the FDC must wait for the howitzer to arrive in the new position and report. If there are problems with the new position (for example, proximity to another howitzer or other friendly element), the FDC must immediately notify the howitzer to move. An unforeseen mask may disrupt communications. Difficulty in coordinating platoon defense increases under decentralized control. The probability of two or more howitzers locating in close proximity, or occupying a position recently vacated by another section, increases without an effective reconnaissance and movement plan. Regardless of the method of control, the FDC must develop tools and procedures for controlling movement.

SURVIVABILITY MOVEMENT TRACKING TECHNIQUES

2-16. The battery commander and tactical standard operating procedures provide the guidance necessary to track movement of platoon personnel and equipment. Preparing a howitzer tracking chart and a howitzer position chart are two means of movement tracking.

HOWITZER TRACKING CHART

2-17. The howitzer-tracking chart may be prepared on a piece of preprinted chart paper with each grid square representing 200 meters. The howitzer tracking chart may also be overlaid on a large scale (normally 1:10,000) map and used to track the movement of the individual howitzers. It is prepared for each platoon position area and is used to manage the movement of the howitzers within the firing area and the position area so that they do not endanger themselves or other friendly elements. The howitzer-tracking chart will serve as a graphical representation of howitzer locations. See figure 2-1 on page 2-4.

2-18. The howitzer tracking chart operator monitors howitzer movement on the tracking chart by using color-coded tic marks. The upper right quadrant of the tic mark is labeled with the platoon number and the gun number, for example 1/2. A legend with color scheme will indicate that status of locations. An example would be to use the color black to indicate a howitzer's current location, red for a past location, and blue can represent a future location.

2-19. If the platoon is operating under decentralized control, the platoon leader and the fire direction officer monitor the firing positions as reported by the sections as they occupy. The platoon leader and the fire direction officer ensure that the howitzers remain within their assigned firing area and that they do not threaten friendly elements by positioning too closely to them. In the decentralized mode, the POC intercedes only if there is a problem. The platoon sergeants are normally in the best position to select positions based upon guidance received from the platoon leader.

2-20. The use of the howitzer-tracking chart is dependent on mission variables. For example, if the platoon were fighting a deliberate defense the howitzer tracking chart could be very useful; during a movement to contact or hasty attack it would be counterproductive until the firing unit has halted and emplaced.

Chapter 2

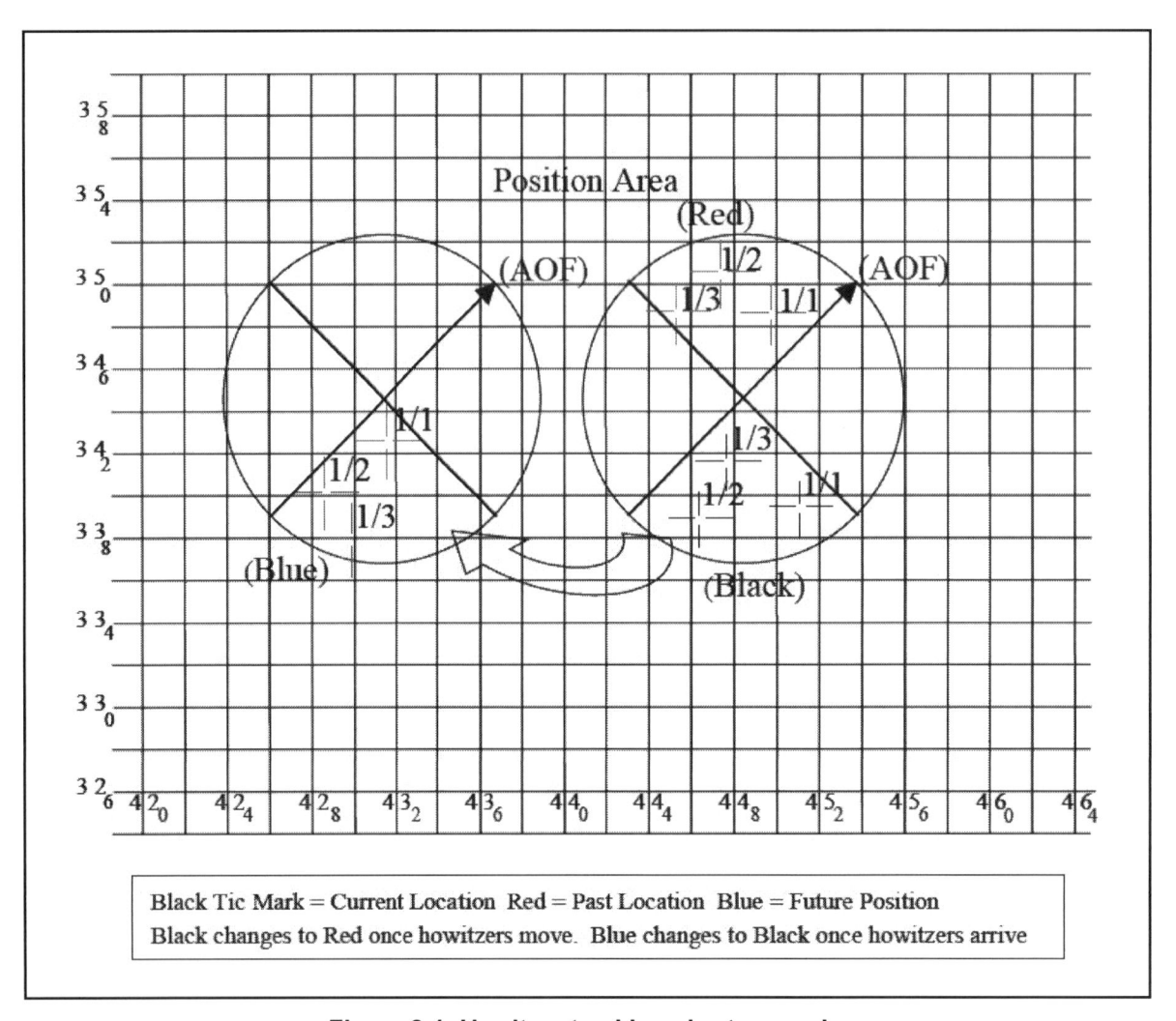

Figure 2-1. Howitzer tracking chart example

HOWITZER POSITION CHART

2-21. While the howitzer tracking chart provides a quick visual reference for past, current, and future planned positions, the howitzer position chart records the actual grid locations reported by the howitzers and those issued in movement orders. When howitzers report emplacement data, the howitzer position chart provides a first line verification of information. If the reported grid and the recorded grid vary, the FDC should immediately plot the grid on the howitzer-tracking chart to determine the discrepancy.

> *Note.* Use the howitzer position chart in conjunction with the howitzer-tracking chart. For information on the use of graphics and symbols, see Army Doctrine Reference Publication (ADRP) 1-02.

SECTION III – TACTICAL AND TECHNICAL FIRE DIRECTION

2-22. Automation systems at the howitzer have caused the FDC to assume a broader role by performing tactical fire control as well as managing movement. Technical fire control by the FDC is now a backup task or is conducted only in special circumstances. The capabilities of the howitzers' computers generate a substantial increase in information management requirements for the FDC. Accurate and timely information management is a necessity. The Advanced Field Artillery Tactical Data System (AFATDS)

software is designed to replicate the decision process that a leader would go through to determine whether a target is appropriate for engagement. However, the recommendation will only be appropriate if commander's guidance is properly input. The FDC has key responsibilities that include:
- Perform AFATDS computer database management.
- Establish internal fire direction networks.
- Control movement of howitzers, to include survivability moves.
- Review fire missions for safety violations (for example; fire support coordination measures or intervening crests).
- Perform tactical and, if required, technical fire direction.

2-23. The FDC performs tactical and possibly technical fire direction for fire missions assigned by the battalion to the battery or platoon. This tactical fire direction includes howitzer selection for missions that do not require the entire firing unit; for example, smoke, illumination, and precision registration missions. The fire direction officer and the FDC chief retain responsibility for tactical and back up technical fire direction while the platoon leader and his designated representative monitor the tactical situation. While tactical fire direction is primarily accomplished at the field artillery battalion command post, the FDC at the battery or platoon ensures that the fire orders received from the battalion are executed properly.

2-24. Technical fire direction during normal operations is normally accomplished by each individual fully digitized howitzer. The leaders at the battery or platoon FDC quickly review each mission as it is received to ensure that it is safe to fire and does not violate maneuver boundaries, restrictive fire support coordination measures, or intervening crests. The FDC also validates the use of precision munitions based on the commander's guidance. After these checks are conducted, the mission is transmitted to the howitzers for processing of individual firing data by the howitzer's computer. This procedure may be modified to accommodate special circumstances. As an example, precision registration missions are computed and controlled by the FDC.

DIRECT CONTROL BY THE FIRE DIRECTION CENTER

2-25. During some types of degraded howitzer operations, the battery or platoon FDC may assume direct control of technical fire direction and send firing data to the howitzer. For example, if the digital control system of an individual howitzer section is degraded or inoperative, the FDC may compute technical firing data for that section.

Note: The preferred method requires an operational howitzer to locate next to the degraded howitzer and the degraded howitzer uses the operational howitzer's firing data.

2-26. In those cases when the FDC is providing technical data down to one or more howitzers, secondary checks by independent means must be used. The secondary independent check for the AFATDS computing data for the degraded howitzer(s) will be by verifying the howitzer location (by the gunnery sergeant, the platoon sergeant, or platoon leader) and target location (from the fire support team, battalion FDC, POC). Once data is verified and correctly input into the AFATDS and no major database change has occurred, then data is good. Safety will be applied to the degraded howitzer the same as on operational howitzers.

PLATOON OPERATIONS CENTER CONTROL OF ALL BATTERY HOWITZERS

2-27. Each platoon FDC must be prepared to simultaneously control all of the battery's howitzers. POCs must develop charts and techniques that let them control the entire battery. The battery commander may designate one of the POCs as the battery operations center when both platoons are collocated in a single battery position as discussed earlier in this chapter.

2-28. The situation map is one of the most important tools in the POC to track operations. The map displays maneuver graphics, battery and platoon operations, and any other information thought necessary.

2-29. <u>Maneuver graphics for the force being supported</u>. Friendly and enemy unit locations, front line of own troops, and observer locations. The battalion operations section should provide this information. The fire direction officer must be proactive in ensuring that the information is current.

2-30. <u>Platoon and battery operations overlay.</u> This overlay includes the current position areas of both the battery headquarters and the platoons in the battery.

2-31. Other overlay information:
- Anticipated future position areas of the battery and platoon, including the locations of the battery headquarters and the other battery POC.
- Battery sustainment assets.
- Survey control information.

SECTION IV – CLIMATE AND TERRAIN

2-32. Climate and terrain can vary widely between operational areas and even within the same operational area. Cannon batteries frequently adjust their tactics, techniques, and procedures to account for these differences. This section briefly discusses some of the climate and terrain techniques and associated considerations unique to specific types of geography.

MOUNTAINS

2-33. Military operations in mountainous terrain are characterized by rugged, compartmented terrain with steep slopes, treacherous mobility, and poor road networks. Additional ammunition may be required to support the maneuver force in mountainous terrain because of reduced munitions effectiveness. Cross-country restrictions force threat forces to use roads and trails, which will enhance friendly interdiction fires. Movement control is more difficult on winding mountain roads. Because of the closeness of terrain masks, fewer suitable platoon positions are available. Maximize use of terrain for cover and concealment to compensate for limited hardening potential. Position units in defilade, if possible. Position observation posts, listening posts, and crew-served weapons to provide early warning and defensive fires. Plan for defensive cannon direct fire missions. Displacement is limited to the use of available roads, which generally are narrow and twisting. Survey may not be as accurate and terrain masks may limit target acquisition. Emplacing on hills increases the range of howitzer weapons systems. For more information on mountain operations, see FM 3-97.6.

JUNGLE

2-34. Military operations in jungle terrain are characterized by high humidity and dense vegetation. Position units for mutual defense, especially when thick vegetation increases vulnerability to ground attack. Humidity may degrade the ability of propellant to achieve desired ranges and may reduce equipment operability. Employ measures to keep powder increments dry. Dense vegetation degrades munitions effects. In thick canopy, variable time and improved conventional munitions are ineffective. Point detonating fuzes may be set on delay to penetrate to the ground and achieve the desired results. Communications degrade because of high humidity, vegetation density, and electronic line of sight. Antennas may have to be elevated to overcome line of sight restrictions. Soft terrain and thick vegetation hamper selection of firing positions. The battery must be prepared to clear fields of fire. Firebase operations are viable means of providing battery defense and 6,400 mil firing capability. Soft ground on the available roads reduces mobility and restricts the use of terrain march. Reduced mobility hampers sustainment resupply. Survey control is more difficult to establish, and survey parties need more time to complete their tasks. Heavy foliage degrades target acquisition accuracy. Position howitzers closer together to provide security of the position. For more information on jungle operations, see FM 90-5.

COLD REGIONS

2-35. Military operations in cold regions are characterized by frozen earth, snow covered terrain, intense sunlight, and prolonged darkness. Obscurants last longer and travel farther in cold weather; however, snow usually smothers the smoke canisters. White phosphorus particles remain active in the area longer and restrict use of that terrain. In all types of terrain, particles of white phosphorus can remain within the charred wedges and can reignite if the felt is crushed and the unburned white phosphorus is exposed to the air. Use artillery fires to start snow slides or avalanches as a munitions effects multiplier. Radio communications can be unreliable in extreme cold, and equipment may become inoperative. Frozen, snow covered terrain may limit the number of available positions for emplacement. Wheeled vehicles and trailers are generally not suited for operations in northern areas due to reduced mobility. Snowstorms and intense cold adversely affect target acquisition equipment. Without the use of improved position azimuth determining system, survey may be more time consuming. For more information on cold region operations, see Army tactics, techniques, and procedures (ATTP) 3-97.11.

URBAN

2-36. Military operations in urban areas are characterized by densely populated areas. High angle fires are most effective in attacking the defiladed areas between buildings. Control of a firing platoon operating in an urban area is demanding. Using existing structures (for example, barns, auto repair shops, and warehouses) as firing or hiding positions provides maximum protection and minimizes the camouflage effort. Additional time must be allotted for the reconnaissance of these positions. The use of aerial imagery could aid in identifying potential locations. Depending on the density of buildings in the area, the reconnaissance party may need to use cordon and search techniques to clear and check buildings. Special techniques for emplacing howitzers may be required if the ground is not suitable for normal emplacement. Consider placing howitzer spades against curbs, rubble, or building walls. Because of the expanded occupation required in the urban area, platoon displacement may be impossible. In this case, displacement may be by howitzer section. Battery personnel must be prepared to use hasty survey techniques to establish directional and positional control. Magnetic instruments are impaired when operating in a built up area and their accuracy is degraded. For more information on urban operations, see FM 3-06.

DESERT

2-37. Military operations in desert regions are characterized by rapid, highly mobile warfare conducted over great distances. Considerations vary according to the type of desert; however, considerations common to all include munitions effects due to the temperature extremes and a lack of identifiable terrain features. The mountain desert has barren, rocky ranges separated by flat basins that may be studded by deep gullies created during flash floods. This terrain will support all types of artillery but is best suited for self-propelled artillery. The rocky plateau desert has slight relief with extended flat areas and good visibility. It has steep-walled eroded valleys (wadis). These areas are suitable for artillery positions, but are subject to flash flooding. The sandy or dune desert has extensive flat areas covered with dunes subject to wind erosion. The dune size, the texture of sand, and the leeward gradient may prohibit terrain movement entirely. For more information on desert operations, see FM 90-3.

Chapter 3
Reconnaissance, Selection, and Occupation of a Position

This chapter discusses the techniques and associated considerations necessary for a rapid and orderly movement to and occupation of a firing position. Section I begins by discussing reconnaissance techniques and associated considerations. Section II discusses the selection techniques and associated considerations for the new position. Section III closes with a discussion on occupation techniques and associated considerations.

SECTION I – RECONNAISSANCE

3-1. The primary purpose of reconnaissance, selection, and occupation of a position (RSOP) is to determine the suitability of a position in terms of providing the necessary fire support, maneuverability, defensibility, trafficability, and communications. The battery commander must issue clear guidance for an effective reconnaissance of battery and platoon positions. The battery commander assembles the reconnaissance elements from one or both platoons. The platoon reconnaissance element is normally the gunnery sergeant and his driver, augmented with additional personnel, as required. The primary function of the reconnaissance element is to determine the suitability of routes and in what general areas the unit can operate. The key to a successful RSOP is discipline and team effort. Reconnaissance examines the terrain to determine its suitability for use in accomplishing the mission.

3-2. The battery commander's guidance to the reconnaissance elements should include:
- Reconnaissance method.
- Positioning options.
- Positioning of support assets, as applicable.
- Considerations for offensive and defensive tasks.

Note. There are no major differences between the reconnaissance, selection, and occupation techniques of a platoon position and a battery position. The platoon survives with a combination of movement and dispersion. The battery commander issues movement criteria to the platoon leader for displacement and survivability moves. Base platoon movement criteria on mission variables and tactical standard operating procedures. Managing survivability moves requires teamwork between the howitzers and the fire direction center.

CONSIDERATIONS

3-3. On the battlefield, a sophisticated threat can locate and engage field artillery in various ways. To survive, field artillery units move often. An artillery unit is most vulnerable to threat action while moving into or out of a position. To minimize movement time, key personnel must be able to perform reconnaissance, selection, occupation, and movement tasks quickly and efficiently. The battery commander must clearly understand the tactical situation of both friendly and threat forces while planning and executing movement. The basic considerations for RSOP are when to move, where to move, and how to move.

3-4. Field artillery units usually conduct moves in response to either tactical or survivability considerations. The three factors driving most unit movements are fire support to maneuver forces, timing, and survival. A unit must be able to move to provide fire support to the supported force. Some tasks require the unit to reach a certain position or phase line to range the target. A unit may also be forced to move when a position becomes untenable due to threat counterfire, attack, or natural disturbances (for example, flooding). The battery commander issues movement criteria to the platoon leader for displacement and survivability moves. Base movement criteria on mission variables and unit tactical standard operating procedures. Some triggers for movement may include number of rounds fired in current location, duration of firing, and time in position. Managing survivability moves requires teamwork between the howitzers and the fire direction center (FDC).

RECONNAISSANCE TECHNIQUES

3-5. The battery commander will conduct a reconnaissance of the proposed position as time allows. Ideally, the reconnaissance will consist of a ground reconnaissance with identification of proposed routes, obstacles, ambush sites, survey locations, and howitzer positions. Reconnaissance allows the battery commander to traverse the terrain that the battery (platoons) will cover en route to the position. Reconnaissance can also accomplish survey coordination, engineer support, route security, adjacent unit coordination, and fire support.

3-6. The three methods of reconnaissance available to the battery commander are map, air, and ground. All reconnaissance methods should begin with a map inspection, supplemented by photomaps, aerial photographs and digital imagery, if available. The best reconnaissance uses a combination of all three methods. The map reconnaissance method is very fast, but there are disadvantages. For example, terrain and other features may have been altered and surface conditions of the route and position cannot be determined. Aerial photographs should be used to supplement maps, as they are usually more recent and present a clearer picture of the terrain. If time and resources are available, an air reconnaissance may be beneficial, but true surface conditions may be indistinguishable. Be careful that the flight plan does not compromise the route or new position area. The best single reconnaissance method is the ground reconnaissance. For this reason, the primary focus for the remainder of this chapter will be on ground reconnaissance.

PLANNING THE RECONNAISSANCE

3-7. <u>Mission</u>. The mission is the governing factor in planning the RSOP. The unit must remain able to perform its mission with minimal degradation as a result of tactical or survivability moves. The battery commander must perform, or have previously done, his mission analysis with respect to his current and subsequent positions. Then the battery commander can identify the battery's critical tasks in each of these positions, and determine a list of movement and positioning criteria.

3-8. Movement Criteria examples:
- The battery cannot lose firing capability. Therefore, the battery must move by platoon.
- Battery is out of range to execute their portion of the tire support plan. Therefore, move by battery using fastest movement technique.
- Battalion has two batteries moving at the same time. The battery could receive an emergency mission. Therefore, the battery must consider an internal platoon order of march and perform a reconnaissance of areas along the planned route to assist the battery on meeting this contingency.

3-9. <u>Enemy Situation</u>. The current enemy situation must be thoroughly understood. The disposition, intentions, and capabilities of enemy forces must be analyzed before the RSOP, particularly their local capabilities as revealed in current combat information.

3-10. Enemy Situation examples:
- If the most likely enemy action during the battery's movement is from air attack, then:
  - The battery commander requests a change to the given route to support a terrain march for certain segments of the planned route where there is not adequate concealment for the battery.
  - The route must allow the march units to conduct their immediate action drills for air attack.
  - A route reconnaissance must be performed to determine easily identifiable features to serve as air target reference points.
  - If a terrain march is too slow, move in an open column.

Reconnaissance, Selection, and Occupation of a Position

3-11. If the most dangerous enemy action during the battery's movement is ambush, then:
- Each march element, to include the reconnaissance and advance parties, must lead with an armored vehicle or crew served weapon.
- Coordinate with higher headquarters to determine possible ambush sites and clear those areas so that advance parties or main bodies can conduct reconnaissance by fire.

3-12. Positioning criteria considerations:
- If the most likely threat in the subsequent position is enemy counterbattery fire, then the battery commander must ensure position areas support maximum dispersion and hardening.
- If the most dangerous threat to the battery in the subsequent position is from ground attack, then the battery commander must::
  - Ensure the position is not located on platoon-size or larger avenues of approach.
  - Locate possible observation posts to provide for early warning to execute hasty displacements or the activation of howitzer direct fire and tank-killer teams.
  - Locate the position area for supplemental positions for howitzer direct fire and tank-killer teams.
  - Determine if the position provides adequate defilade and terrain masking.

3-13. Terrain and Weather. The battery commander and platoon leaders must analyze the routes to be used by the unit assets and the time and distance required to make the move. The ability to move one firing platoon while keeping the other in position and firing is critical to the platoon-based operations and the accomplishment of the battery mission. Moving the battery over long, difficult routes requires well planned, coordinated movement orders and unit standard operating procedures. The effects of the weather on the terrain to be crossed must be analyzed to facilitate rapid movement. Weather affects visibility (fog, haze) and trafficability (ice, rain-softened ground).

3-14. Troops. The current troop strength and level of training must be considered. The mission may not change; but the troops available to accomplish it will. As the other mission variables change, so will the number of troops necessary to perform the mission. Because of casualties and these varying conditions, adjustments must be made during the planning phase.

3-15. Time. The amount of time available for the RSOP will affect all phases of its accomplishment. The time factor will change due to events on the battlefield. Whether minutes or hours are allowed for the RSOP, adjustments must be made.

THE RECONNAISSANCE PARTY

3-16. The reconnaissance party should consist of enough individuals to accomplish successful RSOP. An example of a reconnaissance party is the commander, the gunnery sergeant, and representatives from each howitzer, FDC, and support section. The commander of a firing battery chooses position areas for the platoons or the battery and determines the azimuth of fire. The gunnery sergeant then performs detailed position area RSOP.

ASSEMBLE THE ADVANCE PARTY

3-17. For either a deliberate or a hasty occupation, a prearranged signal or procedure should be used to alert and assemble the advance party. The signal should be in the unit standard operating procedures, which will also list the personnel, equipment, vehicles, and place of assembly. The advance party is normally assembled no later than the prepare-to-march-order phase.

TAKE A FIRING CAPABILITY FORWARD

3-18. Depending upon the mission and tactical situation, the commander may direct that a howitzer section go forward with the advance party. Reasons for taking howitzers forward may be to:
- Confuse enemy moving target locating radars, as part of the infiltration plan.
- Determine the suitability of the route and firing position when conditions are doubtful.

Chapter 3

- Conduct a registration or an offset registration.

MOVEMENT BRIEFING

3-19. Before departing to reconnoiter the new position, the commander briefs the platoon leaders and other key personnel on the movement information:
- Situation:
  - Enemy situation. Rear area activity. Major avenues of approach. Air activity. Potential ambush sites. locations of friendly maneuver units and supporting artillery.
- Mission: Changes in the mission of the supported maneuver unit and supporting artillery.
- Execution:
  - Concept of the operation. General location of the battery and platoon positions, azimuth of fire, routes, order of march, location of start point, release point and times.
  - Mission-oriented protective posture status.
  - Areas of known chemical or nuclear contamination.
- Sustainment: When and where to feed unit personnel, priority for maintenance, recovery, ammunition resupply, and refuel location.
- Command and signal:
  - Changes in location of the battalion command post and battalion support operations and the location of battery commander. It also includes a contingency plan if the commander does not return or report back by a predetermined time or event.
  - Movement radio frequencies and net control restrictions. Signals for immediate actions at the halt and during movement.

3-20. After being briefed by the commander, the platoon leader or executive officer briefs the remaining key personnel. See Table 3-1.

Table 3-1. Reconnaissance Movement Order Briefing

1. Situation:	i. Emergency missions.
2. Mission:	4. Sustainment:
3. Execution:	a. Ammunition.
a. General.	b. Fuel.
b. Organization.	c. Food.
c. Composition of column.	d. Maintenance.
d. Instructions.	5. Command and Signal.
(1) Air observers.	a. Location of executive officer, platoon leader and fire direction officer.
(2) Reconnaissance element.	b. chief of firing battery's or platoon sergeant's location.
(3) Route markers.	c. Battery commander's location.
(4) Start point.	d. Battalion and battery headquarters location.
(5) Check points.	e. Other locations.
(6) Rally points.	f. Signals:
(7) Release points.	(1) Unblocked ambush.
(8) Route of march.	(2) Blocked ambush.
(9) Alternate routes.	(3) Air attack.
(10) Lights.	(4) Emergency mission.
e. Unblocked ambush.	(5) Chemical, biological, radiological, nuclear attack.
f. Blocked ambush.	(6) Artillery attack.
g. Air attack.	(7) Radio.
h. Artillery attack.	

ROUTE RECONNAISSANCE

3-21. After making a map inspection, planning the reconnaissance, and briefing the necessary personnel the commander is now ready to make a ground reconnaissance. Accompanied by the advance party, the commander or his representative departs on the route reconnaissance. The primary purpose of this reconnaissance is to determine the suitability of the route of the units' movement. Items to be analyzed include possible alternate routes, cover, concealment, location of obstacles, likely ambush sites, contaminated areas, route marking requirements, and the time and distance required to traverse the route. Once these areas are analyzed, any information considered pertinent should be sent back to the firing unit.

SECTION II – SELECTION

3-22. Based on the reconnaissance conducted earlier, the battery commander selects the battery or the platoon positions or firing areas. Once the general locations are determined, the gunnery sergeant(s) conduct a detailed preparation of their respective positions.

CONSIDERATIONS

3-23. The mission is the most important consideration for selection of the position. The position must facilitate fires throughout the maximum area of the supported maneuver force. The azimuth of fire is determined with this in mind. **The *azimuth of fire* is the direction, expressed in mils, that a firing unit is laid (oriented) on when it occupies a position.** Communications is a key consideration for position selection. The position must enable communications with higher headquarters. Defensibility is another key consideration for position selection. The position should use existing terrain features to hinder threat forces from targeting the unit. A position that provides protection against the effects of counterfire is very desirable. The position should offer effective cover and concealment with emphasis on concealment. The position should also avoid high-speed avenues of approach and have more than a single entrance and exit. Consider personnel and weapon systems when selecting positions to maximize capabilities in responding to and defeating a physical attack. Trafficability and maneuverability are other key considerations for position selection. The terrain should facilitate movement within the position. An established track plan specifies the routes vehicles take within the position. The weapon systems that will occupy the position dictate the position requirements. For example, units with medium howitzers and associated prime movers require a larger area with stable soil to support the increased weight than with light howitzer units.

POSITIONING TECHNIQUES

3-24. There are three types of positions available for cannon battery occupation. These include the primary position, alternate position, and supplementary position.

3-25. The primary position is one where the firing battery accomplishes its assigned mission. This position includes general locations for the FDC, howitzer sections, support vehicles, entrance point(s), and exit point(s), at a minimum. The battery commander issues general guidance to the gunnery sergeant for the track plan, scheme of defense, and location of ground guide pickup point.

3-26. An alternate position is one where the unit moves to if the primary position becomes untenable. The alternate position must meet the same requirements as the primary position and be located to allow for rapid and orderly occupation. If the unit comes under attack, a prepared alternate position will facilitate rapid movement and continued fires to maneuver forces. Each section chief must know the location and route to the alternate position, because movement to that position may be by section.

Note. The alternate position should be reconnoitered or prepared for occupation as part of position improvement activities for the gunnery sergeant. The position should be far enough away to escape the effects of enemy indirect fire on the primary position.

3-27. A supplementary position is one selected to accomplish a specific mission. For example, a supplementary position for an offset registration should be far enough away that counterfire will not affect the primary position. A supplementary position for defense could be located within the primary position and cover likely threat avenues of approach.

DISPERSION TECHNIQUES

3-28. Threat forces pose a general hazard from counterfire, air attack, ground attack, and electronic warfare. To counter this danger, the battery commander or platoon leader must consider techniques of dispersion, movement, hardening, and concealment when selecting howitzer positions.

Chapter 3

3-29. Consider the use of terrain gun positioning (figure 3-1) to disperse howitzers over a large area when the threat is from threat counterfire or air attack. Terrain gun positioning maximizes the use of natural cover and concealment.

Note. The following examples are for illustration purposes only. Vehicles and equipment differ based on unit configuration and authorizations.

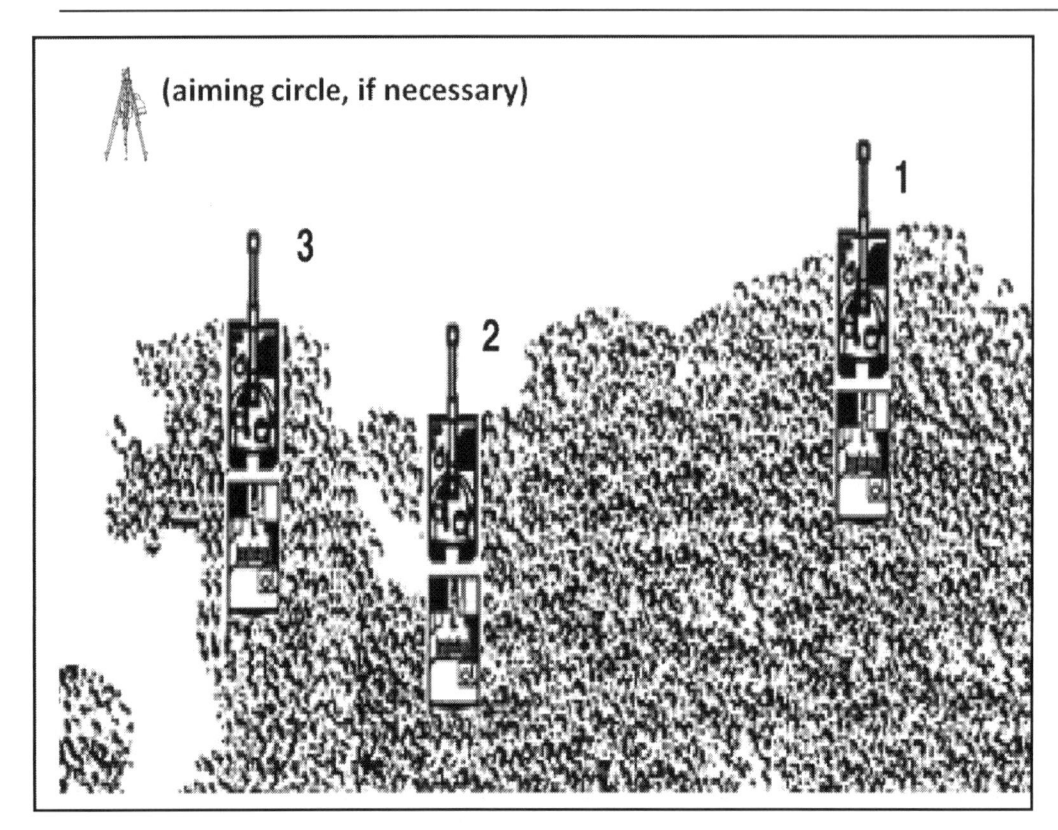

Figure 3-1. Example terrain gun positioning

3-30. Consider the use of wedge and star type formations (figures 3-2 and 3-3) for a tight and defensible position when the threat is from ground attack, guerilla, and special forces. These position formations provide excellent firing and unit defense capabilities as the howitzers can be traversed for all-around defense. In a star formation, the center gun can fire self-illumination missions over the position if necessary.

Reconnaissance, Selection, and Occupation of a Position

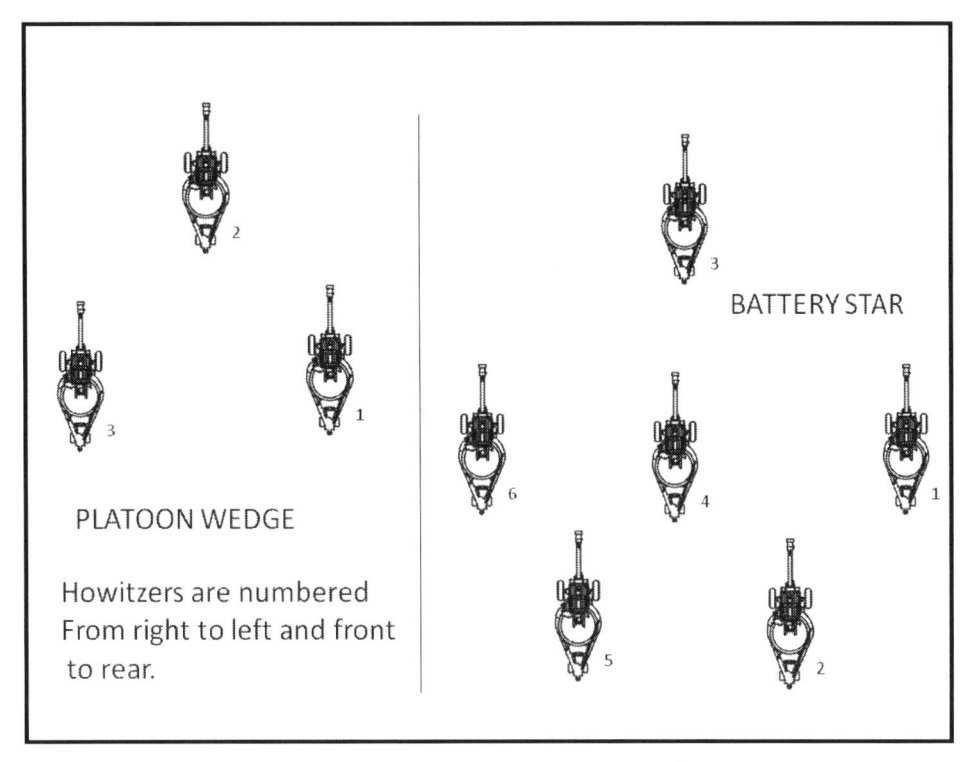

PLATOON WEDGE

Howitzers are numbered From right to left and front to rear.

BATTERY STAR

Figure 3-2. Platoon in wedge and battery in star formation example

3-31. Consider the use of other formations (for example, line or lazy-W in figure 3-3) in situations that require immediate fire support (for example, emergency or hasty occupations). These formations offer excellent control but are vulnerable to air attack.

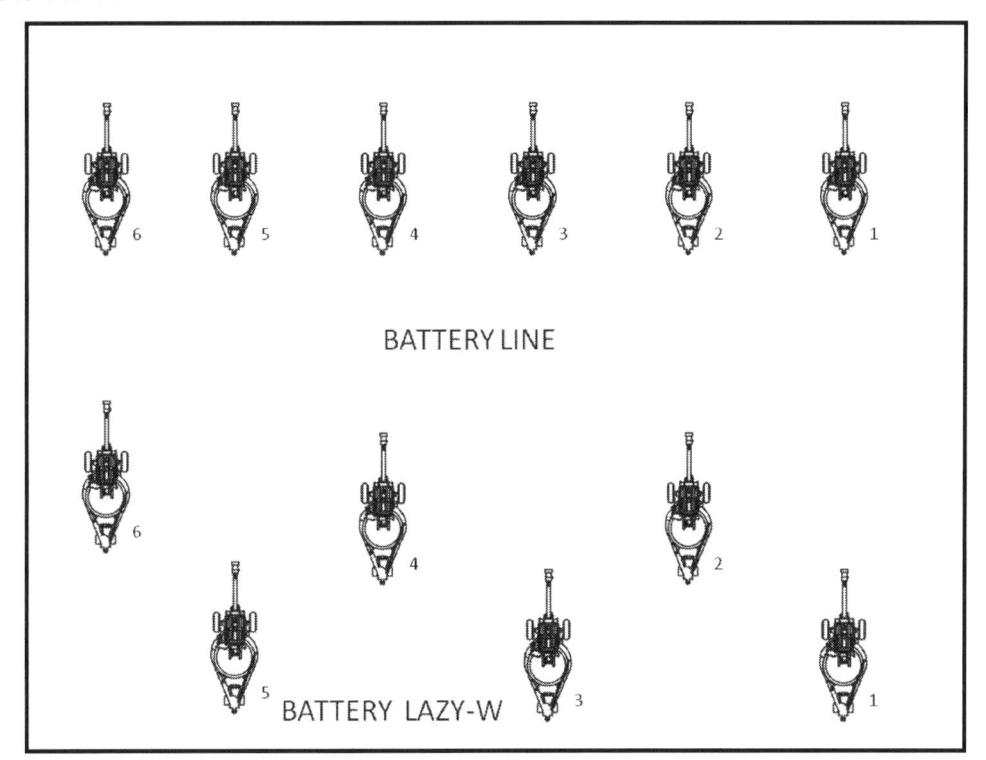

BATTERY LINE

BATTERY LAZY-W

Figure 3-3. Battery in line or in lazy-w formation example

3-32. The type of position and dispersion technique used for emplacement will depend on mission variables and unit tactical standard operating procedures. The main factors to consider are the mission and the threat.

SECTION III – OCCUPATION

3-33. Once the reconnaissance and selection of the new position is complete, the advance party confirms the suitability of the position and organizes the position for occupation. The battery commander finalizes the preparations for occupation to include priorities of work.

CONSIDERATIONS

3-34. Upon arrival at the new location, the advance party conducts a security sweep of the position. The sweep will identify the presence of threat forces; mines; improvised explosive devices; chemical, biological, radiological, or nuclear (CBRN) hazards; and other threats. If these threats are present, the advance party will break contact with threat forces or mark hazards and relocate to another location. The intent is to move stealthily, avoid threat contact, and accomplish the tasks assigned without engaging in close combat. The security sweep should be well trained and rehearsed. Security is continuous throughout advance party operations. For more information on reconnaissance patrols, see ATP 3-21.8.

OCCUPATION TECHNIQUES

3-35. The following paragraphs briefly discuss occupation techniques and associated considerations used in the occupation of a position. Regardless of the type of occupation chosen, local security must be maintained throughout the occupation.

DELIBERATE

3-36. A deliberate occupation is one that is planned. During a deliberate occupation, the advance party precedes the main body and prepares the position for occupation. The deliberate occupation may be during the hours of daylight or after darkness falls. Preparations for the occupation can occur during the day or at night, depending on the tactical situation and time available. Minimize the number and composition of the advance party to preclude observation by threat forces and risking detection. A preferred method for a deliberate occupation at night would be to prepare the position during daylight hours. The nighttime reconnaissance and subsequent movement are often necessary and can be time consuming. The primary considerations for a deliberate occupation are time available and time of day for preparation of the position. Additional planning and preparation time are required for movements conducted at night.

HASTY

3-37. A hasty occupation differs from a deliberate occupation mainly in time available for reconnaissance and subsequent preparation of the position. Generally, a hasty occupation results from unforeseen circumstances. A hasty occupation begins as a deliberate occupation, but due to limited time available for advance party preparations, it then becomes a hasty occupation. The considerations for a hasty occupation include time available and training level of advance party personnel. During a hasty occupation, clear and concise direction is necessary to establish priority tasks.

EMERGENCY

3-38. An emergency occupation is one that results from a call for fire received during a tactical movement. An emergency occupation requires a modification to the normal occupation procedures. Emergency occupation procedures apply to all artillery units, both towed and self-propelled. The battery commander should consider suitable locations for emergency missions along the route during reconnaissance. This information is issued to platoons during the movement briefing. The key to a successful emergency fire mission is well-rehearsed tactical standard operating procedures.

PREPARATION TECHNIQUES

3-39. The following paragraphs briefly discuss the techniques and associated considerations for an orderly occupation with respect to time of day and time available. For more information on emplacement procedures for standard and emergency fire missions, see applicable howitzer technical manuals.

DAYTIME

3-40. The first sergeant or gunnery sergeant establishes the track plan to include the vehicle dispersal area and positions for support vehicles. Considerations for a daytime occupation include:
- Use existing roads.
- Select separate entrance and exit routes.
- Follow natural terrain features (for example, gullies, or tree lines) that take advantage of natural overhead cover and concealment.
- Dictate exact routes for each vehicle if concealment is critical.
- Identify the vehicle pickup point.

3-41. The gunnery sergeant prepares the position for occupation, to include:
- Select howitzer locations.
- Select FDC location.
- Issue priorities of work to advance party members.
- Select orienting equipment location, as required.
- Establish survey, as required.
- Determine deflection (DF), distance, and vertical angle to each howitzer location.
- Record howitzer information on weapons location data card.
- Obtain site to crest (see Appendix E) and piece to crest range from each howitzer representative.
- Determine minimum quadrant elevation, as required.
- Initiate perimeter sketch and defense diagram.
- Supervise advance party personnel in the execution of their duties.

3-42. Advance party personnel prepare their positions for occupation. Each howitzer representative determines the site to crest and piece to crest range. Information is relayed to the gunnery sergeant. Advance party personnel walk the track plan to confirm the path is free of obstacles. The FDC representative selects a position that is located to the rear or flank, as far as possible from the gun line as feasible. The communications representative establishes radio and, if available, wire communications. Upon completion, the advance party personnel report to the pickup point to wait for vehicles, and assume a defensive posture. The loss of space-based communications due to enemy activity remains a major concern for cannon batteries conducting military operations. Whether the interruption of the communications is caused by enemy action against satellites or through the use of intermittent jamming or spoofing, the resulting communications black-out will require deployed forces to adapt and adjust until the capability is restored. Short term losses or disruptions of satellite communications will have to be mitigated through alternative communications methods and courier networks. For more information on preparations for occupation, see the digital training management system website.

LIMITED TIME

3-43. The advance party may not always have enough time to accomplish every task. For this reason, the gunnery sergeant will dictate activities for the advance party emphasizing those tasks in priority, including howitzer positions, orienting equipment, and essential communications. Due to the limited time available, the duties of the advance party are decentralized.

NIGHT

3-44. Preparations for a night occupation are similar to those for a daytime occupation. The main differences are an increased emphasis on noise and light discipline. At night, additional planning, time, and techniques are required to ensure an orderly occupation. Any tasks that can be performed prior to nightfall will be beneficial. Personnel must exercise noise and light discipline. Noise travels much farther at night due to atmospheric conditions, so it is critical that noise be kept to a minimum. Light sources can be detected from greater distances, which can disrupt attempts at an undetected occupation.

3-45. During a night occupation, the gunnery sergeant is especially concerned with noise and light discipline, security, and communication between advance party members. Considerations for a night occupation include:
- Install light sets and generators before dark.
- Shield fire control instruments.
- Install filters on flashlights.
- Mark obstacles with engineer tape or light source (for example, chemical light).
- Secure wire communications, if available.
- Determine site to crest information prior to sunset.
- Brief advance party personnel on nighttime ground guide procedures.

WARNING

Drivers must stop their vehicles whenever they cannot see the light from the vehicle guide's flashlight. Death or serious injury may result.

3-46. Once the occupation is complete and the unit is ready to answer calls for fire, sustaining actions begin. The battery commander or the platoon leader determines sustainment actions in priority, to include:
- Improve position defenses (for example, camouflage, concealment, and fighting positions).
- Harden critical elements.
- Perform maintenance.
- Rehearse reaction forces.
- Conduct resupply.
- Conduct training.

Chapter 4
Laying, Measuring, and Reporting

This chapter discusses the techniques and associated considerations for laying the firing element for direction when a howitzer's onboard system is inoperative, measuring the azimuth of fire, and reporting data. Section I begins with a brief discussion on orienting equipment. Section II discusses the techniques and associated considerations for laying the unit for direction. Section III closes with a discussion on techniques and associated considerations for measuring and reporting data.

SECTION I – ORIENTING EQUIPMENT

4-1. Orienting equipment is used to establish common direction for the unit. Two of the five requirements for accurate fires are an accurate firing unit location and updated weapon information. The following sections discuss the techniques and associated considerations for satisfying those requirements when using backup systems such as the M2A2 aiming circle or the M67 gun laying and positioning system.

AIMING CIRCLE

4-2. The M2A2 aiming circle is a 4-power, fixed focus instrument used to measure azimuth and elevation angles of a ground or aerial target with respect to a preselected base line. The aiming circle orients the howitzer on a designated azimuth of fire. *Azimuth* **is a horizontal angle measured clockwise from a north base line that could be true north, magnetic north, or grid north.** The azimuth is the most common military method to express direction. When using an azimuth, the point where the azimuth originates is the center of an imaginary circle. The circle related to an azimuth of fire is divided into 6400 mils (360 degrees).

4-3. For more information on the aiming circle (such as on instrument controls, setup and takedown, and maintenance), see Technical Manual (TM) 9-6675-262-10. For information on declinating the aiming circle, see Appendix E and the digital training management system.

GUN LAYING AND POSITIONING SYSTEM

4-4. The M67 Gun Laying And Positioning System (GLPS) is a 10-power, fixed focus instrument used to provide accurate directional control and position data to howitzers. The GLPS is used much the same way as the aiming circle, but does not require external survey support. The GLPS has a Class I eye safe laser rangefinder to measure distances to forward stations while providing optics for the system.

> **CAUTION**
> The laser range finder is eye safe when operated according to the operator's manual. Unauthorized handling (for example, opening the cover or using an unauthorized power supply) may exceed established eye safe laser exposure levels. Under these circumstances, radiant exposure may cause eye injury to the operator and bystanders. Corneal and retinal damage can occur.

4-5. The GLPS has a theodolite, which is a digital electronic angle-measuring device used to measure horizontal and vertical angles. The *vertical angle* is the angle measured up or down (in mils) in a vertical plane from the horizontal to a straight line joining the observer and target (ATP 3-09.30). The GLPS has a gyroscope to measure the direction to grid north. **The *vertical interval* is the difference in altitude between the unit or observer and the target or point of burst.** Determine vertical interval by subtracting the altitude of the unit or observer from the altitude of the target or point of burst.

4-6. The GLPS works in concert with companion global positioning system devices, which provide data to the system. Two examples of these are the AN/PSN-11 Precision Lightweight Global Positioning System Receiver and AN/PSN-13A Defense Advanced Global Positioning System Receiver. For more information on the GLPS, see TM 9-6675-347-13&P. See TM 11-5825-291-13 for information on the AN/PSN-11 and TM 11-5820-1172-13&P for the AN/PSN-13, AN/PSN-13A, and AN/PSN-13B.

M2 COMPASS

4-7. The M2 compass is an alternate instrument for orienting or laying howitzers. The unmounted magnetic compass is a multipurpose instrument used to obtain angle of site and azimuth readings. Like the M2A2 aiming circle, the M2 compass requires declination.

4-8. For more information on the M2 compass, see TM 9-1290-333-15. For information on declinating the M2 Compass, see the digital training management system and Appendix E.

SECTION II – LAYING FOR DIRECTION

4-9. This section discusses techniques and associated considerations for laying the battery or platoon howitzers for direction.

Note: Steps for laying with the GLPS differ slightly from the aiming circle. However, the principles are alike. For more information on laying procedures for the GLPS, see the unit standard operating procedures and TM 9-6675-347-13&P. See also TM 9-6675-262-10 for the aiming circle.

RECIPROCAL LAYING

4-10. In reciprocal laying, the 0-3200 line of one instrument and the 0-3200 line of another instrument are laid parallel. Figure 4-1 on page 4-3 provides a graphic representation of reciprocal laying with the GLPS or aiming circle serving as the primary instrument and the howitzer panoramic telescope serving as the secondary instrument.

4-11. Reciprocal laying is based on the geometric theorem that given two lines cut by a common transversal whose alternate interior angles are equal, then those two lines are said to be parallel. The parallel lines are the 0-3200 lines of the aiming circle and the line of fire and rearward extension of the line of fire of the howitzer. The common transversal is the line of sight established between the aiming circle and the panoramic telescope. The alternate interior angles are the deflections as read from the instruments.

4-12. When the 0-3200 line of the instrument (aiming circle or GLPS) is parallel to the azimuth of fire, the instrument operator sights on the lens of the panoramic telescope and reads the deflection. The instrument operator announces the deflection to the gunner on the howitzer.

4-13. The gunner sets the announced deflection on the panoramic telescope. The gunner orders the howitzer to be shifted or traverses the tube until the line of sight through the panoramic telescope is again on the laying instrument (aiming circle or GLPS).

Note: Because the panoramic telescope (pantel) is not directly over the pivot point of the cannon's tube, the pantel displaces horizontally. When the telescope has been sighted on the laying instrument, the gunner reports "**READY FOR RECHECK**".

Laying, Measuring, and Reporting

4-14. The instrument operator again sights on the lens of the pantel and reads and announces the deflection. This procedure is repeated until the gunner reports a difference of 0 mils between successive deflections. The howitzer has then been laid.

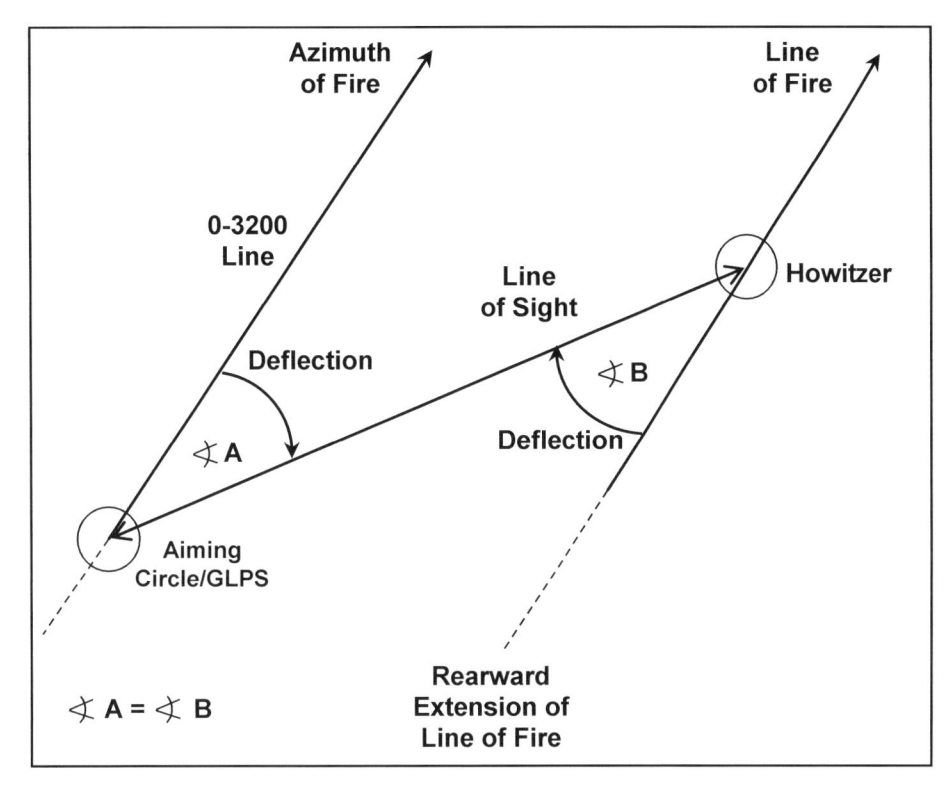

Figure 4-1. Example reciprocal laying

4-15. The operator must first understand several definitions and concepts to grasp the principle behind reciprocal laying:

- The *back-azimuth* is the direction equal to the azimuth plus or minus 3200 mils. For mils, if the azimuth is less than 3200 mils, add 3200 mils to obtain the back-azimuth; if the azimuth is more than 3200 mils, subtract 3200 mils. See TC 3-25.26 for additional discussion of the types of azimuths
- The *line of fire* is 1. as it relates to the principle of the reciprocal laying of field artillery weapons, any line parallel to the azimuth of fire. 2. the direction of the line established by the tube or any line parallel to that line in the firing battery. The line of fire is an imaginary line extending through the central axis of the tube when looking through the breech to the muzzle of the weapon.
- The *rearward extension of the line of fire* is an imaginary line in the exact opposite direction of the line of fire that extends through the center axis of the tube when looking down through the muzzle to the breech of the weapon.
- The *orienting angle* is a horizontal, clockwise angle measured from the line of fire to the orienting line.
- The *orienting line* a line of known direction in the firing unit's area that serves as a basis for laying the firing unit for direction.
- The *azimuth of the orienting line* is the direction from the orienting station to a designated end of the orienting line.
- The *orienting station* is 1. A point established on the ground that has directional control. 2. An orienting device, such as an aiming circle or gun laying and positioning system, set up over a point to lay the weapons by the orienting angle method.

Chapter 4

- A *deflection* is a horizontal clockwise angle measured from the line of fire or the rearward extension line of fire to the line of sight to a given aiming point with the vertex of the angle at the instrument.
- The *common deflection* is the deflection, which may vary based on the weapon's sight system, corresponding to the firing unit's azimuth of fire.
- The *referred deflection* is the deflection measured to an aiming point without moving the tube of the weapon.
- *Refer* is to measure, using the panoramic telescope, the deflection to a given aiming point without moving the tube of the weapon.

4-16. The GLPS or aiming circle measures horizontal clockwise angles from the line of fire to the line of sight of a given aiming point. The panoramic telescope measures horizontal clockwise angles from the line of fire or the rearward extension of the line of fire to the line of sight of a given aiming point. Therefore, the angular measurements taken when reciprocally laying with the GLPS or aiming circle and the howitzer panoramic telescope are always deflections.

TECHNIQUES FOR LAYING

4-17. *Common grid* refers to all firing and target-locating elements within a unified command located and oriented, to prescribed accuracies, with respect to a single three–dimensional datum (FM 3-09). Common grid enables units to mass fires more accurately. Survey data will not always be available; therefore, all efforts should be made to establish directional control as early as possible. Position data provided by battalion and used either in the GLPS "INPUT POSITION/BACK POLAR PLOT" options or on the aiming circle will place the battalion firing assets on a common grid. Hasty survey techniques will be discussed later in chapter 6.

GUN LAYING AND POSITIONING SYSTEM STEPS

4-18. Select the GLPS position during the advance party security sweep. If the GLPS lases to determine grid location data, the minimum distance of the laser range finder is 30 meters. If the precision lightweight global positioning system receiver is used to provide location data to the GLPS, ensure the electronic line of sight between the precision lightweight global positioning system receiver and the satellites is not masked.

4-19. Position the precision lightweight global positioning system receiver on the selected GLPS position and determine the location. Allow the precision lightweight global positioning system receiver sufficient time to update the position data and be available for further use as needed.

> **CAUTION**
> When live firing with precision lightweight global positioning system receiver location data input in the GLPS, the precision lightweight global positioning system receiver Figure of Merit reading must be a Figure of Merit 1 when used for artillery positioning.

4-20. Set-up and level the GLPS in accordance with the procedures outlined in TM 9-6675-347-13&P. Determine what position data is available for the GLPS. The GLPS needs position data that allows the North-seeking gyroscope the ability to accurately orient itself on Grid North. There are three means of providing position data to the system – global positioning system position, input position, and back polar plot.

Global Positioning System

4-21. Global positioning system location data comes from either survey data or from the precision lightweight global positioning system receiver. The precision lightweight global positioning system receiver is the alternate method for determining the position of the GLPS when survey data is not available.

Input Position

4-22. Input Position is normally used when operating at an orienting station, survey control point, or survey location. If survey is available, the point will be tagged with important information, to include:
- Unit.
- 4 May 2016.
- Grid.
- Altitude.
- Azimuth of the orienting line.
- Distance to end of the orienting line.
- Description of the end of the orienting line.

Back Polar Plot

4-23. Back Polar Plot is used when GLPS location data is not known, but distant known location data is available. The GLPS will measure the direction and distance from the current position to a known reference point in order to calculate the current position data. The reference point must be within 2500 meters and have line of sight with the orienting location.

Note: Position data provided by battalion and used in the GLPS Input Position and Back Polar Plot options will place the battalion firing assets on a common grid. Use of the precision lightweight global positioning system receiver location for positioning does not meet the definition of common grid in as far as the separate firing elements having the same location error.

4-24. Orient the GLPS for direction. Once positioning data is provided to the system, there are two methods used to orient the system on grid North. The most accurate means is by running the survey North-seeking gyroscope; the second means is to use existing directional control already established on the ground. This method saves the 210-second gyroscope spin time.

4-25. Prepare the position to receive the howitzers. After the GLPS orientation is complete, the operator selects the "LAY BY DEFLECTION" option and establishes each howitzer location. The operator inputs the azimuth of fire and then sights on each position to determine an initial deflection, range, and vertical angle to each gun location and stores the data. The GLPS calculates the Universal Transverse Mercator/ Universal Polar Stereographic grid coordinates of each gun and stores them. The operator then passes the information to the fire direction center (FDC) and the gun guides to assist during the occupation of position to enhance the unit's ready to fire time. If not already done and time permits before the arrival of the howitzers, use the "LAY BY AZIMUTH" option to establish an orienting station with grid and altitude, an azimuth of the orienting line, and a description of the end of the orienting line. Then use the GLPS's capability to conduct a graphic traverse to establish an alternate position for the unit.

4-26. Lay of the platoon (battery) during the occupation of position. Use the "LAY BY DEFLECTION" option to lay the firing element to a zero mil tolerance. Store the final lay data in the GLPS and pass the information to the FDC to update the center's computer. See TM 9-6675-347-13&P for information on the operation of the GLPS.

M2A2 AIMING CIRCLE STEPS

4-27. Although the aiming circle is normally used as a safety circle to verify the lay of the platoon (battery), the aiming circle may also be used to lay the platoon (battery).

Laying by Orienting Angle (Common Grid)

4-28. This method of laying requires the use of a common grid. If survey is available, the orienting station will be tagged with the same information previously identified to manually input position data into the GLPS.

Chapter 4

4-29. The instrument operator will set up the aiming circle using a plumb bob, and position the aiming circle over the orienting station. Table 4-1 depicts the steps for orienting the aiming circle by orienting angle. An illustration of the computation of the orienting angle is in Figure 4-2.

Table 4-1. Laying by orienting angle (aiming circle)

SEQUENCE	MEMORY AID – TFOOL (if survey is available)	STEPS
Do this first.	TFOOL (Take the azimuth of fire out of the orienting line)	Math step: Subtract the azimuth of fire from the azimuth of the orienting line (add 6400, if necessary). This is the orienting angle (OA).
Do this second.	U	Use the azimuth knob (upper motion) to set the OA.
Do this third.	L	With the orienting knob (lower motion), sight on the EOL.
Do this last.	U	With the azimuth knob (upper motion), sight on the weapon panoramic telescope. Announce the deflection to the weapon(s) and lay, using proper commands.
Note. You must use the azimuth of the orienting line and the azimuth of fire.		
OA = orienting angle EOL = end of the orienting line U = upper motion L = lower motion		

AZIMUTH OF OL   2000
AZIMUTH OF FIRE -0600
ORIENTING ANGLE   1400

EOL – end of the orienting line   GN – grid North
OA – orienting angle   OL – orienting station
OS – orienting station

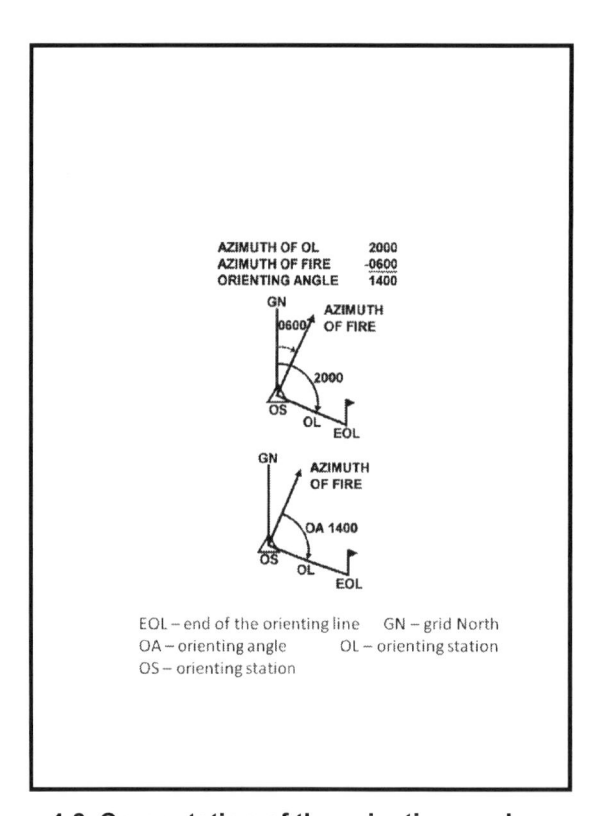

Figure 4-2. Computation of the orienting angle example

Laying by Grid Azimuth

4-30. If survey data is not available and hasty survey is not possible, then the next best method is laying by grid azimuth. Table 4-2 depicts the steps for orienting the aiming circle by grid azimuth. Figure 4-3 shows an example of the computation of the grid azimuth.

Laying, Measuring, and Reporting

Note: Laying by grid azimuth involves the use of the magnetic needle of the aiming circle. The instrument must be set up where it is free from magnetic attractions. The minimum distances are:

Power lines and electronic equipment – 150 meters

Railroad tracks, artillery, tanks, and vehicles – 75 meters

Small metal objects (for example, barbed wire or personal weapons) – 10 meters.

Table 4-2. Laying by grid azimuth (aiming circle)

SEQUENCE	MEMORY AID – SADULU (if survey is not available)	STEPS
Do this first.	SAD (Subtract the azimuth of fire from the declination constant)	Math step: Subtract the azimuth of fire from the declination constant. Add 6400, if necessary. This gives the instrument reading. See figure 4-3.
Do this second.	U	Set the instrument reading using the azimuth knob (upper motion).
Do this third.	L	With the orienting knob (lower motion), float and center the magnetic needle.
Do this last.	U	With the azimuth knob (upper motion), sight on the panoramic telescope of the howitzer. Announce the deflection to the weapon(s) and lay, using proper commands.

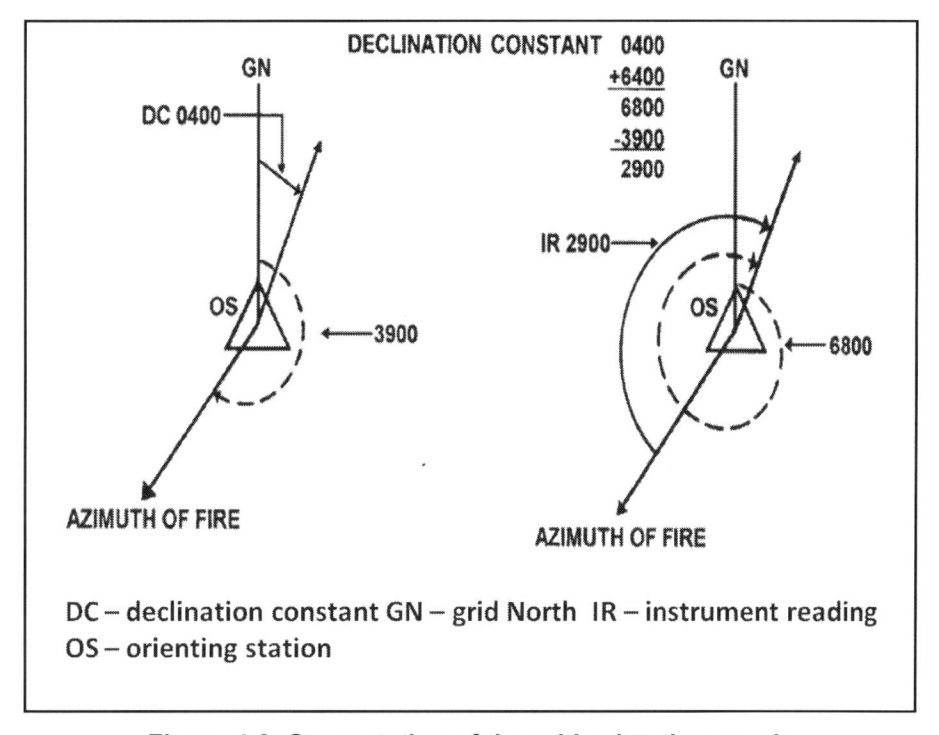

Note. You must use the declination constant and the azimuth of fire.
U = upper motion   L = lower motion

Figure 4-3. Computation of the grid azimuth example

COMMANDS

4-31. Circumstances may arise when the howitzers are not able to orient themselves. Use the commands in the following example to lay a platoon (battery) with a GLPS or an aiming circle.

Chapter 4

> **Example**
> (For brevity, only the exchange between the aiming circle operator and the gunner of howitzer number 3 are given. <u>The deflections announced are only examples.</u> Digital fire control instruments have other gunner actions that must be accomplished during the laying procedure. See the appropriate technical manual for those steps.)
>
> Instrument operator: **"PLATOON (BATTERY) ADJUST, AIMING POINT THIS INSTRUMENT."**
>
> Gunner of number 3: **"NUMBER 3, AIMING POINT IDENTIFIED."**
>
> Instrument operator: (Using the aiming circle azimuth knob [**upper** motion], the instrument operator turns the aiming circle until the line of sight is on the panoramic telescope of howitzer number 3. The instrument operator reads and announces the deflection to howitzer number 3.) **"NUMBER 3, DEFLECTION 3091."** See TM 9-6675-347-13&P for steps using the GLPS.
>
> Gunner of number 3: **"NUMBER 3, DEFLECTION 3091."**
> (The gunner sets the deflection on the panoramic telescope and traverses the tube until the gunner is sighted on the aiming circle.)
> Gunner of number 3: **"NUMBER 3, READY FOR RECHECK."**
>
> Instrument operator: (The instrument operator again turns the head of the aiming circle until the line of sight is on the panoramic telescope of number 3 and reads and transmits the deflection.) **"NUMBER 3, DEFLECTION 3093."**
>
> Gunner of number 3: **"NUMBER 3, DEFLECTION 3093, 2 MILS."**
> (This indicates a difference of 2 mils from the previous deflection of 3091. The gunner sets 3093 on the panoramic telescope and traverses the tube until the gunner is sighted on the aiming circle.)
> The gunner then transmits: **"NUMBER 3, READY FOR RECHECK."**
>
> Instrument operator: (The instrument operator again turns the head of the aiming circle until the line of sight is on the panoramic telescope of number 3 and reads and transmits the deflection.) **"NUMBER 3, DEFLECTION 3093."**
>
> Gunner of number 3: **"NUMBER 3, DEFLECTION 3093, 0 MILS."**
>
> Instrument operator: **"NUMBER 3 IS LAID."**
>
> Instrument operator (once the entire platoon or the battery is laid): **"THE PLATOON (BATTERY) IS LAID."**

Note. Normally, howitzers are laid in the order of their readiness. <u>When the gunner of any howitzer transmits a difference of 10 mils or less, the instrument operator normally continues to lay that particular howitzer until it is laid.</u> When the deflection announced by the instrument operator and the deflection on the panoramic telescope are identical the howitzer is laid.

LAYING BY ALTERNATE METHODS

4-32. Based on an ever changing tactical environment, situations could arise that would make it impractical or impossible to use the primary methods of lay (orienting angle and grid azimuth). In such cases, the alternate methods of lay will provide the firing unit with other options to establish common direction. The following paragraphs will briefly discuss the alternate methods available and procedures for laying the battery or platoon howitzers for direction.

M2 Compass Method

4-33. This method of laying is normally used during an occupation when a GLPS or an aiming circle is not available or in an emergency fire mission. The instrument operator sets up the M2 compass on a stable object (for example, collimator cover or mattock handle) away from magnetic attractions. The M2 compass should be positioned at least 55 meters from high-tension power lines, 10 meters from large metal objects (for example, railroad tracks, artillery, tanks, and vehicles), 10 meters from small metal objects (for example, barbed wire or telephone), 2 meters from crew-served weapons, and 0.5 meters from personal weapons. Table 4-3 depicts the steps for laying a howitzer when using the M2 compass.

Table 4-3. Laying by M2 compass

SEQUENCE	MEMORY AID – SAM	STEPS
Do this first.	SAM (Subtract the azimuth of fire from the measured azimuth)	Measure the azimuth to the weapon pantel. Math step: Subtract the azimuth of fire from the azimuth measured to the panoramic telescope of the howitzer. Add 6400, if necessary).
Do this second.		Using the proper commands, announce the resulting deflection to the howitzer.
Do this last.		The howitzer that was laid by the M2 compass will lay the rest of the unit reciprocally.
Note. You must use the azimuth to the howitzer measured with the compass and the azimuth of fire.		

4-34. The advantage for this method of lay is that all howitzers will be oriented parallel. The disadvantages are the compass is graduated every 20 mils and can only be read to an accuracy of 10 mils. The accuracy will depend on the ability of the instrument operator. Use the following commands to lay a battery or platoon with the M2 compass.

> **Example**
> The exchange is between the instrument operator and the gunner of howitzer number 3, which was selected to lay the rest of the battery. The deflection announced and the howitzer selected are examples only.
>
> Instrument operator: **"NUMBER 3 ADJUST, AIMING POINT THIS INSTRUMENT, DEFLECTION 3020."**
> (The gunner sets the deflection on the panoramic telescope and traverses the tube until the gunner is sighted on the compass.)
>
> Gunner of number 3: **"NUMBER 3, AIMING POINT IDENTIFIED, DEFLECTION 3020."**
>
> Instrument operator: **"NUMBER 3 IS LAID, PLATOON ADJUST, AIMING POINT NUMBER 3."**
> (The gunner of number 3 will then reciprocally lay the remaining howitzers in the platoon using commands outlined in the example in paragraph 4-31 and recalling to add or subtract 3200 mils as noted in paragraph 4-39).

Aiming Point Deflection Method

4-35. This method of laying is normally used during an emergency fire mission when the need to expedite the mission outweighs the need for first round accuracy. A distant aiming point is required and must be at least 1,500 meters from the position. A compass, or a map and protractor are the only equipment needed. Table 4-4 on page 4-10 depicts the steps for orienting on the distant aiming point.

Chapter 4

Table 4-4. Laying by aiming point deflection method

SEQUENCE	MEMORY AID – AP-BAF	STEPS
Do this first.	AP-BAF (Azimuth to the aiming point minus the back-azimuth of fire)	Subtract the back-azimuth of fire from the azimuth to the aiming point. Add 6400, if necessary.
Do this last.		Using the proper commands, announce the resulting deflection to the unit.
Note. You must use the azimuth to the distant aiming point (at least 1,500 meters away) and the azimuth of fire.		

4-36. The advantage for this method of lay is a very rapid method of lay with only one command required to lay the entire firing element. The disadvantages are a suitable distant aiming point must be available, line of sight may be obscured (for example, smoke, fog, or darkness), and howitzers will not be laid parallel when oriented with a common deflection to an aiming point. Use the following commands to lay a battery or platoon by the aiming point deflection method.

> **Example**
> For brevity, only the exchange between the instrument operator and the gunner of howitzer number 3 are given. In this example, a water tower is selected as the distant aiming point. The deflection announced is an example only.
>
> Instrument operator: **"PLATOON (BATTERY) ADJUST, AIMING POINT WATER TOWER, LEFT FRONT, DEFLECTION 3091."**
>
> (Each gunner sets the deflection on the panoramic telescope and traverses the tube until the gunner is sighted on the distant aiming point.)
> Gunner number 3: **"NUMBER 3, AIMING POINT IDENTIFIED, DEFLECTION 3091."**
>
> Instrument operator: **"NUMBER 3 IS LAID."**
> (When all sections have reported, command: **"THE PLATOON IS LAID."**)

Howitzer Back-Lay Method

4-37. This method of laying is normally used during an emergency fire mission or adjust fire mission. This method should only be used if the grid azimuth and aiming point deflection methods are not possible. A compass and aiming circle are the only equipment needed. Table 4-5 depicts the steps for orienting the aiming circle by howitzer back-lay method.

Table 4-5. Laying by howitzer back-lay method

SEQUENCE	MEMORY AID – ULU	STEPS
Do this first.		Set up the aiming circle where it is visible by all howitzers, and level it.
Do this second.		After the adjusting howitzer fires the first round, command the gunner to refer to the aiming circle.
Do this third.	U	With the azimuth knob (upper motion), place the referred deflection on the aiming circle.
Do this fourth.	L	With the orienting knob (lower motion), sight on the panoramic telescope of the adjusting howitzer.
Do this last.	U	With the azimuth knob (upper motion), lay the rest of the unit.
Note. Using the M2 compass, align engineer tape (a wooden stake at one end and an eyebolt lifting plug at the other) on the azimuth of fire and position the adjusting howitzer alongside (SP) or over (towed) and parallel to the tape. All other howitzers pull on line. The aiming circle is typically emplaced to the left rear of the position area.		
U = upper motion L = lower motion SP = self-propelled		

4-38. The advantages for this method of lay are an immediate firing capability with the adjusting howitzer and the position requires minimal preparation. The disadvantages are the laying process is not as timely as other methods, and if boresight errors exist at the adjusting howitzer, they will be passed along to the remaining howitzers. Use the following commands to lay a battery or platoon by the howitzer back-lay method.

> **Example**
> For brevity, only the exchange between the instrument operator and the gunner of howitzer number 3 are given. The deflection announced is an example only.)
>
> (The FDC transmits firing data to the adjusting howitzer (number 3), and the first round is fired.)
> Instrument operator: "NUMBER 3 IS LAID, NUMBER 3 REFER, AIMING POINT THIS INSTRUMENT."
>
> Gunner number 3: "NUMBER 3, AIMING POINT IDENTIFIED, DEFLECTION 3091."
> (The instrument operator sets the referred DF on the azimuth knob (upper motion) of the aiming circle and with the orienting knob (lower motion) sights on the panoramic telescope of the adjusting piece. The instrument operator will now lay the remaining howitzers using the azimuth knob (upper motion).
>
> Instrument operator: "PLATOON (BATTERY) ADJUST, AIMING POINT THIS INSTRUMENT."
> (The instrument operator will then lay the remaining howitzers. Normally, only one deflection will be read to each howitzer and the howitzer is laid.)

4-39. If all howitzers are not able to see the aiming circle, one howitzer can lay another (reciprocal laying). The commands for laying reciprocally from another howitzer are the same as those given when laying with the aiming circle or gun laying positioning system. When equipped with the M100-series panoramic telescopes, the readings between any two weapons will be 3,200 mils apart. To prevent confusion, the gunner on the laying howitzer adds or subtracts 3,200 mils to or from his reading before announcing it to another howitzer. If the howitzer to which the laying gunner is referring is on his left, the gunner must add 3200. If it is on his right, the gunner must subtract 3200 (left, add; right, subtract rule). See Figure 4-4.

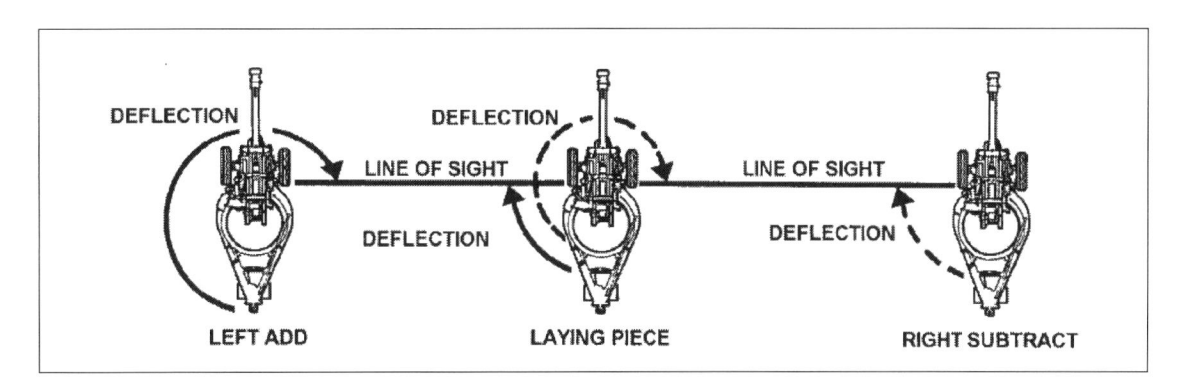

Figure 4-4. Reciprocal laying from another howitzer (M100-series sight)

4-40. Regardless of the method selected to lay the battery, the deflection to each weapon should be recorded by the instrument operator for use by the FDC.

Note: The chief of section supervises the laying process and verifies all data after the gunner lays the howitzer.

SAFETY AND VERIFYING THE LAY OF THE PLATOON (BATTERY)

4-41. Safety and leader verification of tasks exist in the field artillery, regardless of whether operations are in combat or in peacetime. For every task, someone in a leadership position (for example, section chief, platoon sergeant or platoon leader, fire direction officer, or battery commander) verifies the accuracy of the action performed. This system of double checks is inherent in all operations and is not considered a limiting factor in providing timely fire support. Therefore, commanders must ensure that their units have a system of independent safety checks. These safety checks ensure that another individual checks tasks affecting firing (for example, mission processing and orienting howitzers for direction). Although most independent checks take place before firing, performing independent checks is a continuous process that must be rigidly enforced to ensure fires are timely, accurate, and safe. Unit standard operating procedures will dictate what checks are performed. For more information on field artillery safety, see TCs 3-09.8 and 3-09.81.

4-42. The lay of the unit is verified immediately following a deliberate or hasty occupation. The platoon leader or designated safety officer sets up a verification (safety) circle using a method other than that of the lay GLPS or aiming circle. The safety aiming circle must be located where all howitzers can see it and should not be any closer than 10 meters to the lay circle. Care must also be taken not to position the safety circle along the line of sight between a howitzer and the GLPS or aiming circle used to lay the battery.

4-43. After the safety circle is established, command the instrument operator on the GLPS to measure a deflection to the safety circle. The instrument operator on the GLPS determines a deflection to the safety circle and then announces that deflection to the safety circle operator. This procedure serves to verify that the GLPS was oriented properly when it laid the platoon. The tolerance allowed between the deflections of the lay circle and the safety circle must be within 10 mils or can be found in the local range regulations for the firing range in use. Use the stricter tolerance for verification of lay. The unit standard operating procedures will specify the method and sequence of verifying lay (for example, M2 compass) during an emergency occupation.

4-44. If the lay GLPS or lay circle and the safety circle deflections are within tolerance, as specified by the stricter figure of 10 mils or local range regulations, the safety circle instrument operator places the deflection read by the lay circle on the azimuth knob (upper motion) of the safety circle. With the orienting knob (lower motion), the safety circle operator sights back in on the GLPS or lay circle. This aligns the 0-3200 line of the safety circle parallel to the 0-3200 line of the GLPS or lay circle. Table 4-6 depicts the steps for verifying the lay of the platoon or battery.

Note. When an aiming circle is used to orient another aiming circle for direction, the readings between the two circles will be 3200 mils apart because both circles measure horizontal clockwise angle from the line fire. Remember, if the lay circle is a GLPS it does not have a red scale! If the safety circle operator after sighting on the GLPS remembers that, "if you see red, read red" or if the deflection given is greater than 3200 the safety circle operator will have to subtract 3200 the deflection given by the GLPS. The safety circle commands: "**LAY CIRCLE REFER, AIMING POINT THIS INSTRUMENT.**" The lay circle sights on the safety circle, reads the deflection and replies, "**AIMING POINT IDENTIFIED, DEFLECTION XXXX (Lay circle determined instrument reading).**" If the deflection on the safety circle and the aiming circle are within the specified tolerance, set the announced deflection on the safety circle and, using the safety circle's orienting knob (lower motion), sight in on the lay circle.

Table 4-6. Verifying the lay (aiming circle)

SEQUENCE	MEMORY AID – ULU	STEPS
Do this first.	U	With the azimuth knob (upper motion), place the referred deflection on the verification circle.
Do this second.	L	With the orienting knob (lower motion), sight on the lay circle.
Do this last.	U	With the azimuth knob (upper motion), sight on the panoramic telescope of the howitzer.
Note. When an aiming circle is used to verify another aiming circle for direction, the readings between the two circles will be 3,200 mils apart because both circles measure horizontal clockwise angles from the line of fire. To prevent confusion, remember—if you see red, read red.		
U = upper motion L = lower motion		

4-45. The platoon leader or platoon sergeant should walk the gun line and visually check the tubes to ensure they are parallel. An M2 compass should also be used to ensure that the tubes are on the azimuth of fire. The following commands are used to verify the lay of a platoon (battery).

Laying, Measuring, and Reporting

> **Example**
> (The deflection announced is an example only.)
>
> Instrument operator on <u>verification (safety)</u> circle: "**GLPS (OR LAY CIRCLE) REFER, AIMING POINT THIS INSTRUMENT.**"
>
> Instrument operator on GLPS or <u>lay</u> circle: "**AIMING POINT IDENTIFIED, DEFLECTION 3091.**"
>
> Instrument operator on <u>verification (safety)</u> circle: "**PLATOON (BATTERY) REFER, AIMING POINT THIS INSTRUMENT.**"
> (If the deflection referred by a howitzer is within the tolerance given in the standard operating procedures or local range regulations, the instrument operator on the verification (safety) circle transmits that the howitzer is safe: **(example)** "**NUMBER 3 IS SAFE**". When all sections have reported and are within tolerance, command: "**THE PLATOON (BATTERY) IS SAFE.**")

VERTICAL ANGLES

4-46. Normally, vertical angles are measured during advance party operations. The vertical angle and distance from the orienting station to each howitzer are required by the FDC for fire mission processing. The vertical angle to a point is measured from the horizontal plane passing through the horizontal axis of the instrument. The vertical angle is expressed as plus or minus, depending on whether the point is above (plus) or below (minus) the horizontal plane. On an M2A2 aiming circle this correction factor is determined by using the elevation knob to center the tubular leveling vial, then read and record the result (black numbers are plus and red numbers are minus) for use in determining the vertical angle. The vertical angle is measured to the height of the instrument—about chest high on the average individual at the howitzer position. When measuring the vertical angle, elevate or depress the telescope to place the horizontal cross hair on the instrument. Read and record the value on the elevation and elevation micrometer scales to the nearest mil. Apply correction factors and report measurements to the FDC.

SECTION III – MEASURING AND REPORTING DATA

4-47. The accuracy of lay is directly related to the method used to orient the howitzers on the azimuth of fire and the alignment of the fire control equipment. Measuring and reporting data provides a means of correction for errors in the lay. The FDC may require a check of direction. Normally, this check is made after registration or establishing survey control to check the data fired and the accuracy of lay. Verify direction by reporting the correct deflection, measuring the azimuth, or measuring the orienting angle. Reporting will reveal improper procedures used by the gun crews (for example, failure to center bubbles or improper sight picture). Measuring will check the accuracy of the lay. **The *registering piece* is the howitzer that is designated by the fire direction center to conduct a registration fire mission**.

Note. These checks must be made before "END OF MISSION" is received at the howitzer.

BACKWARD AZIMUTH RULE

4-48. The backward azimuth rule is a mathematical relationship used to apply equal changes in angles used in the laying process. This rule establishes the relationship between deflection, azimuth, and orienting angle. Therefore, an increase in deflection causes an equal decrease in azimuth and an equal increase in orienting angle. Conversely, a decrease in deflection causes an equal increase in azimuth and an equal decrease in orienting angle.

REPORTING THE CORRECT DEFLECTION

4-49. Upon completing a mission and before announcing "END OF MISSION", the FDC may request that the platoon leader or platoon sergeant report the correct deflection. The platoon leader or platoon sergeant goes to the howitzer and verifies the sight picture. It may be necessary to center the bubbles or correct the sight picture. The deflection read from the panoramic telescope is reported to the FDC. The azimuth, orienting angle, and deflection announced are examples only. Table 4-7 depicts the steps for reporting the correct deflection.

Table 4-7. Reporting the correct deflection

SEQUENCE	STEPS
Do this first.	Go to the howitzer.
Do this second.	Check to ensure that the bubbles on the sight mount are centered. If they are not, center them with the pitch and cross level control knobs.
Do this third.	Check the sight picture. If incorrect, correct it by moving the head of the panoramic telescope only. **Do not traverse the tube**.
Do this last.	Read and report the deflection on the panoramic telescope.

4-50. The following command is used to report the correct deflection. The deflection announced is an example only.

> **Example**
> The platoon is laid on azimuth 5,000 (orienting angle 0600) with a common deflection of 3,200. After firing a registration, the FDC requests that the platoon leader report the correct deflection. The platoon leader completes the required checks, and reports **"CORRECT DEFLECTION 3250."**

MEASURING THE AZIMUTH OF THE LINE OF FIRE

4-51. If a howitzer fires out of safe, the platoon leader or battery commander may wish to determine the azimuth at which the round was fired. This is the most common reason for measuring the azimuth of the line of fire. There are two methods of measuring the azimuth of the line of fire. The method used depends on the availability of survey control. If measuring the line of fire following a firing incident, the crew of the howitzer in question will not move the tube, but simply refer. Otherwise, the tube of the howitzer being measured is at lay deflection.

> **Example using an M2A2 aiming circle**
> Instrument operator: (Orients the 0-3200 line generally parallel with the tube of the weapon.)
> Commands: "**NUMBER (number of howitzer) REFER, AIMING POINT THIS INSTRUMENT.**"
>
> Howitzer gunner: (Measures with the panoramic telescope the deflection to the aiming circle without moving his tube.) Announces: "**NUMBER (number of howitzer), AIMING POINT IDENTIFIED, DEFLECTION 0963 (example number).**"
>
> Instrument operator: (Sets the announced deflection on the upper [recording motion] of the aiming circle. With the lower (non-recording) motion, sights in on the panoramic telescope.
> *Note:* The 0-3200 line of the aiming circle is now parallel to the tube of the firing weapon.)
>
> The final step at the aiming circle depends on whether survey control is available.
> If survey control is not available:
> (1) The platoon leader, with the azimuth knob (upper motion), floats and centers the magnetic needle. *Note*: Since the magnetic needle is being used, the aiming circle must be declinated and set up away from magnetic attractions.
> (2) The value now on the azimuth knob (upper motion) is the instrument reading. Subtract the instrument reading from the declination constant. The difference is the azimuth of the line of fire.
>
> If survey control is available, the following is the final step:
> (1) The platoon leader with the azimuth knob (upper motion), sights in on the end of the orienting line.
> (2) The value now on the azimuth knob scale (upper motion) is the orienting angle. Subtract the orienting angle from the azimuth of the orienting line. The difference is the azimuth of the line of fire.
>
> You have two options at this point:
> •Leave the platoon laid on the determined azimuth of the line of fire based on the reported deflection (in this case, **0963**) and have the FDC correct its computer entries for azimuth of fire and piece locations.
> •Re-lay the platoon on the originally intended azimuth.
> *Note.* The first option requires less time and effort and is thus normally preferred if the tubes were laid parallel. However, if the unit was laid by an alternate method of lay where the tubes are not truly parallel, then re-laying would be preferred.

CORRECTING BORESIGHT ERROR

4-52. If the battery or platoon is to deliver accurate fire, the boresight of the weapon must be correct. Boresighting is the process of ensuring that the optical axis of the weapon sights are parallel to the cannon tube. The primary methods of boresighting are the distant aiming point, test target, and standard angle.

4-53. If a howitzer is not in boresight, the tube is disoriented in relation to the amount of boresight error. If the sight is off to the right, the tube is disoriented by that amount to the left. If the sight is off to the left, the tube reflects that error to the right.

4-54. Once a weapon is properly boresighted, the deflection to an aiming point (aiming circle, GLPS, or collimator) is reestablished. The angle (deflection) between aiming point and pantel has not changed from when the weapon was laid. The entire angle has simply rotated by the amount of boresight error. Since the angle has not changed, the deflection recorded to the aiming point is set off on the pantel and the tube is traversed onto the aiming point. The relationship made at the time of lay is now reestablished. It is improper, after correcting for boresight error, to move (or fine tune) the aiming point to the tube in relation to the deflection (numbers) originally established at the time of lay.

4-55. Emergency occupation of a firing position may require firing before boresight is verified and any error is corrected. In such cases, the howitzers must verify boresight as soon as possible. If this verification discloses an error (the 0-3200 line of the pantel and the howitzer tube are not parallel) the platoon leader takes corrective actions after measuring the error and reporting it to the fire direction center (FDC).

Chapter 4

4-56. When a deflection is read from the pantel or when an azimuth is measured, the deflection or azimuth determined is that of the 0-3200 line of the pantel as read from the azimuth counter. When the FDC requests the platoon leader to "**MEASURE THE AZIMUTH**", the azimuth requested is that of the howitzer tube. If the howitzer is out of boresight, the data derived is inaccurate by the amount of the error.

> *Note.* If the howitzer in question was used to lay the aiming circle or the rest of the howitzers, the other howitzers are out of lay by the amount of error found. The platoon leader should take immediate corrective action to orient them on the correct azimuth of lay (after all howitzers have verified boresight).

Verifying boresight

4-57. Verify howitzer boresight. This can be done with an alignment device or other means such as distant aiming point or test target.

Howitzers with an alignment device

4-58. The azimuth counter (not the reset counter) and the appropriate alignment device are used when verifying boresight. The numerical error of boresight can be determined from the azimuth counter. The amount of error is the difference between the required deflection for the alignment device (according to the operator's manual) and the deflection read (on the azimuth counter) once the vertical hairline has been aligned.

4-59. Use the backwards azimuth rule to determine the correct azimuth of the howitzer tube. Once the error has been measured and reported, the platoon leader directs the following actions to be taken to correct the error:
- Boresight the weapon.
- Correct the azimuth of lay and piece location in the FDC or re-lay the piece.

Howitzers without an alignment device

4-60. Use the azimuth scale during boresighting. The tube is pointed at the aiming point when a DAP or test target is used. If the sight is pointed to the right of the aiming point the tube is pointed to the left of the 0-3200 line of sight. Before this correction is made, any azimuth measured will be greater than the azimuth of the tube and any orienting angle will be smaller than the true orienting angle. (The opposite relationship also exists.)

4-61. The amount of error is determined by referring the sight to the aiming point and reading the deflection. This deflection is compared with the deflection used for boresighting and the difference is the amount of error in boresight. The orienting station operator applies the appropriate correction for the boresight error to the measured azimuth or orienting angle prior to reporting to the FDC. The orienting station operator corrects the lay of the pieces as required.

MEASURING WITH THE GUN LAYING AND POSITIONING SYSTEM

4-62. Perform these steps with the GLPS and the howitzer panoramic telescope. The GLPS operator obtains the howitzer's referred deflection to measure the azimuth of fire, line of fire or measured azimuth of the howitzer tube. Table 4-8 depicts the steps for using the GLPS to measure the azimuth.

Laying, Measuring, and Reporting

Table 4-8. Measuring the azimuth with a gun laying and positioning system

SEQUENCE	MEMORY AID	STEPS
Note. With survey control – the GLPS uses the "Input Location" or "Back Polar Plot" option to enter the GLPS location at an orienting station, survey control point, or survey location provided from battalion.		
Do this first.		Select the Lay by Azimuth option on the GLPS and measure an azimuth to the identified howitzer's panoramic telescope.
Do this second.		Command the howitzer to refer to the GLPS.
Do this third.		Subtract the referred deflection from measured azimuth (adding 6400 mils If necessary). The remainder is the measured azimuth.
Do this fourth.		Math step: Subtract the howitzer's referred deflection from the gun laying and positioning system's measured azimuth to the howitzer's panoramic telescope. *The GLPS measured azimuth to the howitzer minus (-) the howitzer's referred deflection = the measured angle (the azimuth of fire or line of fire).*
Do this last.		Report the measured azimuth to the FDC.
Note. You must use the deflection given to you from the howitzer.		
Note. Without survey control – global positioning system data from the precision lightweight global positioning system receiver is the primary method for determining the position of the gun laying and positioning system when survey data is not available.		

MEASURING WITH AN AIMING CIRCLE

4-63. Table 4-9 depicts the steps for measuring the azimuth. Steps both with and without survey control are provided.

Table 4-9. Measuring the azimuth with an aiming circle

SEQUENCE	MEMORY AID	STEPS
With Survey Control – ULU-SOL		
Do this first.	U	With the azimuth knob (upper motion), place the referred deflection on the aiming circle.
Do this second.	L	With the orienting knob (lower motion), sight on the howitzer panoramic telescope.
Do this third.	U	With the azimuth knob (upper motion), sight on the EOL.
Do this fourth.	SOL (Subtract the orienting angle from the orienting line.)	Math step: Subtract the orienting angle (on the aiming circle) from the azimuth of the orienting line.
Do this last.		Report the measured azimuth to the FDC.
Note. You must use the deflection given to you from the howitzer.		
Without Survey Control – ULU-SID		
SEQUENCE	MEMORY AID	STEPS
Do this first.	U	With the azimuth knob (upper motion), place the referred deflection on the aiming circle.
Do this second.	L	With the orienting knob (lower motion), sight on the howitzer panoramic telescope.
Do this third.	U	With the azimuth knob (upper motion), float and center the magnetic needle.
Do this fourth.	SID (Subtract the instrument reading from the declination constant.)	Math step: Subtract the instrument reading (on the aiming circle) from the declination constant.
Do this last.		Report the measured azimuth to the FDC.
Note. You must use the deflection given to you by the howitzer and the declination constant recorded for the instrument.		
EOL - end of the orienting line U = upper motion		L = lower motion

4-64. The following commands are used with either the GLPS or the aiming circle to measure the azimuth of the line of fire. Steps to follow when measuring with the pantel are in table 4-10 on page 4-18.

Chapter 4

> **Example**
> Instrument operator: "NUMBER 3 (number of howitzer) REFER, AIMING POINT THIS INSTRUMENT."
> Gunner Number 3: "NUMBER 3, AIMING POINT IDENTIFIED, DEFLECTION (so much)."

Table 4-10. Measuring deflection with the panoramic telescope

SEQUENCE	STEPS
Do this first.	Go to the howitzer.
Do this second.	Check to ensure the bubbles on the sight mount are level. If they are not, level them with the leveling knobs.
Do this third.	Check the sight picture. If incorrect, correct it by moving the head of the panoramic telescope only. Do not traverse the tube.
Do this last.	Read and report the deflection on the panoramic telescope.

BORESIGHT VERIFICATION

4-65. If the battery or platoon is to deliver accurate fires, the boresight of the howitzer must be correct. Boresighting is the process of ensuring that the optical axis of the weapon sights is parallel to the cannon tube. The primary methods of boresighting are distant aiming point, test target, and standard angle. If a howitzer is not in boresight, the tube is disoriented in relation to the amount of boresight error. If the sight is off to the right, the tube is disoriented by that amount to the left. If the sight is off to the left, the tube reflects that error to the right. Howitzer sections verify boresight as part of occupation procedures. Howitzers sections will follow the boresight procedures outlined in the applicable howitzer TM. Emergency occupation of a firing position may require firing before the boresight is verified. In such cases, the howitzers must verify boresight as soon as possible. If this verification discloses an error (for example, the 0-3200 line of the panoramic telescope and the howitzer tube are not parallel), immediate corrective action is taken after measuring the error and reporting it to the FDC.

> *Note.* If the howitzer in question was used to lay the aiming circle or the rest of the howitzers, the other howitzers are out of lay by the amount of error found. The platoon leader should take corrective action to orient them on the correct azimuth of lay after all howitzers have verified boresight.

SECTION IV – FDC-HOWITZER COMMUNICATIONS

4-66. Although the AFATDS now conducts primarily tactical fire control, circumstances may arise where the FDC still provides technical fire control for the howitzers. The FDC uses fire commands to provide howitzer sections with information necessary to initiate and cease firing. Fire commands can be issued digitally or by voice. The communications used will be based on unit standard operating procedures and mission variables.

TYPES OF COMMUNICATIONS

4-67. Digital communications are the primary method of field artillery communications. Voice communications are available as a back-up means.

Laying, Measuring, and Reporting

DIGITAL

4-68. Units equipped with advanced digitized equipment at the FDC and howitzers use digital fire missions. The AFATDS or equivalent transmits the digital fire missions from the FDC to the howitzers. The howitzer's digital fire control system receives and displays the fire mission data. The fire mission display contains the menu, information, and data entry areas required for operating the howitzer's digital fire control system. The specific data shown in this area is dependent on the functions being performed. Various instructions and warnings will appear in this area, as necessary. See TMs 9-2350-314-10-1 and 9-2350-314-10-2 for the M109-series howitzer, TM 9-1025-215-10 for the M777-series howitzer, and TM 9-1015-260-10 for the M119-series howitzer for further information on use of the howitzers' digital fire control systems.

4-69. Establishing digital communications is vital. Initialization and howitzer database checks occur whenever the digital fire control is first turned on, in accordance with procedures found in the howitzer operators manual. These include entering communications parameters and navigation system initialization. Unit standard operating procedures should list explicitly those settings to be made at the howitzer. The platoon leaders assisted by the gunnery sergeants and platoon sergeants will verify each howitzer's initialization data base and at a minimum, these leaders will verify the initialization grid Easting, Northing, azimuth, and communication parameters. They will report this information to the FDC and ensure verification that the correct data has been sent.

4-70. To ensure the FDC and howitzer sections have the correct digital fire control and radio settings, the FDC should prepare a communications parameter card (see table 4-11) for each howitzer during pre-combat checks. Parameter cards should then be treated similar to safety T's, with any changes reported to all subscribers. Platoon leadership checks to ensure changes are recorded and applied.

Table 4-11. Howitzer parameter card example.

Net Access	Net Address
Communication configuration: _____. Number of stations: _____. Use net busy detect: No (default) Yes (Circle desired setting). Intranet relayer: Disable (default) Enable (Circle desired setting). N-layer pass through: Enabled (default) Disabled (Circle desired setting).	Gun section/platoon: _____/_____. DFC URN: _____. FDC (P) URN: _____. FDC (B) URN: _____. DFC Rank: _____. FDC (P) Rank: _____. FDC (B) Rank: _____. Controlling FDC: _____.
Digital net: _____. Voice net: _____. Backup digital net: _____. Backup voice net: _____. Data rate: _____. PT/CT: _____.	Spheroid: _____. Datum: _____. Time zone: _____.
B – backup CT – cipher text DFC – digital fire control FDC – fire direction center	N-layer – software logical architecture division of components or functionality P – primary PT – plain text URN – uniform resource name

4-71. The FDC initializes the AFATDS in accordance with the applicable technical bulletin and the standard operating procedures. The fire direction officer will verify that all entries made by the AFATDS operator are correct.

4-72. The FDC ideally will be operational before the howitzers are initialized. Then once the howitzers have initialized the first check of digital communications will be the howitzer transmitting its position and status to the FDC and the resultant acknowledgement. If this does not work, the howitzer crew, FDC, and platoon leadership must begin communications troubleshooting procedures. Once the position and status message is successfully passed, the FDC should verify that the location data is what was expected.

VOICE

4-73. Units without a digital capability must use voice fire commands. Units also use voice fire commands if the digital equipment malfunctions. To facilitate voice commands, the FDC provides the fire command standards to the section chief after occupation of the position. Fire command standards are discussed in the main paragraph below.

DEGRADED DIGITAL

4-74. Digital communications are the primary means for transmitting fire commands. If digital communication is lost or degraded, digital communications must be reestablished as soon as possible. An alternative to voice communications is degraded digital communication. Degraded digital communication uses the AFATDS purely as a technical fire direction computer and transmits the fire command by voice. If one howitzer in the battery or platoon loses digital communications, the FDC will issue voice commands to that howitzer. If two or more howitzers lose digital communications, the FDC may direct all howitzers to use degraded mode. The howitzers will then ignore gun display unit data and take fire commands by voice only.

4-75. See ATP 3-09.23 for information on the communications nets in which the field artillery operates. See chapter 7 for information on the fire commands used by the howitzers.

RECORD OF MISSIONS FIRED

4-76. The Department of the Army (DA) Form 4513 is used by the howitzer section to record fire commands (digital or voice), ammunition (for example, on hand, fired, transferred, or resupplied), and any standardized data. After this form is completed, the information is used primarily for computing remaining tube life on the DA Form 2408-4. All elements of this form must be recorded neatly and accurately. For more information on the record and maintenance of fire mission data on DA Form 4513, see Appendix D.

Chapter 5
Battery Defense

This chapter discusses techniques and associated considerations for battery defense. Section I begins with a discussion of threat capabilities and battery responsibilities for the defense. Section II discusses techniques and associated considerations for the defense. Section III closes with a discussion on techniques and associated considerations unique to specific threats.

SECTION I – CONSIDERATIONS

5-1. The reconnaissance, selection, and occupation of the position are complete. Now the battery must prepare an adequate defense in order to survive and provide continuous fire support to the maneuver commander. A defense is more effective when there is adequate time to thoroughly plan and prepare defensive positions. For more information on defense or security operations, see Field Manual (FM) 3-90-1 or ATP 3-21.8

THREAT CAPABILITIES

5-2. Threat forces direct actions against the field artillery to affect the ability to deliver fires. Threat forces may try to detect field artillery elements through the study of doctrine and the processing of information collected by using reconnaissance and surveillance as sources of information. Personal communication devices, such as cellular phones, permit untrained observers or irregular forces to report unit positions for targeting. In addition to visual observation, predicted activities, bumper markings, and leftover rubbish add to the collection of information supporting the threat targeting effort. However, the greatest threats to the field artillery battery come from counterfire, air attack, and ground attack. The battery commander must analyze the intelligence preparation of the battlefield and develop an overall defensive plan to mitigate these threats.

BATTERY RESPONSIBILITIES

5-3. The battery commander is responsible for general planning, coordination, and execution of the battery defense. By thoroughly analyzing mission variables, the battery commander gains an understanding of the tactical situation and identifies potential friendly and threat weaknesses. The battery commander must graphically portray to his subordinate leaders how the commander intends to defend the position. This information will aid the platoon leaders in developing a plan to defend the platoon. The first sergeant is responsible for the overall execution of the battery defense. The first sergeant integrates the platoon defense plans into an overall battery defense. This may not be feasible if the platoons disperse over a significant distance (distributed unit). The battery defense plan must be submitted to the battalion headquarters so the operations sergeant can integrate all firing battery defense plans into the overall battalion defense plan. A unit defense checklist may aid in the defense preparations. A sample unit defense checklist is discussed in appendix B of this publication.

SECTION II – DEFENSE

5-4. The battery commander will undertake actions to provide for early and accurate warning of threat activities. This will protect the battery from surprise and reduce the unknowns in any situation. Unit

Chapter 5

standard operating procedures must contain provisions for battery self-defense. These include gunnery techniques such as firing Killer Junior (time fuzed, high explosive rounds fired in direct fire) on dismounted avenues of approach and flechette (antipersonnel-tracer) rounds for perimeter defense. This section briefly discusses techniques and associated considerations for battery defense. See chapter 9 and appendix F for information on Killer Junior.

TECHNIQUES FOR THE DEFENSE

5-5. A battle will never go exactly as planned, so the battery commander and platoon leaders must remain flexible and respond quickly to the unexpected. They must continuously evaluate mission variables and be prepared to deal with unplanned situations. Battery and platoon standard operating procedures should be developed and followed to maintain control during the defense. The battery commander or platoon leader should consider the amount of time required to prepare the defense and issue priorities of work to the Soldiers. The tasks assigned and their priority will depend on requirements to defend the position or displace in the event of an attack. Unit tactical standard operating procedures should dictate actual work priorities involved in position improvement. Position improvement is a continuous process. The following paragraphs will briefly discuss the techniques available and associated considerations for executing a battery defense.

USE TERRAIN

5-6. A concealed or unrecognizable battery has greater odds of survival. Occupying positions that offer cover and concealment will aid the battery in avoiding detection. Use any terrain and natural concealment available to blend into the surroundings. Use available camouflage (for example, trees, shrubs, buildings, and lightweight screening systems) to hide equipment and not contrast with the natural surroundings. Maintain noise and light discipline throughout operation. Use the track plan, because the most common signs of military activity in an otherwise well camouflaged area are tracks, disrupted soil, and debris associated with movement. Use the terrain by occupying positions that have natural advantages for the defense (for example, interior tree lines and ravines). Harden battery positions and dig in whenever possible. If possible, construct obstacles to delay, stop, divert, or canalize an attack force. Once emplaced, these obstacles should be covered by fire. In fast moving situations, or when emergency displacement is anticipated, hardening might be limited to digging fighting positions on the perimeter, placing sandbags around sensitive equipment (for example, collimators and tires), and constructing survivability positions.

PROVIDE FOR EARLY WARNING

5-7. Plan the unit's defense laterally and in depth so the unit is warned of an impending attack soon enough to displace or defend the position. Coordinate with adjacent units to provide early warning of enemy attacks. Observation posts and listening posts are key elements for providing early warning. When determining the location for observation posts and listening posts, consider terrain, visibility, likely threats, and the time required by the battery or platoon to displace or occupy preselected fighting positions. Observation posts should allow observation of likely avenues of approach, so personnel can engage the threat at maximum ranges. Observation posts must allow for quick identification of target reference points and targets in avenues of approach and communication to higher headquarters.

DEFEND IN DEPTH

5-8. The howitzer battery or platoon is most vulnerable to attack during the occupation of and displacement from a position. The first consideration for either is establishing security. Each section will have a predetermined sector of responsibility. This sector of fire must maximize the use of primary weapons and ensure there is a coordinated 6,400-mil defense with interlocking fires. The defense plan is visually depicted by a defense diagram, to be discussed later in this section. The defense diagram includes the fields of fire for the howitzer cannon, antitank weapons, crew served weapons, and individual weapons. If howitzer sections are dispersed over great distances, the section may become responsible for its own defense. This requires the section to defend itself until help arrives. If the unit is attacked or penetrated by threat forces, a reaction force may be required. This reaction force responds by assembling at a predetermined location to assess the situation and deploys to augment the existing perimeter. The reaction force deploys using fire and maneuver techniques to expel or destroy the threat and reestablish the perimeter. Composition of the reaction force is mission variable dependent and tactical standard operating procedures driven. Based on personnel strength levels, the unit may not be able to fully man an effective defensive perimeter and provide continuous fires. Battery personnel should be trained on basic and advanced warfighting skills that were formally exclusive to the infantry. For more information on warfighting skills, see Soldier Training Publication (STP) 21-1-SMCT and STP 21-24-SMCT.

DISPERSE

5-9. Dispersion laterally and in depth minimizes the effects of an air attack or counterfire, but the unit becomes more susceptible to dismounted infantry and individual threat combatants. The battery commander will determine the method of employment and formation for howitzers and other support vehicles, based on mission variables. Howitzer sections should be positioned at least 100 meters apart, with the fire direction center (FDC) an even greater distance to the rear or either flank of the formation.

DEFENSE DIAGRAM

5-10. Another technique used in the conduct of a defense, is the defense diagram. The defense diagram graphically portrays the position with respect to the azimuth of fire. The defense diagram displays section positions, defensive positions (for example, sectors of fire, target reference points, and adjacent units), and key terrain. The defense diagram illustrates 6,400-mil coverage for the battery. The defense diagram identifies terrain, vehicles, weapon systems, and sectors of fire, which include:

- Dominant terrain features.
- Dead space.
- Target reference points.
- Range markers.
- Observation and listening posts.
- Howitzer direct fire sectors.
- Crew served weapons sectors of fire.
- Fire direction centers.

5-11. The platoon sergeant establishes the sectors of fire for the platoon. When these sectors have been determined and assigned, each section will construct a range card for each weapon system position (for example, howitzer, machine gun, grenade launcher, or antitank team). The sections will continually update and revise range cards throughout the occupation of a position. Battery leaders should verify that range cards are properly constructed and maintained.

Note. A sample Department of the Army (DA) Form 5699, *Howitzer Range Card*, is at Appendix D (Figure D-6 on page D-12). For information on DA Form 5517, *Standard Range Card*, for other weapons and sector sketches, see ATP 3-21.8.

5-12. Once the range cards are completed, the information is used to construct the sectors of fire on the defense diagram. The objective is a completed defense diagram with pertinent data for the platoon defense. The methods for constructing a matrix on which to draw the diagram vary. The key is to pick a scale suitable for plotting the grid locations for the unit. The matrix may be a commercially produced item, or one developed by the user. The most important thing to remember is that the matrix should accurately reflect conditions on the ground. The FDC has preprinted grid sheets, which are scaled to 1:25,000. Each grid square represents 1,000 meters on these sheets. Other map scales are available for use in constructing a matrix. For example, each grid square may represent 500 meters (1:12,500) or each square may represent 200 meters (1:5,000). For the purposes of this discussion, the matrix scales in the following examples are 1:5,000 (figure 5-1 on page 5-4).

Chapter 5

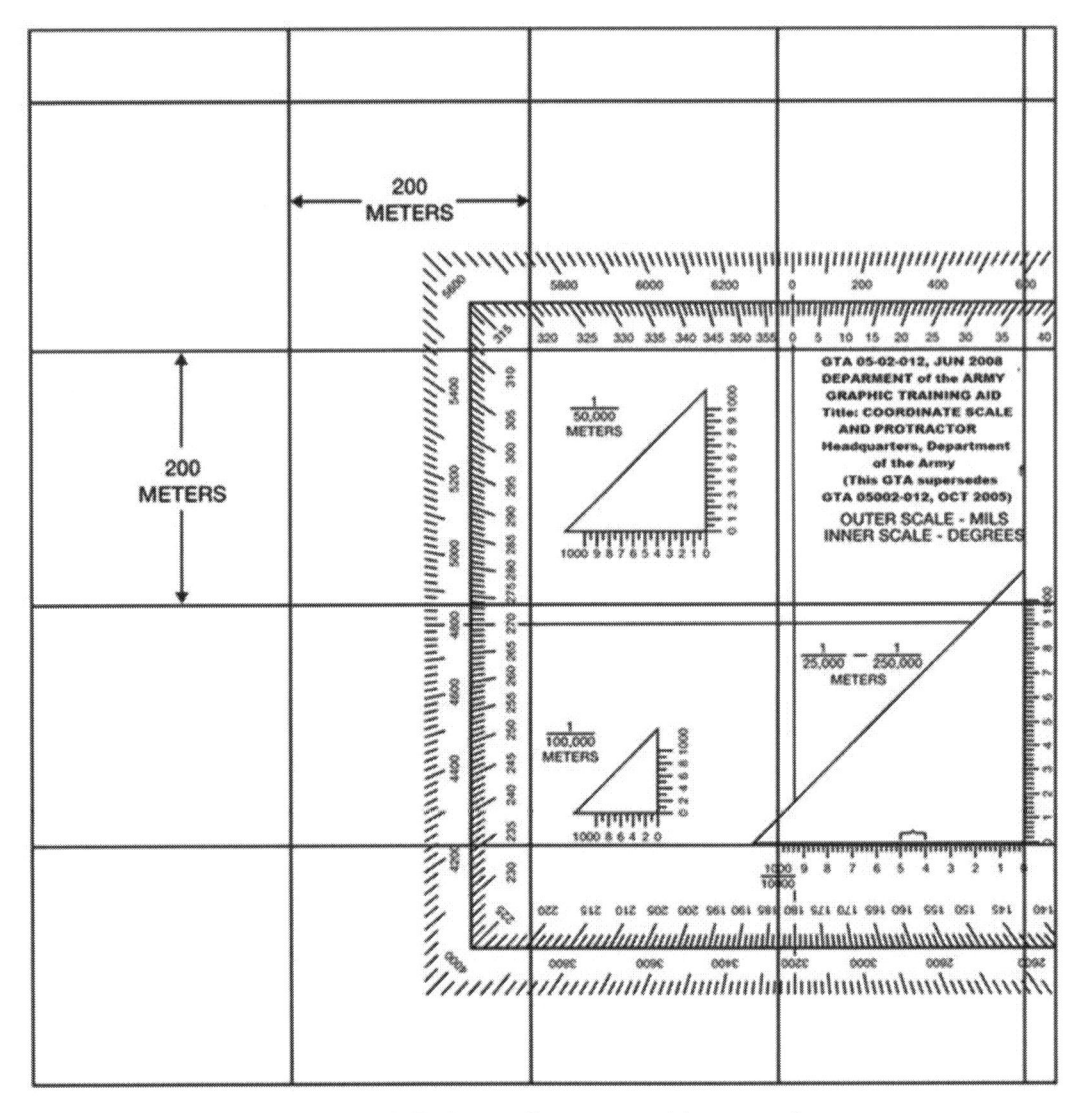

Figure 5-1. Defense diagram matrix example

5-13. The steps used in constructing a defense diagram are based on user preference and experience level. These steps may or may not be done in sequential order, for example:
- Add easting and northing grid line identifications (figure 5-2).
- Add terrain features, to include dead space.
- Draw the azimuth of fire to orient the diagram.
- Plot the required positions (for example, howitzers, FDC, observation and listening posts, target reference points, crew-served weapons, tank-killer team positions, and Killer Junior targets).
- Draw sectors of fire for howitzers and crew-served weapons (figure 5-3 on page 5-6).

- Record related information with grid locations on the back of the defense diagram (table 5-1 on page 5-7).
- Verify that the defense diagram graphically portrays the battery commander's defensive plan.

Note. Grid coordinates may be obtained from the FDC computer, global positioning system receivers, or a map spot.

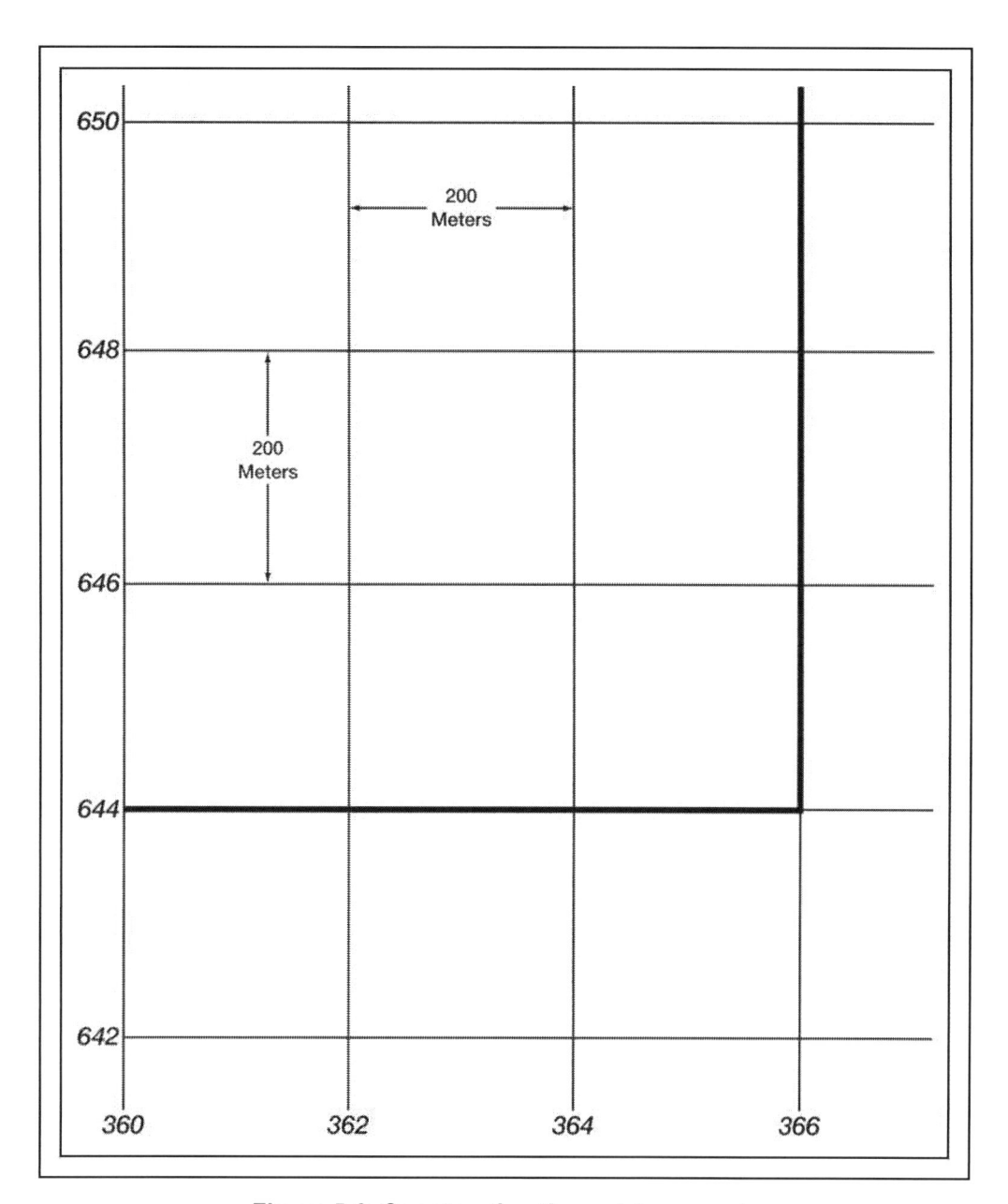

Figure 5-2. Constructing the matrix example

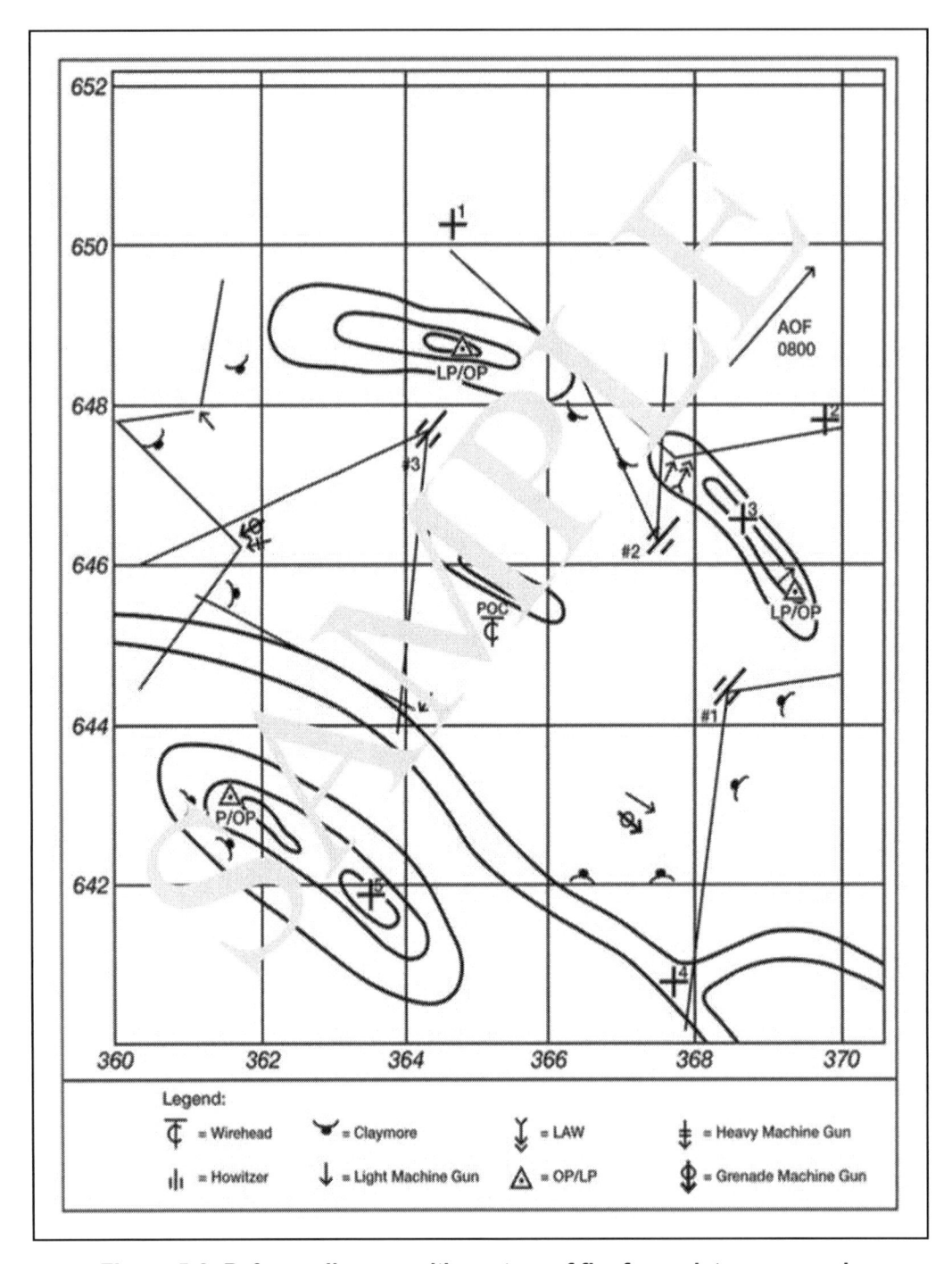

Figure 5-3. Defense diagram with sectors of fire for a platoon example

Note. The legend is customized for user preference, to include symbols and their associated description (for example, M136 AT4 or similar light antitank weapon; azimuth of fire; POC; observation posts and listening posts). For more information on symbols and graphics, see Army Doctrine Reference Publication (ADRP) 1-02.

Table 5-1. Example related information

\multicolumn{4}{c}{Unit: 1/A/2-81 FA 4}
\multicolumn{4}{c}{May 2016: 12 March}
\multicolumn{4}{c}{2014 Scale: 1:5,000}
\multicolumn{4}{c}{*Platoon Fire Support Defensive Targets*}
GRID	ALTITUDE	DESCRIPTION	REMARKS
1 - 36476504	400	Dead Space	Killer Junior #3
2 - 36986478	400	Dead Space	Killer Junior #1
3 - 36876468	450	Hilltop	HE/Q
4 - 36776408	400	Road Junction	DPICM
5 - 36356419	470	Hilltop	HE/Q
6 -			
7 -			
8 -			
9 -			
10 -			

Notes
Air defense team located at grid 388642.

Legend:
HE = high explosive
Q = fuze quick
DPICM = dual purpose improved conventional munitions

5-14. The defense diagram is completed based on guidance from the battery commander or first sergeant and unit tactical standard operating procedures. The gunnery sergeant initiates the defense diagram, to include howitzer locations, terrain sketch, and initial defensive positions, during the advance party operations. Once the main body occupies the new position, the gunnery sergeant submits the defense diagram to the platoon sergeant for completion or verification. The first sergeant collects completed platoon diagrams and integrates them into the overall battery defense diagram. The defense diagrams are continuously updated as the battery improves the defenses. The completed battery defense diagram and updates are forwarded to the battalion command post for use in development of a battalion defense plan.

SECTION III – THREAT

5-15. This section briefly discusses techniques and associated defensive preparations and considerations unique to specific threats. Those actions unique to a specific type of threat are addressed in the appropriate paragraph below. The battery commander and subordinate leaders must understand the differences in these threats and the implications for the battery. Any action or response to a threat will be based on mission variables and unit tactical standard operating procedures.

5-16. For examples of sample mission checklists, see Appendix B. For more information on defensive control measures or defensive planning considerations, see FM 3-90-1 and ADRP 3-90.

DEFENSE AGAINST ARMORED OR MECHANIZED FORCES

5-17. The preferred defense technique against an armored or mechanized ground attack is for the battery or platoon to displace to an alternate position and continue the mission. Direct confrontation with this type of force is not advised. In some circumstances, this may be unavoidable. When attack is imminent, direct all howitzer crews to prepare for direct fire. The unit tactical standard operating procedures should address the method of control for direct fire engagements. Consider the use of illumination during periods of limited visibility. The perimeter security must be alert to defend against lightly armored vehicles (for example, light trucks with armed threat personnel) with crew served weapons. Tank-killer teams should be used in pairs for increased lethality against heavier armored vehicles. Actions to defend against armored and mechanized forces should be exercised to maintain proficiency.

DEFENSE AGAINST AIR ATTACK

5-18. The preferred defense technique against air attack is for the battery or platoon to remain undetected. If detected and attacked, the key to survival is dispersing and engaging the attacking aircraft with a large volume of fire. Accuracy is not as important as mass during the attack. When attack is imminent, direct all sections to prepare for air attack. The unit tactical standard operating procedures should address the method of control for air engagements. Consider the use of air target reference points (for example, dominant terrain features, or identifiable objects) to mass crew served weapons and provide a wall of fire against the threat. Actions to defend against air attack should be exercised to maintain proficiency.

DEFENSE AGAINST DISMOUNTED ATTACK

5-19. The preferred defense technique against a dismounted attack is for the battery or platoon to engage the threat outside the perimeter. When attack is imminent, direct all howitzer crews to prepare for ground attack. The unit tactical standard operating procedures should address the method of control for engagements. Consider the use of illumination during periods of limited visibility. The perimeter security must be alert to defend against ambushes, dismounted infantry, and guerilla type attacks. These types of attacks are normally preceded by a diversionary attack, followed by the main attack. The use of mines, barbed or concertina wire, and other obstacles will aid in the defense effort. Plan for Killer Junior missions on dismounted avenues of approach. Verify fighting positions provide interlocking sectors of fire. Actions to defend against dismounted attacks should be exercised to maintain proficiency.

DEFENSE AGAINST INDIRECT FIRE

5-20. Indirect fire is the greatest threat to the field artillery. The preferred defense technique against indirect fire is a combination of dispersion, hardening, and survivability movements. Dispersion requires the least effort and time. If the ground threat or terrain makes dispersion impractical, then hardening the position will increase survivability. Survivability moves decrease vulnerability to counterfire, but take time and may limit the unit's ability to provide fire support. The unit tactical standard operating procedures should address the method of control and movement criteria for movement within the position. Actions to defend against indirect fire should be exercised to maintain proficiency.

DEFENSE AGAINST CHEMICAL, BIOLOGICAL, RADIOLOGICAL, AND NUCLEAR ATTACK

5-21. The preferred defense technique against a chemical, biological, radiological, and nuclear (CBRN) hazard is to practice avoidance. If avoidance is not possible, protection should be the focus. The unit tactical standard operating procedures should address CBRN operations. The battery and platoon should rehearse CBRN reconnaissance and surveillance tasks, protective measures, immediate action, decontamination procedures, and warning and reporting procedures as time permits. Actions to defend against CBRN attack should be exercised regularly to maintain proficiency. For more information on CBRN operations, see FM 3-11 or FM 3-11.3 respectively.

Chapter 6
Hasty Survey Techniques

This chapter discusses techniques and associated considerations for hasty survey. Section I begins with a brief discussion of the elements of survey control. Section II discusses techniques and associated considerations available to establish directional control. Section III closes with a discussion on techniques and associated considerations for determining location.

SECTION I – SURVEY CONTROL

6-1. Common grid reduces the amount of survey error between firing units, and is required to accurately mass fires. However, accurate survey data may not always be available due to mission variables. Registration can eliminate errors in firing caused by a lack of survey control, but registration may not be possible or practical due to security or ammunition requirements. Consequently, battery leaders must be proficient in the hasty survey techniques discussed in this chapter.

> *Note.* Units equipped with the gun laying and positioning system (GLPS) have an organic capability to establish an orienting station and end of the orienting line for the unit.

6-2. The three elements of survey control are direction, location, and altitude. The survey section should survey the firing unit's position before the unit arrives, if the tactical situation permits. The survey section will provide coordinates and height of the orienting station and grid azimuth from the orienting station to the end of the orienting line. The hasty survey techniques discussed in this chapter fall into two categories–directional control and location determination.

SECTION II – DIRECTION

6-3. Direction is the most important element of survey control. The mil relation formula states that one mil of error in direction at 1,000 meters will result in a one meter lateral deviation from the target. Therefore, as the range increases, so does the deviation. This section discusses techniques available to establish or transfer directional control with the M2A2 aiming circle.

SIMULTANEOUS OBSERVATION

6-4. Simultaneous observation of a celestial body is a fast and easy method of transferring directional control. Simultaneous observation is ideally suited for field artillery units because multiple units can be placed on common directional control in minutes. The principle of simultaneous observation is that any given celestial body is so far away that, for practical purposes, the lines of sight to it from two or more points on the surface of the earth are parallel. During daylight hours, the sun will serve as the celestial object, at night any clearly defined object will suffice. There are certain requirements for a simultaneous observation, to include:
- Clear weather that permits observation of the celestial object.
- Communications between the master and flank stations.
- Known directional control to a known point.
- Distance between master and flank stations does not exceed 26 kilometers.

Chapter 6

Note. Distances greater than 26 kilometers may result in exceeding hasty survey tolerances of direction.

6-5. The point having known directional control (a grid azimuth to a known point) becomes the master station. It can be occupied by survey personnel or personnel from the firing unit. All positions requiring the establishment of directional control become flank stations.

> **CAUTION**
> Place the sun filter over the aiming circle eyepiece before tracking the sun.

6-6. The M2A2 aiming circle at the flank station is set up to observe the prearranged celestial object. It becomes the orienting station for the firing unit. The instrument operator of the flank station will set up the aiming circle using a plumb bob, and position the aiming circle over a user defined orienting station marker. If the simultaneous observation is prearranged, the flank station can maintain radio silence during the procedure. Table 6-1 depicts the steps for performing a simultaneous observation. For more information on procedures and commands for simultaneous observation, see the digital training management system and Army Techniques Publication (ATP) 3-09.02.

Table 6-1. Example simultaneous observation

MASTER STATION	FLANK STATION(S)
Step 1. Use the azimuth knob (upper motion) to set the known azimuth value on the instrument azimuth scale (upper motion), and sight on the known point or azimuth marker with the orienting knob (lower motion).	Step 1. With the azimuth knob (upper motion), set 0.0 mils on the instrument.
Step 2. Using the azimuth knob (upper motion), identify and sight on the predetermined celestial object.[1] **"This is November 38, ready, start tracking, out."**	Step 2. Contact the master station, and report that you are ready to observe. **"November 38, this is November 37, ready to observe, over."**
Step 3. Using the azimuth knob (upper motion), track the celestial object and announce, "TIP."[2] **"This is November 38, tracking, tracking, tracking (countdown), TIP, out."**	Step 3. With the orienting knob (lower motion), sight on and track the celestial object until the master station announces, "TIP."
Step 4. Read the azimuth to the celestial object from the azimuth scale, and announce it to the flank station(s). **"This is November 38, azimuth 3741.5, over."**	Step 4. Depress the telescope of the instrument, and place the end of the orienting line squarely along the line of sight at least 30 meters away from the orienting station. Record the azimuth that is announced by the master station.
Step 5. Repeat steps 2 and 3, and determine a second angle for verification. **"This is November 38, tracking, tracking, tracking, TIP, out."**[3]	Step 5. With the azimuth knob (upper motion), track the celestial object until the master station announces, "TIP."
Step 6. Determine the clockwise angle (check angle) between the first and second azimuths. Announce the check angle to the flank station(s).	Step 6. Read the angle that was measured, and copy the check angle from the master station.
	Step 7. Ensure the check angle from the master station and the angle measured agrees within ±2 mils; the azimuth to the end of the orienting line is the azimuth that was recorded in step 4. If the check angle is out of tolerance, repeat the entire procedure.

1 Sight on the center mass of the celestial object. With the M2A2 aiming circle, you can see celestial objects when they are only half-visible to the naked eye.
2 TIP - telescope in place.
3 The second TIP on the celestial object verifies the accuracy of the orienting line.
Bold text indicates commands between master station and flank station. (Call signs and azimuths depicted are examples only)

DIRECTIONAL TRAVERSE

6-7. The directional traverse transfers directional control from one point to another using measurements and directions to a series of straight lines connecting a series of points. The directional traverse should only be used when conditions prohibit the use of simultaneous observation or other methods. The advantage of this method is improved accuracy versus floating the magnetic needle of an aiming circle or scaling an azimuth from a map. The disadvantages are the loss of accuracy (0.5 mils) for each angle turned during the traverse, and time consumption due to overall distance traveled. For more information on steps for directional traverse, see the digital training management system and ATP 3-09.02.

SECTION III – LOCATION

6-8. Accurate location of the firing unit is the second most important element of survey control. Using the improved position azimuth determining system or GLPS to establish the firing unit location assures a high degree of accuracy. The alternative methods for determining the location of the firing unit are map spot and global positioning system. If the unit's position is incorrect, the initial rounds will have little, if any effect on the target. This section briefly discusses alternate techniques available to determine location and corresponding altitude in the absence of survey support.

TECHNIQUES FOR LOCATION

6-9. When survey or global positioning system equipment are not available, the desired location may be determined through a graphic resection or graphic traverse. The following paragraphs will briefly discuss the techniques available and associated considerations for determining location. For more information on procedures for determining location, see the digital training management system, and ATP 3-09.02.

GRAPHIC RESECTION

6-10. The graphic resection is a quick method of determining location, but requires coordinates to known aiming points (for example, water tower, church steeple, or trigonometric markers). The advantage of a graphic resection is the relative ease in determining location. The disadvantages include visibility and more than one known aiming point must be available.

GRAPHIC TRAVERSE

6-11. A graphic traverse is a means of transferring direction and location control from one point to another using angle and distance measurements. This procedure is similar to a directional traverse, with the exception of distance to each forward station is included in the measurements. The data needed to begin a graphic traverse include the coordinates to a known aiming point and the direction to an azimuth mark.

TECHNIQUES FOR DISTANCE

6-12. During a graphic traverse, the distance of each traverse leg is measured. This distance measured is the horizontal distance along the traverse leg, not the slope distance obtained by measuring along the contour of the earth. This horizontal distance can be easily measured by pacing, subtense, or using a premeasured length. The following paragraphs will briefly discuss techniques available and associated considerations used in measuring distance.

SUBTENSE

6-13. With the exception of the GLPS, the subtense method is the fastest. Subtense is based on a principle of visual perspective, where the farther away an object is, the smaller it appears. An advantage of subtense is that a horizontal distance is obtained indirectly; that is, the distance is computed rather than measured. This allows subtense to be used over terrain where obstacles (for example, streams, ravines, or steep slopes) may prohibit pacing. The subtense base (for example, 2-meter bar, or rifle) may be any desired length. The instrument operator sights on one end of the object and measures the horizontal clockwise angle to the other end. If a 2-meter bar or rifle is used, the Soldier facing the aiming circle must hold the rifle or 2-meter

Chapter 6

bar perpendicular to the line of sight. Repeat the process twice and then determine the mean angle. The subtense method uses precise values with a trigonometric solution. Use the computation below or appropriate subtense table to extract the distance.

> **Example**
> You are using a 2-meter subtense bar and you measure an angle of 10.5 mils. Determine the horizontal distance using the following formula:
>
> Distance = $\frac{½ \text{ base}}{\tan ½ (\text{angle})}$ = $\frac{1}{\tan (5.25)}$ = $\frac{1}{0.005154}$ = 194 meters

Note. You must convert mils to degrees by dividing 17.778 into the angle determined. To determine the tangent (tan) of an angle, you will need a calculator.

6-14. For ease of measurement and speed of action, the subtense method is preferred. Tables 6-2, 6-3, and 6-4 on pages 6-5 through 6-10 are provided that calculate distances for measured angles.

Table 6-2. Subtense using a 2-meter base (bar)

ANGLE	DISTANCE	ANGLE	DISTANCE	ANGLE	DISTANCE
6.0	340	18.5	110	31.0	66
6.2	329	18.8	108	31.2	65
6.5	313	19.0	107	31.5	65
6.8	300	19.2	106	31.8	64
7.0	291	19.5	104	32.0	64
7.2	280	19.8	103	32.2	63
7.5	272	20.0	102	32.5	63
7.8	261	20.2	101	32.8	62
8.0	255	20.5	99	33.0	62
8.2	248	20.8	98	33.2	61
8.5	240	21.0	97	33.5	61
8.8	231	21.2	96	33.8	60
9.0	226	21.5	95	34.0	60
9.2	221	21.8	93	34.2	60
9.5	214	22.0	93	34.5	59
9.8	208	22.2	92	34.8	59
10.0	204	22.5	91	35.0	58
10.2	200	22.8	89	35.2	58
10.5	194	23.0	88	35.5	57
10.8	189	23.2	88	35.8	57
11.0	185	23.5	87	36.0	57
11.2	182	23.8	86	36.2	56
11.5	177	24.0	85	36.5	56
11.8	173	24.2	84	36.8	55
12.0	170	24.5	83	37.0	55
12.2	167	24.8	82	37.2	55
(continued)					

Hasty Survey Techniques

Table 6-2. Subtense using a 2-meter base (bar) (continued)

ANGLE	DISTANCE	ANGLE	DISTANCE	ANGLE	DISTANCE
12.5	163	25.0	81	37.5	54
12.8	159	25.2	81	37.8	54
13.0	157	25.5	80	38.0	54
13.2	154	25.8	79	38.2	53
13.5	151	26.0	78	38.5	53
13.8	148	26.2	78	38.8	52
14.0	146	26.5	77	39.0	52
14.2	143	26.8	76	39.2	52
14.5	140	27.0	75	39.5	52
14.8	138	27.2	75	39.8	51
15.0	136	27.5	74	40.0	51
15.2	134	27.8	73	40.2	51
15.5	131	28.0	73	40.5	50
15.8	129	28.2	72	40.8	50
16.0	127	28.5	71	41.0	50
16.2	126	28.8	71	41.2	49
16.5	123	29.0	70	41.5	49
16.8	121	29.2	70	41.8	49
17.0	120	29.5	69	42.0	48
17.2	118	29.8	68	42.2	48
17.5	116	30.0	68	42.5	48
17.8	114	30.2	67	42.8	48
18.0	113	30.5	67	43.0	47
18.2	112	30.8	66		

Table 6-3. Subtense using rifle or carbine as base

ANGLE	DISTANCE		ANGLE	DISTANCE		ANGLE	DISTANCE	
	M16A2/3/4	M4/4A1		M16A2/3/4	M4/4A1		M16A2/3/4	M4/4A1
6.0	171	128	17.5	59	44	29.0	35	27
6.2	165	124	17.8	58	43	29.2	35	26
6.5	158	118	18.0	57	43	29.5	35	26
6.8	151	113	18.2	56	42	29.8	34	26
7.0	146	110	18.5	55	42	30.0	34	26
7.2	142	107	18.8	55	41	30.2	34	25
7.5	137	103	19.0	54	41	30.5	34	25
7.8	131	99	19.2	53	40	30.8	33	25
8.0	128	96	19.5	53	39	31.0	33	25
8.2	125	94	19.8	52	39	31.2	33	25
8.5	121	91	20.0	51	39	31.5	33	24
8.8	116	88	20.2	51	38	31.8	32	24
9.0	114	86	20.5	50	38	32.0	32	24

(continued)

Chapter 6

Table 6-3. Subtense using rifle or carbine as base (continued)

ANGLE	DISTANCE		ANGLE	DISTANCE		ANGLE	DISTANCE	
	M16A2/3/4	M4/4A1		M16A2/3/4	M4/4A1		M16A2/3/4	M4/4A1
9.2	111	84	20.8	49	37	32.2	32	24
9.5	108	81	21.0	49	37	32.5	32	24
9.8	105	79	21.2	48	36	32.8	31	23
10.0	102	77	21.5	48	36	33.0	31	23
10.2	100	75	21.8	47	35	33.2	31	23
10.5	98	73	22.0	47	35	33.5	31	23
10.8	95	71	22.2	46	35	33.8	30	23
11.0	93	70	22.5	46	34	34.0	30	23
11.2	91	69	22.8	45	34	34.2	30	23
11.5	89	67	23.0	45	33	34.5	30	22
11.8	87	65	23.2	44	33	34.8	29	22
12.0	85	64	23.5	44	33	35.0	29	22
12.2	84	63	23.8	43	32	35.2	29	22
12.5	82	62	24.0	43	32	35.5	29	22
12.8	80	60	24.2	42	32	35.8	29	22
13.0	79	59	24.5	42	31	36.0	28	21
13.2	78	58	24.8	41	31	36.2	28	21
13.5	76	57	25.0	41	31	36.5	28	21
13.8	74	56	25.2	41	31	36.8	28	21
14.0	73	55	25.5	40	30	37.0	28	21
14.2	72	54	25.8	39	30	37.2	28	21
14.5	71	53	26.0	39	30	37.5	27	21
14.8	69	52	26.2	38	29	37.8	27	20
15.0	68	51	26.5	38	29	38.0	27	20
15.2	67	51	26.8	37	29	38.2	27	20
15.5	66	50	27.0	37	29	38.5	27	20
15.8	65	49	27.2	37	28	38.8	26	20
16.0	64	48	27.5	37	28	39.0	26	20
16.2	63	48	27.8	36	28	39.2	26	20
16.5	62	47	28.0	36	28	39.5	26	19
16.8	61	46	28.2	36	27	39.8	26	19
17.0	60	45	28.5	35	27	40.0	26	19
17.2	60	45	28.8	35	27			

Note. Measure the rifle or carbine from the top of the butt to the end of the flash suppressor.

Table 6-4. Subtense using a 60-meter base

ANGLE	DISTANCE	ANGLE	DISTANCE	ANGLE	DISTANCE	ANGLE	DISTANCE
60.0	1,018	95.8	637	131.5	464	204.8	297
60.2	1,015	96.0	636	131.8	463	205.0	297
60.5	1,010	96.2	635	132.0	462	205.2	297

(continued)

Table 6-4. Subtense using a 60-meter base (continued)

ANGLE	DISTANCE	ANGLE	DISTANCE	ANGLE	DISTANCE	ANGLE	DISTANCE
60.8	1,005	96.5	633	132.2	462	205.5	296
61.0	1,002	96.8	631	132.5	461	205.8	296
61.2	998	97.0	630	132.8	460	206.0	296
61.5	993	97.2	628	133.0	459	206.2	295
61.8	989	97.5	626	133.2	458	206.5	295
62.0	985	97.8	624	133.5	457	206.8	295
62.2	982	98.0	623	133.8	456	207.0	294
62.5	978	98.2	622	134.0	455	207.2	294
62.8	973	98.5	620	134.2	454	207.5	294
63.0	970	98.8	618	134.5	453	207.8	293
63.2	967	99.0	617	134.8	452	208.0	293
63.5	962	99.2	616	172.5	353	208.2	293
63.8	958	99.5	614	172.8	353	208.5	292
64.0	955	99.8	612	173.0	352	208.8	292
64.2	952	100.0	611	173.2	352	209.0	291
64.5	947	100.2	609	173.5	351	209.2	291
64.8	943	100.5	608	173.8	351	209.5	291
65.0	940	100.8	606	174.0	350	209.8	290
65.2	937	101.0	605	174.2	350	210.0	290
65.5	933	101.2	603	174.5	349	210.2	290
65.8	928	101.5	602	174.8	349	210.5	289
66.0	925	101.8	600	175.0	348	210.8	289
66.2	923	102.0	599	175.2	348	211.0	289
66.5	919	102.2	597	175.5	347	211.2	288
66.8	915	102.5	596	175.8	347	211.5	288
67.0	912	102.8	594	176.0	346	211.8	288
67.2	909	103.0	593	176.2	346	212.0	287
67.5	905	103.2	592	176.5	345	212.2	287
67.8	901	103.5	590	176.8	345	212.5	287
68.0	898	103.8	588	177.0	344	212.8	286
68.2	895	104.0	587	177.2	344	213.0	286
68.5	892	104.2	586	177.5	343	213.2	286
68.8	888	104.5	584	177.8	343	213.5	285
69.0	885	104.8	583	178.0	342	213.8	285
69.2	883	105.0	582	178.2	342	214.0	285
69.5	879	105.2	580	178.5	342	214.2	284
69.8	875	105.5	579	178.8	341	214.5	284
70.0	873	105.8	577	179.0	341	214.8	283
70.2	870	106.0	576	179.2	340	215.0	283
70.5	867	106.2	575	179.5	340	215.2	283

(continued)

Table 6-4. Subtense using a 60-meter base (continued)

ANGLE	DISTANCE	ANGLE	DISTANCE	ANGLE	DISTANCE	ANGLE	DISTANCE
70.8	863	106.5	573	179.8	339	215.5	283
71.0	860	106.8	572	180.0	339	215.8	282
71.2	858	107.0	571	180.2	338	216.0	282
71.5	854	107.2	570	180.5	338	216.2	282
71.8	851	107.5	568	180.8	337	216.5	281
72.0	848	107.8	566	181.0	337	216.8	281
72.2	846	108.0	565	181.2	336	217.0	281
72.5	843	108.2	564	181.5	336	217.2	280
72.8	839	108.5	563	181.8	335	217.5	280
73.0	837	108.8	561	182.0	335	217.8	280
73.2	835	109.0	560	182.2	335	218.0	279
73.5	831	109.2	559	182.5	334	218.2	279
73.8	828	109.5	558	182.8	333	218.5	279
74.0	826	109.8	556	183.0	333	218.8	278
74.2	823	110.0	555	183.2	333	219.0	278
74.5	820	110.2	554	183.5	332	219.2	278
74.8	817	110.5	553	183.8	332	219.5	277
75.0	815	110.8	551	184.0	331	219.8	277
75.2	812	111.0	550	184.2	331	220.0	277
75.5	809	111.2	549	184.5	330	220.2	276
75.8	806	111.5	548	184.8	330	220.5	276
76.0	804	111.8	546	185.0	329	220.8	276
76.2	802	112.0	545	185.2	329	221.0	275
76.5	799	112.2	544	185.5	329	221.2	275
76.8	795	112.5	543	185.8	328	221.5	275
77.0	793	112.8	541	186.0	328	221.8	274
77.2	791	113.0	540	186.2	327	222.0	274
77.5	788	113.2	539	186.5	327	222.2	274
77.8	785	113.5	538	186.8	326	222.5	274
78.0	783	113.8	536	187.0	326	222.8	274
78.2	781	114.0	536	187.2	326	223.0	273
78.5	778	114.2	535	187.5	325	223.2	273
78.8	775	114.5	533	187.8	325	223.5	272
79.0	773	114.8	532	188.0	324	223.8	272
79.2	771	115.0	531	188.2	324	224.0	272
79.5	768	115.2	530	188.5	323	224.2	271
79.8	765	115.5	529	188.8	323	224.5	271
80.0	764	115.8	527	189.0	322	224.8	271
80.2	762	116.0	526	189.2	322	225.0	271
80.5	759	116.2	525	189.5	322	225.2	270

(continued)

Table 6-4. Subtense using a 60-meter base (continued)

ANGLE	DISTANCE	ANGLE	DISTANCE	ANGLE	DISTANCE	ANGLE	DISTANCE
80.8	756	116.5	524	189.8	321	225.5	270
81.0	754	116.8	523	190.0	321	225.8	270
81.2	752	117.0	522	190.2	320	226.0	269
81.5	749	117.2	521	190.5	320	226.2	269
81.8	747	117.5	520	190.8	319	226.5	269
82.0	745	117.8	518	191.0	319	226.8	268
82.2	743	118.0	517	191.2	319	227.0	268
82.5	740	118.2	516	191.5	318	227.2	268
82.8	738	118.5	515	191.8	318	227.5	268
83.0	736	118.8	514	192.0	317	227.8	267
83.2	734	119.0	513	192.2	317	228.0	267
83.5	732	119.2	512	192.5	317	228.2	267
83.8	729	119.5	511	192.8	316	228.5	266
84.0	727	119.8	510	193.0	316	228.8	266
84.2	725	120.0	509	193.2	315	229.0	266
84.5	723	120.2	508	193.5	315	229.2	266
84.8	720	120.5	507	193.8	314	229.5	265
85.0	718	120.8	505	194.0	314	229.8	265
85.2	717	121.0	504	194.2	314	230.0	265
85.5	714	121.2	504	194.5	313	230.2	264
85.8	712	121.5	502	194.8	313	230.5	264
86.0	710	121.8	501	195.0	312	230.8	264
86.2	709	122.0	500	195.2	312	231.0	263
86.5	706	122.2	500	195.5	312	231.2	263
86.8	704	122.5	498	195.8	311	231.5	263
87.0	702	122.8	497	196.0	311	231.8	263
87.2	700	123.0	496	196.2	311	232.0	262
87.5	698	123.2	495	196.5	310	232.2	262
87.8	696	123.5	494	196.8	310	232.5	262
88.0	694	123.8	493	197.0	309	232.8	261
88.2	692	124.0	492	197.2	309	233.0	261
88.5	690	124.2	491	197.5	308	233.2	261
88.8	688	124.5	490	197.8	308	233.5	261
89.0	686	124.8	489	198.0	308	233.8	260
89.2	685	125.0	488	198.2	307	234.0	260
89.5	682	125.2	488	198.5	307	234.2	260
89.8	680	125.5	486	198.8	306	234.5	259
90.0	679	125.8	485	199.0	306	234.8	259
90.2	677	126.0	484	199.2	306	235.0	259
90.5	675	126.2	484	199.5	305	235.2	259
(continued)							

Table 6-4. Subtense using a 60-meter base (continued)

ANGLE	DISTANCE	ANGLE	DISTANCE	ANGLE	DISTANCE	ANGLE	DISTANCE
90.8	673	126.5	483	199.8	305	235.5	258
91.0	671	126.8	481	200.0	305	235.8	258
91.2	670	127.0	481	200.2	304	236.0	258
91.5	667	127.2	480	200.5	304	236.2	258
91.8	665	127.5	479	200.8	303	236.5	257
92.0	664	127.8	478	201.0	303	236.8	257
92.2	662	128.0	477	201.2	303	237.0	257
92.5	660	128.2	476	201.5	302	237.2	256
92.8	658	128.5	475	201.8	302	237.5	256
93.0	657	128.8	474	202.0	302	237.8	256
93.2	655	129.0	473	202.2	301	238.0	256
93.5	653	129.2	472	202.5	301	238.2	255
93.8	651	129.5	471	202.8	300	238.5	255
94.0	650	129.8	470	203.0	300	238.8	255
94.2	648	130.0	469	203.2	300	239.0	255
94.5	646	130.2	469	203.5	299	239.2	254
94.8	644	130.5	468	203.8	299	239.5	254
95.0	643	130.8	467	204.0	299	239.8	254
95.2	642	131.0	466	204.2	298	240.0	253
95.5	639	131.2	465	204.5	298		

PACING

6-15. Soldiers who have measured their pace should be able to pace 100 meters to an accuracy of ±1 meter over level ground. However, the paced distance follows the contour of the earth and can provide inaccurate measurements over great distances. Therefore, in sloping or rough terrain, determining a horizontal distance with accuracy becomes more difficult. Soldiers can try to adjust their pace length to the degree of slope being paced, but accuracy will decrease. Pacing should be used only over relatively flat terrain, when other methods are unavailable.

MEASURING

6-16. A measured and marked length of wire or substitute may be used as a means to measure distance. This method is substantially more accurate than pacing, but it requires that two Soldiers hold the ends of the wire. The wire may be any length, although a length of 60 meters is recommended. The wire should be marked with the same color-coded tape at every meter increment throughout its entire length, and with a different color-coded tape at every 10-meter increment. The Soldiers will measure in a straight line from one point to the other and count the number of whole lengths measured. The distance of the leg is determined by multiplying the number of whole wire lengths by 60 (the length of the wire) and adding the partial length.

TECHNIQUES FOR ALTITUDE

6-17. Altitude is the last of the three elements of survey control. The location data, to include altitude is provided by the survey section. If not provided, determine altitude using a global positioning system device or directly from the map. Normally, altitude can be considered accurate to half of the contour interval on the map. The contour interval is expressed as elevation in meters (for example, contour interval 10 meters, supplementary contours 5 meters).

Chapter 7
Fire Commands

This chapter discusses the types, elements, and sequence of fire commands. The fire direction center (FDC) uses fire commands to provide howitzer sections with information necessary to initiate and cease firing. Fire commands can be issued digitally or by voice. Initial fire commands include all elements necessary for orienting, loading, and firing the howitzer. Subsequent fire commands include only those elements that have changed, except quadrant elevation. Quadrant elevation is given in every fire command.

MEANS OF TRANSMITTING FIRE COMMANDS

7-1. The means of transmitting fire commands between the FDC and the howitzers will be based on unit tactical standard operating procedures and mission variables (mission, enemy, terrain and weather, troops and support available, time available, and civil considerations (METT-TC)). The possible means are digital, degraded digital, and voice. See chapter 4 for further discussion.

Note. Section chiefs must view the digital fire command for each mission in its entirety. This will preclude errors in firing when the fire for effect is entered or if the shell, charge, fuze type, or fuze setting changes.

ELEMENTS OF FIRE COMMANDS

7-2. Elements of fire commands may be transmitted digitally or by voice from the FDC. The howitzer section chief announces the fire commands to the section members.

WARNING ORDER

7-3. A warning order alerts the firing element to an impending fire mission. When the FDC transmits the warning order digitally, the gun display unit emits a steady alarm signal indicating the start of the fire mission. The howitzer section chief acknowledges receipt and prepares for action. When using voice commands, a warning order of "**FIRE MISSION**" is announced.

Note: The warning order is not given in subsequent commands.

PIECES TO FOLLOW, PIECES TO FIRE, AND METHOD OF FIRE

7-4. This information provides the basic information for the fire mission. These commands designate the firing element that will follow the mission; the howitzer(s) that will initially fire; and how the howitzer(s) will engage the target.

Pieces to Follow

7-5. Pieces to follow designates the firing element that will follow the commands given for an adjust fire mission. "**PLATOON (BATTERY) ADJUST**" indicates the mission will be an adjust-fire mission and that all howitzers will copy the commands, follow the mission, and participate in the fire for effect phase. Any howitzer or number of howitzers may be announced in this element; for example, "**PLATOON ADJUST**" or "**NUMBER 1 AND NUMBER 3 ADJUST**."

Pieces to Fire

7-6. Pieces to fire designates which howitzer(s) will fire the data given in the initial fire command. "**PLATOON ADJUST, NUMBER 3**" indicates that during an adjust fire mission, number 3 will fire the initial round of adjustment. Piece(s) to fire may be standardized. A voice command would be "**NUMBER 3, 1 ROUND**". If the mission were fire for effect, then "**PLATOON**" would be sent.

Method of Fire

7-7. Method of fire designates how many rounds to fire. "**PLATOON ADJUST, NUMBER 3, 1 ROUND**" indicates that during this adjust fire mission, number 3 will fire 1 round. "**PLATOON 1 ROUND**" indicates a fire for effect mission with all howitzers firing 1 round. Method of fire may be standardized.

SPECIAL INSTRUCTIONS

7-8. This element designates specific actions that differ from normal. "**DO NOT LOAD**" or "**AT MY COMMAND**" signify restrictive commands. Other special instructions include high angle, use gunner's quadrant, azimuth, zone, sweep, zone and sweep fire, and special corrections. When more than one special instruction applies, announce restrictive commands first.

Do Not Load

7-9. "**DO NOT LOAD**" is a restrictive fire command that prohibits loading and firing. The section may prepare the projectile, charge, and fuze (if applicable); lay the howitzer for deflection; and set the quadrant elevation or loading elevation, as required.

At My Command

7-10. The restrictive fire command "**AT MY COMMAND**" prohibits the firing element from firing until directed by the FDC. "**AT MY COMMAND**" remains in effect until the FDC commands "**CANCEL AT MY COMMAND**" (or "**BY PIECE**" or "**BY ROUND AT MY COMMAND**"). "**AT MY COMMAND**" may be cancelled at any time. If the FDC has announced "**QUADRANT**", the command would be "**CANCEL AT MY COMMAND, QUADRANT (so much)**".

HIGH-ANGLE

7-11. "**HIGH-ANGLE**" alerts the firing element that the fire mission requires an angle of elevation greater than 800 mils. Light artillery weapons can be elevated before loading. Medium artillery weapons normally must be loaded at loading elevation.

USE GUNNER'S QUADRANT

7-12. "**USE GUNNER'S QUADRANT**" alerts the firing element that the gunner's quadrant must be used to set or check the quadrant elevation. This procedure is more often used when firing danger close or precision fire missions, which require greater accuracy.

AZIMUTH

7-13. "**AZIMUTH**" alerts the element to a large shift in the direction of fire. The azimuth in mils follows the command of azimuth. ***Direction of fire* is the direction on which a fire unit is laid to the most significant threat in the target area, to the chart direction to the center of the zone of fire, or to the target.**

SWEEP-MILS-DEFLECTIONS

7-14. "**SWEEP (so many) MILS, (so many) DEFLECTIONS**" commands a seldom-used method of fire when the standard sheaf does not adequately cover the target and more width is required. Sweep fire provides for firing several deflections with 1 quadrant. The howitzer section chief computes the required deflections and, after firing the initial deflection, fires the remaining deflections in any order, or as directed by unit tactical standard operating procedures.

> **Example**
> "SPECIAL INSTRUCTIONS, SWEEP 15 mils, 3 DEFLECTIONS"
>
> 3246   *3231*   3216
> 306   *306*   306
>
> The howitzer section chief computes deflections 3216 and 3246 by subtracting 15 mils from and adding 15 mils to the displayed deflection.
>
> **Bold italicized text indicates the displayed or commanded deflection and quadrant elevation**

7-15. **The *sheaf* is the lateral distribution of the bursts of two or more pieces fired together.** The width of the sheaf is the lateral distance (perpendicular to the direction of fire) between the centers of flank bursts. A sheaf may be formed in any of the following patterns: converged, open, parallel, or special.

ZONE-MILS-QUADRANT

7-16. "ZONE (so many) MILS, (so many) QUADRANTS" commands another method of fire used when the standard sheaf does not adequately cover the target and more depth is required. Zone fire provides for firing 1 deflection with several quadrants. The howitzer section chief computes the required quadrants, fires the initial quadrant, and fires the remaining quadrants in any order, or as directed by unit tactical standard operating procedures. Zone fire always includes an odd number of quadrants fired.

> **Example**
> "SPECIAL INSTRUCTIONS, ZONE 10 mils, 3 QUADRANTS"
>
> 3295   *3295*   3295
> 399   *409*   419
>
> The howitzer section chief computes quadrants 399 and 419 by subtracting and adding 10 mils to the displayed quadrant elevation.
>
> **Bold italicized text indicates the displayed or commanded deflection and quadrant elevation**

SWEEP-MILS-DEFLECTIONS-ZONE-MILS-QUADRANTS

7-17. "SWEEP (so many) MILS, (so many) DEFLECTIONS, ZONE (so many) mils, (so many) QUADRANTS" commands a method of fire combining sweep fire and zone fire. Sweep and zone fire provides for firing several deflections and quadrants. The howitzer section chief fires the initial commands for deflection and quadrant first, and then fires all combinations of computed deflections and quadrants in any order, or as directed by unit tactical standard operating procedures.

Chapter 7

> **Example**
> "SPECIAL INSTRUCTIONS, SWEEP 10 mils, 3 DEFLECTIONS, ZONE 4 mils, 3 QUADRANTS"
>
> | 3210 | 3200 | 3190 |
> |------|------|------|
> | 314 | 314 | 314 |
> | 3210 | *3200* | 3190 |
> | 310 | *310* | 310 |
> | 3210 | 3200 | 3190 |
> | 306 | 306 | 306 |
>
> The howitzer section chief computes deflections 3190 and 3210, and quadrants 306 and 314.
>
> **Bold italicized text indicates the displayed or commanded deflection and quadrant elevation**

SPECIAL CORRECTIONS

7-18. "**SPECIAL CORRECTIONS**" alerts the crew that separate data will be transmitted to one or more sections. The command "**SPECIAL CORRECTIONS**" should precede any special corrections that apply to the fire command. This command prevents misunderstanding and unnecessary repetition of missed special corrections. Unit tactical standard operating procedures and level of training dictate the use of special corrections.

PROJECTILE

7-19. This element designates the type of projectile (often high explosive (HE)) required in the fire mission, for example "**SHELL HE**." The projectile must be announced when it differs from standard.

AMMUNITION LOT

7-20. This element designates the ammunition lot required in the fire mission, for example "**LOT XY**" Code ammunition lot numbers for simplicity. Separate loading ammunition has two designators. The first letter is for the projectile and the second letter is for propellant. Semi-fixed ammunition has a one letter designation. The lot designator(s) must be announced when it differs from standard.

CHARGE

7-21. This element designates the amount of propellant required and allows the section to prepare the propellant charge, for example "**CHARGE 5**."

Note: The charge is never standardized!

FUZE

7-22. This element designates the fuze type required in the fire mission, for example "**FUZE QUICK**." The fuze must be announced when it differs from standard.

FUZE SETTING

7-23. This element designates the corresponding fuze setting required in the fire mission, for example "**FUZE TIME, TIME 17.6**." If fuze quick is to be fired on the delay mode, "**DELAY**" is displayed digitally or announced by the FDC.

DEFLECTION

7-24. This element designates the 4-digit deflections required for the fire mission, for example "**DEFLECTION 0320**." With voice commands, deflection is always announced as four digits; for example, "**DEFLECTION 0321 (zero three two one)**".

QUADRANT ELEVATION

7-25. This element designates the quadrant elevation required in the fire mission, for example "**QUADRANT 471**." When the section chief announces deflection, the gunner reads back the deflection. After the assistant gunner (AG) has reported "**QUADRANT (so much), SET**", the gunner will verify his sight picture, ensure that his bubbles are centered, and reports "**DEFLECTION (so much), READY**".

Note: The quadrant elevation is never standardized and is always announced for subsequent fire commands.

METHOD OF FIRE FOR EFFECT

7-26. This element designates the number of rounds and type of ammunition to be used in effect, for example "**2 ROUNDS IN EFFECT**." When applicable, method of fire for effect is announced in the initial fire command after the quadrant, and then must be announced before the last subsequent command in an adjust fire mission. Receiving the method of fire for effect allows the section to prepare the appropriate propellant charges and fuze the projectiles.

SEQUENCE OF FIRE COMMANDS

7-27. The elements of a fire command are always given in the same sequence (table 7-1 on page 7-6). This saves time and eliminates confusion. Each member of the section knows the sequence and can anticipate what will come next. This sequence allows actions to occur simultaneously. For example, the propellant charge and shell fuze combination are prepared while the deflection and quadrant are being set.

7-28. Certain elements of the fire command may be designated as standard, and these need not be sent on each subsequent fire command. If the FDC decides to vary from fire command standard data, the existing standard data must be cancelled to issue replacement data. Only one set of standard data can be in effect at any particular time.

Table 7-1. Fire command sequence

ELEMENT	WHEN ANNOUNCED	
	Initial Fire Commands	Subsequent Fire Commands
1. Warning order	Always	Never
2. Pieces to follow[1] Pieces to fire[1] Method of fire[1]	When applicable When other than standard When other than standard	When changed
3. Special Instructions • Do not load • At my command • High angle • Use gunner's quadrant • Azimuth • Special corrections • Sweep or zone fire	When applicable	When changed
4. Projectile[1]	When other than standard	When changed
5. Ammunition lot[1]	When other than standard	When changed
6. Charge	Always	When changed
7. Fuze[1]	When other than standard	When changed
8. Fuze setting[1]	When other than standard	When changed
9. Deflection	Always	When changed
10. Quadrant	Always	Always
11. Method of fire for effect	When applicable	When changed
[1] These elements may be designated as standard. Elements so designated will be announced only when something other than standard is to be fired.		

FIRE COMMANDS FOR DIRECT FIRE

7-29. Fire commands for direct fire are similar to those for indirect fire although much abbreviated. See table 7-2.

Table 7-2. Fire commands for direct fire example

Element	Example
1. Warning Order.	1. "**TARGET ARMORED CAR**"
2. General direction to the target.	2. "**LEFT FRONT**"
3. Lead in mils.	3. "**LEAD, LEFT 5**" (Reference the appropriate weapon technical manual).
4. Range to the target.	4. "**RANGE 500**"
5. Method of fire.	5. "**FIRE AT WILL**".
Note: The shell, fuze, and charge to be fired in direct fire should be standardized in order to save time.	

SPECIAL METHODS OF FIRE

7-30. There are special methods of fire that may include:

- "**CONTINUOUS FIRE**" commands the howitzer crews to continuously fire within the prescribed rates of fire for the howitzer, until the command "**CHECK FIRING**" or "**CEASE LOADING**" is given.

- **"FIRE AT WILL"** commands the howitzer crews to engage targets at will, while under control of the howitzer section chief. This command is used in a direct fire role, primarily for perimeter defense.

CHECK FIRING

7-31. Anyone can give the command "**CHECK FIRING**," but it should be used only in emergencies, or if a safety violation is observed. All firing ceases immediately. This command may be given by voice, displayed digitally, or both. Immediate action is taken to determine the nature of the check firing and to correct the situation.

CEASE LOADING

7-32. The command "**CEASE LOADING**" allows the firing element to fire rounds that are loaded, but no additional rounds may be loaded. This allows howitzers to avoid having HE rounds remaining in a tube that may be hot from repeated firing.

END OF MISSION

7-33. The command "**END OF MISSION**" terminates the current fire mission. The howitzer sections should return to the lay deflection and quadrant, or lay on priority target data, as required.

PLANNED TARGETS

7-34. The battery may be assigned planned targets for which current firing data must be maintained. Each target is assigned a number and each weapon is laid on its assigned priority target. In such cases, unit standard operating procedures usually designate a command or a prearranged signal to fire on the priority target, bypassing the usual sequence of fire commands.

> **EXAMPLE**
> Target AC7343 has been designated as a priority target. Firing data have been computed and have been transmitted to the left firing platoon. On the command "**LEFT, SUPPRESS AC7343**", the left platoon engages Target AC7343 with the previously arranged method of fire

7-35. In defensive operations, the command "**FIRE THE FPF**" causes the firing battery to fire the final protective fires on which it is laid. Firing the final protective fire continues until all ammunition is expended or the FDC commands "**CEASE LOADING**". That command ensures rounds are not left in a hot tube.

REPETITION AND CORRECTION OF FIRE COMMANDS

7-36. During degraded operations (for example, voice), one section of the firing element is designated to read back all voice fire commands to ensure the howitzer sections receive correct fire commands. If a command is unclear or misunderstood, request retransmission from the FDC, for example "**DEFLECTION NUMBER 2**." The FDC replies with the repetition, for example "**NUMBER 2, THE COMMAND WAS DEFLECTION 2768**."

7-37. If an incorrect command is given prior to quadrant, the FDC commands "**CORRECTION**," followed by the correct command and all subsequent elements. If quadrant was announced, the FDC commands "**CHECK FIRING, CANCEL CHECK FIRING**," followed by the corrected element and all subsequent elements.

FIRING REPORTS

7-38. Howitzer section chiefs transmit firing reports to the FDC during firing, as required. These reports notify the FDC of section firing status, for example:

Chapter 7

- When the FDC commands the special instruction "**DO NOT LOAD**," the howitzer section chief reports, "**LAID, NUMBER (so and so)**." The howitzer section chief reports when the projectile, charge, and fuze have been prepared; the howitzer is laid for deflection; and the quadrant has been set.
- When the FDC commands the special instruction "**AT MY COMMAND**" or "**BY PIECE (or BY ROUND) AT MY COMMAND**," the section chief reports, "**READY, NUMBER (so and so)**." The howitzer section chief reports when the section is ready to fire.
- The howitzer section chief submits the report "**SHOT NUMBER (so and so)**" after a round is fired. However, if the method of fire is more than one round, the howitzer section chief reports "**SHOT**" only after the initial round.
- The howitzer section chief reports "**ROUNDS COMPLETE NUMBER (so and so)**" when the final round designated in the method of fire is fired. However, if only one round is to be fired, the section chief does not report rounds complete after shot.
- The section chief reports "**MISFIRE NUMBER (so and so)**" when a misfire occurs (voice only).

Note. The reports above are used primarily during voice communication. For more information on reporting with the gun display unit, see Technical Manual (TM) 11-7440-283-12-2.

7-39. The howitzer section chief reports ammunition status, as required. This report includes the number of rounds expended by type and lot number. This report is submitted in accordance with unit tactical standard operating procedures.

7-40. The howitzer section chief reports data fired in error. The section chief reports the actual data fired in error to the FDC; for example, "**NUMBER 2 FIRED DEFLECTION 3276**."

RECORD OF MISSIONS FIRED

7-41. Howitzer sections use the DA Form 4513 to record fire commands (digital or voice), ammunition (for example, on hand, fired, transferred, or resupplied), and any standardized data. After this form is completed, the information is used primarily for computing remaining tube life on the DA Form 2408-4. Record neatly and accurately all elements of the DA Form 4513. For more information on the record and maintenance of fire mission data on DA Form 4513, see Appendix D.

Chapter 8
Minimum Quadrant Elevation

This chapter provides a summary of the steps for computing minimum quadrant elevation. For more information on methods and procedures for determining minimum quadrant elevation, see TC 3-09.8

RESPONSIBILITIES

8-1. The platoon leader is responsible for determining the lowest quadrant elevation that can be safely fired from a position to ensure that projectiles clear all visible crests.

Note: All references to platoon leader will apply to the executive officer as well when platoons are collocated. Also, the gunnery sergeant is responsible for these same duties prior to the platoon's occupation of position.

ELEMENTS OF COMPUTATION

8-2. Always determine a minimum quadrant for each howitzer. The maximum of these minimum quadrants is the minimum quadrant elevation. Using the rapid fire tables in TC 3-09.8 for 105-mm M67 and 155-mm M3A1 green bag, and M4A1 and M119 white bag powders is the fastest method of computing the minimum quadrant elevation for those powders and specified fuzes. Modular artillery charge system rapid fire tables have not been republished at the time of this writing. The quadrant elevation determined using the rapid fire table is always greater than or equal to manual computations and therefore safer. Figure 8-1 depicts the elements of minimum quadrant elevation.

Note: Manual computations are more accurate than the rapid fire tables and are used if the sum of the site to crest and the angle needed for a 5-meter angle of site is greater than 300 mils.

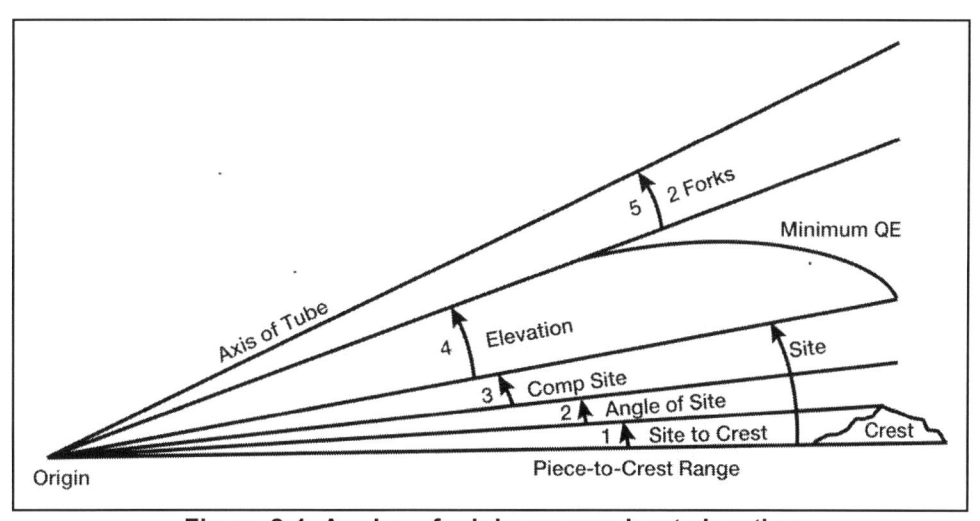

Figure 8-1. Angles of minimum quadrant elevation

8-3. Piece to crest range is the horizontal distance between the howitzer (piece) and the crest, expressed to the nearest 100 meters.

Chapter 8

Note. All angles are determined and expressed to the next higher mil.

8-4. The sum of angles 1 through 5 (figure 8-1 on page 8-3) is the minimum quadrant elevation for the weapon and the charge computed, to include:
- Angle 1 is the angle of site to crest measured by for the weapon. See TC 3-09.8 for the steps to measure angle 1. The largest site to crest will not necessarily yield the largest minimum quadrant.
- Angle 2 is the vertical angle required to clear the top of the crest. For quick, time, and unarmed proximity (variable time) fuzes, a vertical clearance of 5 meters is used. For armed fuzes, reference their technical manual. In most cases for existing artillery fuzes fired over ordinary terrain, it is 70 meters.
- Angle 3 is the complementary angle of site. It is the complementary site factor (tabular firing tables, table G) for the appropriate charge at the piece to crest range multiplied by the sum of angles 1 and 2. Site is the sum of angles 1, 2, and 3.

Note. The entry argument for applicable tabular firing table is the piece to crest range. If not listed, do not interpolate, instead use the next higher listed value.

- Angle 4 is the elevation (from the tabular firing table, table F) for the appropriate charge corresponding to the piece to crest range.
- Angle 5 is a safety factor equivalent to the value of 2 forks (tabular firing table, table F) for the appropriate charge at the piece to crest range.
- The sum of angles 1 through 5 is the minimum quadrant elevation for the weapon and the charge computed.

MEASURING ANGLE OF SITE TO CREST

8-5. During advance party operations, site to crest is measured with the M2 compass, M2A2 aiming circle, or GLPS. During position improvement, the section chief verifies the site to crest and reports this information to the platoon leader. The site to crest and piece to crest range is reported as part of the section chief's report.

MEASURING PIECE TO CREST RANGE

8-6. The methods commonly used to measure the piece to crest range are:
- Automation devices, such as laser range finders, are accurate but should be checked due to possible false readings due to inadvertent reflections.
- Taping is accurate, but is normally too time consuming.
- Subtense is fast and accurate.
- Map measurement is fast and accurate if the obstacle can be accurately located (for example, a building may appear on a map; a lone tree likely will not).
- Pacing is time consuming and depends on the distance and accessibility to the crest.
- Estimation is the least accurate, but used when other methods are not feasible.

8-7. Regardless of the method used to measure the piece to crest range, the platoon leader must verify piece to crest range before computing minimum quadrant elevation.

8-8. Table 8-1 is a summary of the steps for computing the minimum quadrant elevation. It should be used as a reference by the platoon leader and when training individuals to compute minimum quadrant elevation.

Table 8-1. Computing minimum quadrant elevation

COMPUTING ELEMENT	HOW TO DO THE COMPUTATION		
	Fuze PD, fuze MTSQ, or fuze VT with a fuze setting equal to or greater than minimum safe time	Fuze VT with a fuze setting less than minimum safe time	
		PCR greater than minimum arming range	Minimum arming range greater than PCR
Angle 1: Site to crest reported	As reported	As reported	As reported
Angle 2: Angle of site for clearance of crest	5 meters ÷ PCR in thousands x 1.0186 mils	Appropriate vertical clearance divided by PCR in thousands multiplied by 1.0186 mils	Appropriate vertical clearance at the forward line of troops divided by minimum range to the forward line of troops multiplied by 1.0186 mils
Angle 3: Complementary site (comp site)	Comp site factor at PCR (or next greater listed range) multiplied by the sum of angles 1 and 2	Sum of angles 1 and 2 multiplied by comp site factor at PCR (or next greater listed range)	The sum of angles 1 and angle 2 multiplied by the comp site factor corresponding to the range of the forward line of troops (or next greater listed range)
Angle 4: Elevation	At PCR	At PCR	At minimum arming range
Angle 5: 2 forks	At PCR	At PCR	At minimum arming range
Note. All angles above are expressed up to the next higher whole mil. The sum of angles 1 through 5 equals minimum quadrant elevation.			
Attention. Minimum quadrant elevation must be computed for each weapon and charge to be fired. The maximum quadrant of these minimum quadrants is the minimum quadrant elevation for the firing unit.			
MTSQ – mechanical time and superquick PD – point detonating	PCR – piece to crest range VT – variable time		

COMPUTATION FOR FUZES OTHER THAN ARMED VARIABLE TIME

8-9. The platoon leader performs the computations listed in this section if the sum of angles 1 and 2 (figure 8-1 on page 8-1) exceeds 300 mils or if the rapid fire tables are not available. All angles are determined and expressed to the next higher whole mil. The platoon leader performs the computation for all howitzers. One howitzer section may report a sight to crest that is unusually high. If the platoon leader determines that the high sight to crest is due to a single narrow obstruction (for example, a lone tree), that howitzer may be called out of action when deflections that would engage the obstruction are fired. This would enable the platoon to use the next lower minimum quadrant elevation. Other alternatives are to remove the obstruction or move the howitzer. The following special segment on page 8-4 is an example of computations used to determine minimum quadrant elevation for other than armed variable time fuzes.

Chapter 8

> **Example**
> Howitzer number 1 has a range to crest of 1,100 meters. The site to crest reported is +16 mils. Howitzer number 1 is a 155-mm howitzer, and charge 3 green bag will be fired. The platoon leader computes the minimum quadrant elevation, to include:
> - Angle 1: Record the site to crest reported by the chief of section (+16 mils).
>
> - Angle 2: Determine the angle of site in mils and use the following equation to determine angle of site: Vertical interval ÷ range in thousands x 1.0186 mils = angle of site (for example, 5 meters ÷ 1.1 meters x 1.0186 mils = 4.63 mils expressed to the next higher whole mil of +5 mils).
>
> **Note.** The value for angle 2 can also be extracted from the rapid fire tables. See TC 3-09.8 for 105-mm howitzers and M3A1 green bag, and M4A2 and M119 white bag powders for 155-mm howitzers.
> - Angle 3: Determine comp site by multiplying the comp site factor corresponding to the piece to crest range (or the next higher listed range in the tabular firing table, table G, if that range is not listed) by the sum of angles 1 and 2. Angle 1 + angle 2 = +21. The comp site factor corresponding to 1,500 meters (range 1,100 is not listed in the tabular firing table) is +0.010. Therefore, +21 x 0.010 = +0.210. Once a value for comp site is determined, it must be expressed to the next higher whole mil: +1 mil.
>
> - Angle 4: Determine elevation for the piece to crest range (tabular firing table). If this value is not a whole number, it is expressed to the next higher whole mil (74.1 expressed to 75): +75 mils.
>
> - Angle 5: Determine the value of 2 forks (tabular firing table) at piece to crest range (for example, 2 x +2 mils = +4 mils).
>
> Total: Add angles 1 through 5 to determine the platoon leader's minimum quadrant elevation. 16 + 5 + 1 + 75 + 4 = 101.
>
> Therefore, the minimum quadrant elevation for howitzer number 1, charge 3 green bag is 101 mils.
>
> The platoon leader will compute the minimum quadrant elevation for each howitzer in the firing unit. The highest value is the minimum quadrant elevation for the firing unit with this charge.
>
> **Note.** All computations are derived from tabular firing tables, graphical firing tables, and manual computation of angle of site.

COMPUTING FOR ARMED VARIABLE TIME FUZES (LOW-ANGLE FIRE)

8-10. The method of computing the minimum quadrant elevation for firing a projectile fuzed with a proximity fuze depends on the method in which the fuze is used. The proximity (variable time) fuze is designed to arm 3 seconds prior to the time set on the fuze; however, some proximity fuzes arm as early as 5.5 seconds prior to the time set on the fuze. Because of the probability of premature arming, a safety factor of 5.5 seconds is added to the time of flight corresponding to the piece to crest range. Since time on the setting ring is set to the whole second, the time determined is expressed up to the next higher whole second. A proximity fuze is designed to arm two seconds into the time of flight, which makes it a bore-safe fuze.

8-11. In combat situations, the platoon leader determines the minimum safe time and minimum quadrant elevation at the piece to crest range. The quadrant elevation determined for point detonating fuzed rounds is safe for proximity fuzes if the time set is equal to or greater than the minimum safe time determined. If it is necessary to fire a proximity fuze with a time less than the minimum safe time, then increase the angle of site for the minimum quadrant elevation to ensure that the fuze will not function as it passes over the crest.

8-12. If the projectile is to be fired with the proximity fuze set at a time less than the minimum safe time, make an allowance for angle of site of friendly elements. If the projectile is to be fired over marshy or wet terrain, the average height of burst will increase. Therefore, increase the angle of site by 50 percent. If the projectile is to be fired over water, snow, or ice, increase the angle of site shown by 100 percent. When a fuze setting less than the minimum safe time is fired, the minimum quadrant elevation for fuze proximity is based on piece to crest range and a greater angle of site instead of 5 meters. The following special segment is an example of computations used to determine minimum quadrant elevation for armed variable time fuzes.

Example

The site to crest reported by the chief of section is +16 mils. The piece to crest range is 1,700 meters. Howitzer number 1 is a 155-mm howitzer. Charge 4 green bag, and armed variable time fuzes (M732) will be fired. The platoon leader computes the minimum quadrant elevation, to include:

- Angle 1: Record the site to crest reported by the chief of section (+16 mils).

- Angle 2: Determine the angle of site in mils and use the following equation to determine angle of site: Vertical interval ÷ range in thousands x 1.0186 mils = angle of site (for example, 70 meters ÷ 1.7 meters x 1.0186 mils = 41.94 mils expressed to the next higher whole mil of +42 mils).

- Angle 3: Determine comp site by multiplying the comp site factor corresponding to the piece to crest by the sums of angles 1 and 2. Angle 1 + angle 2 = +58. The comp site factor corresponding to 1,700 meters (tabular firing table gives a comp site factor of 0.010 for charge 4 green bag and range 2,000 meters.) Therefore, +58 x 0.010 = +0.580 expressed to the next higher whole mil: +1mils.

- Angle 4: Determine elevation at piece to crest (tabular firing table): +90 mils.

- Angle 5: Determine the value of 2 forks (tabular firing table) at piece to crest range (for example, 2 x +2 mils = +4 mils).

Total: Add angles 1 through 5 to determine the platoon leader's minimum quadrant elevation. 16 + 42 + 1 + 90 + 4 = 153 mils quadrant elevation for charge 4 green bag.

Minimum safe time (time of flight) at piece to crest range (5.6 + 5.5 = 11.1 or 12.0 seconds) is 12.0 seconds.

The minimum quadrant elevation for this howitzer is 153 mils, charge 4 green bag, minimum safe time 12.0 seconds (M732), fuze-armed variable time.

The platoon leader will compute the minimum quadrant elevation for each howitzer in the firing unit. The highest value is the minimum quadrant elevation for the firing unit with this charge.

Note. All computations are derived from tabular firing tables, graphical firing tables, and manual computation of angle of site.

8-13. The minimum quadrant elevation is compared to the minimum quadrant elevation and the minimum point detonating range line as computed by the FDC. The greater of these two values is placed on the DA Form 7353, *Universal Safety T*, (or a locally produced version of that form). See TCs 3-09.8 and 3-09.81 for additional information.

> *Note:* Always compute the platoon leader's (executive officer's) minimum quadrant elevation (QE) for all howitzers and select the largest value as the platoon leader's or battery executive officer's minimum QE.
>
> See TM 43-0001-28-3 for information on the interchangeability among North Atlantic Treaty Organization members' ammunition types.

MARK 399-1 FUZE

8-14. The Mark (MK) 399-1 fuze was developed specifically for combat in urban terrain. It can be used on both 105-mm and 155-mm high explosive rounds. It provides conventional point detonating capability. It also provides a short delay mode which, coupled with its heavy steel penetrator body, allows for improved penetration through wood frame, reinforced concrete, and multilayered brick structures for high-explosive artillery projectiles. In urban operations, one role of the artillery is to supply indirect fire, which will typically be at high angles. Use the MK 399-1fuze's delay mode to penetrate a building or structure and achieve blast effects inside of the target, or use the point detonating mode to rubble the structure.

> **CAUTION**
> If a projectile fired with an MK 399-1 fuze impacts a substantial object (either intentionally or unintentionally), a high-order explosive function may result even when the object is located inside the 400-caliber minimum arming distance from the weapon (138 feet for 105-mm and 203 feet for 155-mm weapon systems).

8-15. TC 3-09.8 describes the steps required to determine the minimum quadrant elevation to safely fire the howitzers. Field artillery units must follow those steps to ensure targets are not engaged (either in the indirect or direct fire mode) before the MK 399-1-fuzed round has reached the 400-caliber minimum arming distance from the weapon. Point detonating fuzes on delay only allow penetration of the first wall or roof. For more information on loading and firing during direct fire missions, see technical manuals (TM) 9-1015-252-10 for M119A2 howitzer, TM 9-1015-260-10 for the M119A3 howitzer, TM 9-1025-215-10 for the M777-series howitzer, and TM 9-2350-314-10-1 and -2 for the M109-series howitzer.

Chapter 9
Composite Units

This chapter provides a brief overview and discussion of techniques and associated considerations unique to cannon units operating as a composite organization. Cannon units operating with weapons of different calibers (105-mm, 155-mm) and sometimes types (towed, self-propelled) characterize composite units. See FM 3-09 for a discussion of light and medium field artillery cannon systems.

OVERVIEW

9-1. The composite cannon structure consists of any combination of howitzer systems, with associated prime movers and ammunition resupply vehicles, which may include:
- Howitzer, Medium, Self-Propelled, 155-mm, M109A6.
- Howitzer, Medium, Towed, 155-mm, M777-series.
- Howitzer, Light, Towed, 105-mm, M119-series.

9-2. Composite units may be organized under tables of organization and equipment or through force tailoring. Although a battalion may be organized with individual firing batteries equipped with only a given type of weapon, a mission's task organization may require that different weapon systems co-exist within the same battery. Under this circumstance, the battery's howitzer crews should train on and, as a goal, be certified to operate both systems for maximum tactical flexibility. This training will be easier if both are similar types of weapon systems. Mixing training on towed and self-propelled systems will be more difficult, for example, due to the added maintenance training on the self-propelled model, air mobile training for the towed model, and differing employment techniques.

9-3. Although cannon battalions in Infantry BCTs are organized as composite units, combat operations have dictated that other units encounter composite unit situations where they might have any combination of howitzer configurations across the battery or battalion. These situations affect personnel, equipment, manning, training, and sustainment among others. Identify considerations associated with composite units as early as possible in the military decisionmaking process.

> **Examples**
> 1. A possible type of composite battalion organization is where Alpha and Bravo batteries are organized with 2 platoons of 3 M109A6 Paladin self-propelled howitzers, while Charlie battery is organized with a platoon of 3 M109A6 Paladin self-propelled howitzers and a second platoon of 3 M777A2 towed howitzers.
>
> 2. A composite cannon battery organization, where the battery organized as a dual unit. In this example, each howitzer section is allocated both an M119A3, 105-mm, towed howitzer and an M777A2, 155-mm, towed howitzer system. This configuration might be seen in combat outposts and forward operating bases.

9-4. Composite battery units present unique challenges and tactical considerations for the cannon battery commander and key leaders. Considerations for composite battery units include—
- Unit composition (howitzer mix).
- Manning levels for howitzer sections, fire direction centers (FDC), and platoon leadership.
- Technical firing solution computation capabilities.

Chapter 9

UNIT COMPOSITION (LIGHT AND MEDIUM HOWITZER MIX)

9-5. The makeup of a composite cannon battery will vary. Unit tables of organization and equipment, task-organization, commander's preference, personnel strength, level of training, individual capabilities, and other factors may require the battery commander to modify unit composition. The battery commander bases this decision on mission variables or unit tactical standard operating procedures. The battery commander issues planning guidance on unit composition to key leaders.

Note. The type of howitzer, associated prime mover (if so equipped), and ammunition resupply vehicle vary among the systems. See the applicable technical manual for general information and equipment description.

9-6. Planning considerations for unit composition include equipment type, quantity, supply, and maintenance associated with different types of equipment. Considerations vary according to the type of howitzer(s) (self-propelled or towed) and quantity of vehicles (wheels and tracks) and associated equipment in the cannon battery, which include:

- Position area requirements that increase with the use of self-propelled howitzers and other tracked vehicles, while decreasing with the use of towed howitzers and other wheeled vehicles.
- Climate and terrain that hampers or restricts movement of track or wheeled vehicles (mountains, jungle, desert, cold regions, and urban population areas).
- Methods of employment (platoon, paired, grouped, or single howitzer) that differ between terrain and distance.
- Method of control (centralized or decentralized) based on method of employment.

Note. Chapter 2 discusses techniques and key considerations for methods of employment and methods of control.

- Movement by alternate means (airborne or air assault), as required.

Note. For more information on airborne or air assault missions, see Field Manual (FM) 3-99.

- Sustainment requirements that increase with the amount of vehicles task-organized to the unit.
- Supply accountability of equipment with hand receipts, shortage annexes, and additional authorization listings.
- Operator level maintenance and records management of howitzers, vehicles, and associated equipment new (not organic) to the unit.
- Maintenance support from forward support company or brigade support battalion.

Note. A maintenance section is not currently authorized at battalion or battery level.

- Operator licensing requirements for organic and task-organized equipment.
- Ammunition (105-mm, 155-mm) management (see Appendix A).

9-7. For more information on sustainment within the cannon battalion, see ATP 3-09.23. For more information on howitzer systems, see Technical Manuals (TM) 9-1015-252-10 for the M119A2, TM 9-1015-260-10 for the M119A3, TM 9-1025-215-10 for the M777-series howitzer, and TMs 9-2350-314-10-1 and 9-2350-314-10-2 for the M109A6 Paladin howitzer.

MANNING LEVELS

9-8. The unit manning levels will vary based on unit composition. Unit tables of organization and equipment, task-organization, commander's preference, personnel strength, level of training, individual capabilities, and other factors may require the battery commander to modify requirements for unit manning levels. The battery commander bases this decision on mission variables or unit tactical standard operating procedures. The battery commander issues planning guidance on minimum safe manning levels for howitzer sections and FDC personnel during firing.

9-9. It is normal to expect howitzer sections and FDCs to reduce to numbers less than prescribed by tables of organization and equipment strength due to illness, casualties, battery tasking, and the need to rest personnel, among others. Combine the duties of section personnel to meet mission requirements and still maintain continuous operation, as required.

9-10. Planning considerations for manning levels include unit composition and minimum safe manning requirements. Considerations vary according to the assigned equipment, which include:
- Experience level (towed, self-propelled) for howitzer section personnel.
- Experience level for FDC personnel.
- Knowledgeable and competent personnel assignments from section level to platoon leadership.

9-11. Determine minimum safe manning requirements or levels as early as possible in the military decisionmaking process. Include these numbers in the unit tactical standard operating procedures, as applicable.

HOWITZER SECTION

9-12. Considerations for howitzer sections include:
- Tactical situation.
- Crew drill on each weapon system (dual assigned).
- Cross training among howitzer platforms to increase proficiency.
- Minimum safe manning requirements for firing.
- Training and certification programs for howitzer crews on each assigned weapon system.

9-13. The purpose of crew drill is to improve the performance of the howitzer section through execution of assigned tasks and cross training of section personnel. Drill howitzer sections until reactions to commands are automatic, rapid, and efficient. Adherence to procedures will prevent injury to personnel or damage to equipment.

9-14. Cross training of section personnel takes on an added importance with the introduction of dual howitzers at the section level. The howitzer section must be ready and capable of executing dual fire missions on both systems near simultaneously. In addition to indirect fires, the need may arise to include direct fires, as well. For more information on howitzer section crew drill and reduced crew drill, see the applicable howitzer technical manual

> **Example**
> Firing sections conducted a dual fire mission, switching between indirect and direct artillery fire modes on M777A2 and M119A3 weapon systems against several threat positions. These Soldiers fired nearly simultaneously in support of nearby troops in contact, while also engaging the forces firing at the combat outpost, switching between systems and modes within mere minutes.

Note. Chapter 11 discusses other considerations for cross training of composite and distributed units.

9-15. Combine howitzer sections to maintain established minimum safe manning requirements. Battery leadership may perform duties as cannoneers with a howitzer section, if required.

Chapter 9

> *Note.* Problems during firing arise due to a lack of training or sacrificing established procedure for speed. Bypassing established procedures can lead to inaccuracies in fires, wasted rounds, and a decrease in the effectiveness of fire support. Careless or improper procedures at the howitzer contribute to these inaccuracies. Proper training is the key to minimizing human error and careless gunnery procedures.

FIRE DIRECTION CENTER

9-16. Considerations for FDC personnel include:
- Military occupational specialty critical shortages.
- Requests for additional military occupational specialty authorizations above tables of organization and equipment.
- Fire request processing.
- Ammunition management.

9-17. The FDC is the primary fire control facility for the cannon battery. Positive and effective fire control depends on well-trained personnel able to process fire requests in a timely manner to support the mission. The FDC is organized and equipped to maintain continuous operation.

9-18. The FDC requires well-trained and properly staffed personnel to determine responsive and accurate firing data. Personnel or equipment shortages will result in a decrease in mission effectiveness. The battery commander may develop an operational needs statement based on mission variables. Identify considerations for critical shortages of military occupational specialties and requests for additional authorizations as early as possible in the military decisionmaking process. For more information on duties and responsibilities of FDC personnel, see TC 3-09.81.

PLATOON LEADERSHIP

9-19. Considerations for platoon leadership include:
- Supervision of gunnery procedures for firing elements, especially those assigned different weapon systems (dual assigned).
- Supervisory responsibilities involving firing safety for the unit.

9-20. The platoon leadership enforces gunnery procedures and safety practices within the unit, with special emphasis on FDC and howitzer section operation. Lack of attention to detail, improper supervision, and failure to make safety checks lead to incidents that result in equipment failure, and can lead to physical injury or death to personnel. Proper supervision of firing units could eliminate or at least reduce the opportunity for common mistakes or malpractices. Leaders at every level should be diligent in enforcement of safety practices and procedures. Each member of the unit is responsible for firing safety.

9-21. The battery commander and key leaders must identify the unique challenges as well as techniques and associated considerations for composite battery units. For more information on firing safety, to include duties and responsibilities of safety personnel in a battery, see the applicable gunnery publication.

Chapter 10
Distributed Units

This chapter provides a brief overview and discussion of techniques and associated considerations unique to cannon batteries operating as distributed units. Distributed units are characterized as small units operating independently over extended distances, with or without additional support. These small, highly capable tactical units spread across a large area to create a tactical advantage over threat forces.

OVERVIEW

10-1. Dispersion assists in disrupting or denying threat access to key terrain and avenues of approach. Extensive dispersion reduces the unit's vulnerability to threat observation and fires but may increase its vulnerability to attack by threat forces.

10-2. Current operations, recent trends, and lessons learned indicate the need for distributed units. Distributed units require effective small unit leaders, decentralized positions, decentralized decisionmaking and well-trained small units. The more distributed units are, the greater the reliance on effective leadership, standardization, and small unit performance. The responsibility of small unit leaders is ever increasing. Today, company grade officers and noncommissioned officers are fully prepared to assume much greater authority and responsibility than was traditionally expected at small unit level.

10-3. There are tactical advantages, disadvantages, and risks associated with small, distributed units. Small units operating independently from each other may require improved external sustainment support from higher headquarters; improved situational awareness; reconnaissance and surveillance support; organic sensors that can survive under fire; and increased local security. Additionally, increasing the distance between units beyond mutually supporting ranges may require support to supplement organic fires. Identify considerations associated with small, distributed units as early as possible in the military decisionmaking process.

10-4. Small, distributed units present unique challenges and tactical considerations for the battery commander and key leaders. Considerations for small, distributed units include:
- Methods of control (centralized or decentralized).
- Methods of employment (platoons, pairs, groups, or individual howitzers).
- Personnel (strength and level of training).
- Communications (equipment availability and level of training).
- Sustainment (supply and maintenance operations).

Note: Chapter 9 discusses other considerations for composite and distributed units.

PERSONNEL

10-5. Distributed units require well-trained and professional small unit leaders that focus training on small unit doctrine, tactics, techniques, and procedures. These small unit leaders motivate, inspire, and influence their Soldiers to work toward a common purpose, compelling them to go beyond their individual interests and work for the common good. Small units achieve success when competence breeds the confidence that cements cohesion. Distributed units will lead to a greater reliance on teamwork, cohesion, and trust.

10-6. Cannon batteries may perform maneuver tasks in addition to firing battery tasks, as required. The cannon battery is not equipped with the equipment, resources, or personnel to conduct standard infantry missions. A traditional infantry company is considerably larger that a cannon battery. All personnel must

Chapter 10

fully understand the mission; cultural impacts, if any; and rules of engagement. Unit tactical standard operating procedures must be developed, rehearsed, and coordinated to effectively deal with these complex situations.

10-7. The considerations for personnel will vary based on unit composition and method of employment. Unit tables of organization and equipment, task-organization, commander's guidance, personnel strength, level of training, individual capabilities, and other factors may require the battery commander to modify personnel assignments for task organization. The battery commander bases this decision on mission variables or unit tactical standard operating procedures. The battery commander issues planning guidance on personnel, to include minimum safe manning levels for firing and priorities for defense of the unit.

BATTERY PERSONNEL

10-8. Considerations for battery personnel include:
- Personnel strength levels.
  - Unit elements (distributed).
  - Unit positions (forward operating base or combat outpost).
- Level of training on defense tactics and procedures.
- Maneuver missions for one or more firing platoons.

Note. Distribution of FDC personnel across multiple locations such as forward operating bases or combat outposts can create a shortage of experience in FDCs. The unit should identify mission requirements (composite or distributed) and expedite operational needs statements, as needed prior to deployment.

10-9. Monitor personnel strength levels for unit elements conducting maneuver missions in addition to firing battery tasks. Monitor personnel strength levels for positions where the unit may not be able to fully maintain an effective defensive perimeter and provide for continuous fires from all howitzers.

MEDICAL SUPPORT

10-10. Considerations for medical support include:
- Medical personnel assigned to the unit.
- Task organization of combat medics to the firing platoons.
  - Augmentation.
  - Allocations.
- Identification of unit combat lifesavers.
  - Criteria.
  - Totals.
- Training of unit combat lifesavers.
  - Sustainment.
  - Requalification.
- Number of combat lifesaver bags.
- Requisition Class VIII supplies for combat lifesaver bags.
- Number of litters (standard collapsible or nonstandard collapsible) for casualty evacuation.
- Precombat checks or inspections for availability and contents of combat lifesaver bags (include in unit tactical standard operating procedures).

10-11. Request additional trained combat medical personnel to augment unit level combat medics to meet mission requirements. Determine the number of combat lifesavers that the unit needs and establish a selection criteria to identify the best qualified Soldiers to attend training. The goal should be to position a combat lifesaver and bag in every section and on every vehicle. Identify and nominate Soldiers to attend emergency medical technician training to enhance first responder care within the units.

COMMUNICATIONS

10-12. Distributed units require more robust communications equipment and assets to operate effectively over great distances. Communications between the howitzers and the FDC is a major concern with increased distances. Develop unit tactical standard operating procedures to establish primary and alternate means of communications and provide for redundancy.

10-13. The battery communication requirements will vary based on unit composition and method of employment. Unit tables of organization and equipment, task-organization, commander's guidance, personnel strength, level of training, individual capabilities, and other factors may require the battery commander to modify the unit communications plan. The battery commander bases this decision on mission variables or unit tactical standard operating procedures. The battery commander issues planning guidance on priorities for voice and data networks, to include redundancy.

10-14. Planning considerations for communications include:
- Communications equipment availability.
  - Tactical radios.
  - Wire communications.
  - Non-organic equipment.
- Information systems availability.
- Network availability.
  - Voice networks.
  - Data networks.
  - Connectivity.
  - Bandwidth.
  - Redundancy.
  - Rehearsals.
- Training.
  - Unit training.
  - New equipment training.
- Certification.
  - Operators.
  - Unit leadership.
- Interference.
- Security measures.

Note. Chapter 9 discusses other considerations for communications.

10-15. Inventory tactical radios and wire communications, if available for accountability and serviceability. In addition, inventory non-organic equipment assigned to the unit, for example, theater provided equipment. Inventory information systems, if available for accountability and serviceability. In addition, inventory peripherals, power supplies, and stand-alone kits, if equipped. Verify systems capability to maintain situational awareness, perform threat analysis, and display imagery analysis. Establish voice and data networks based on availability and operational status of equipment. Verify network connectivity and bandwidth. Request additional bandwidth to support mission requirements, as required. Establish backup plans for each network for redundancy. Conduct rehearsals of communications, to include degraded operation.

10-16. Determine level of training and certification of unit personnel on assigned equipment. Identify training requirements for communications equipment and information system operators. Request new equipment training or mobile training teams, if available. Develop a certification program for communications equipment or information system operators. Include unit leadership in training and certification, if possible.

10-17. Determine locations or terrain that may interfere with communications. Terrain masks may interfere or disrupt lines of communication. Verify communications for future locations, if possible. Relocate to improve communication with all elements or higher headquarters.

10-18. Develop communications security measures to prevent disruption in connectivity. For instance, use secure communications equipment whenever possible. In addition, practice communications discipline by limiting transmission length and frequency of use.

10-19. Mission success depends as much on preparation as it does on planning. Preparation requires leader and Soldier actions. To make a tentative plan, the battery commander must gather information by focusing on battery level mission variables. Mission checklists could be valuable in providing sample topics and questions that may assist the commander in this effort.

10-20. Tables are available, which provide sample mission checklists. These tables include:
- Mission planning.
- Precombat checklists for:
  - Ground threat (mounted and dismounted).
  - Air threat.
  - Counterfire.
  - Chemical, biological, radiological, and nuclear threats and hazards.
  - Medical evacuation.
  - Artillery raid.
  - Scatterable mines.
  - Massing.
  - Inventory of assets.
  - Critical events timeline.
  - Unit defense.
  - Degraded operation.

Note. Appendix B discusses sample mission checklists.

10-21. Develop some version of these checklists for use by battery personnel and incorporate the checklists into the unit tactical standard operating procedures. Develop checklists for composite units as well.

Chapter 11

Other Considerations for Composite or Distributed Units

This chapter discusses techniques and other considerations for cannon batteries operating as composite or distributed units. Section I begins with an overview and discussion of other considerations for training. Section II provides an overview and discussion of other considerations for battery tasks. Section III provides an overview and discussion of other considerations for sustainment. Section IV provides an overview and discussion of other considerations for communications. Section V provides an overview and discussion of other considerations for fire support. Section VI closes with an overview and discussion of other considerations for survey and meteorological tasks.

SECTION I – TRAINING

11-1. Field artillery skills require extensive training to maintain proficiency. These military occupational specialties suffer skills atrophy when weighted down with an increasing operation tempo and non-field artillery missions. In order to maintain field artillery skills, it is crucial that battery commanders and key leaders set aside time and resources for training. Once time is set aside, the focus should be on basic gunnery skills, with particular attention to cross training and reduced crew drill for howitzer sections and fire direction centers (FDC).

Note. Chapter 12 discusses home station training for deployment, mobile training teams, and new equipment training.

11-2. Training for composite or distributed units presents unique challenges and tactical considerations for the battery commander and key leaders. Other considerations for training include:
- Time available.
- Resources available.
- Cross training of howitzer sections on composite equipment.
- Reduced crew drill for howitzer section and FDC personnel.
- Certification of howitzer crews, FDCs, and platoon leadership.

PLANNING CONSIDERATIONS

11-3. Planning considerations for training will vary based on time and resources available. Unit tables of organization and equipment, task-organization, commander's guidance, personnel strength, level of training, individual capabilities, and other factors may require the cannon battery commander to modify the unit training plan. The battery commander bases this decision on mission variables or unit tactical standard operating procedures. The battery commander issues planning guidance to key leaders based on these considerations. This guidance dictates the necessary planning and preparation required to train the unit and ensure future mission success.

TECHNIQUES

11-4. The techniques for training composite and distributed units should be included in the unit's tactical standard operating procedures. Techniques include cross training, reduced size crew drill, and certification.

Chapter 11

CROSS TRAINING

11-5. Planning considerations for cross training include:
- Time available.
- Personnel available.
- Training objective.
- Training end state or desired outcome.

11-6. The Army trains leaders for their next higher position before they assume it. Small unit leaders train their Soldiers in the same way through cross training; preparing them to assume the next higher position within the section, squad, or team. Cross training provides unit depth and flexibility and fosters leader confidence. Sections conduct cross training to increase proficiency among section members. Section members rotate duties during training so that each member can perform all duties within the section. In composite cannon battery organizations, the howitzer sections have an added responsibility to conduct cross training on more than 1 howitzer system. The howitzer sections must be proficient on each howitzer system assigned to the unit, or dual assigned to the individual howitzer section.

Note. Cross training could include training on basic howitzer skills for all battery personnel not assigned to the howitzer sections, so that they could function efficiently with a howitzer section if required.

REDUCED SIZE CREW DRILL

11-7. Planning considerations for reduced crew drill include:
- Personnel available.
- Experience level.
- Level of training.
- Hot, warm, and cold platoon status.

11-8. Combine the duties of howitzer section personnel in order to meet mission requirements and maintain continuous operation. The howitzer section chief combines and assigns duties to the crewmembers. Personnel experience and level of training will dictate the minimum safe levels for manning howitzer sections.

Note. Standardized procedures for operating with a reduced crew were developed under the Army standardization program. For more information on howitzer section reduced crew drill, see applicable howitzer technical manual.

11-9. An alternative to reduced crew drill is the method of rotating personnel at "hot gun" platoon locations. In this scenario, the designated firing platoon maintains continuous manning of howitzers and the FDC. The firing platoon rotates the howitzers between a hot, warm, and cold status. The hot status represents a fully mission capable state of readiness, while the warm status represents a standby near fully mission capable status. The cold status could represent a non-mission capable status due to maintenance, rest, training, or unit tasking. Standardize the terms (hot, warm, cold gun), definitions, and methods mentioned here in the unit tactical standard operating procedures.

CERTIFICATION

11-10. Planning considerations for certification of FDCs, howitzer sections, and platoons include:
- Time available.
- Personnel available.
- Access to equipment.
- Certification level (artillery tables).

11-11. Certification and subsequent qualification of battery elements is the responsibility of the battery commander. Certification focuses on firing safety of howitzer crews and FDCs. This assessment validates the battery commander's recommendation of safety certification. The battery commander certifies his howitzer crews and FDCs, once the commander determines they are qualified to perform duties, as required. Complete certification for each assigned howitzer weapon system. Qualification is a live-fire event completed later at battery level and observed by battery leadership.

11-12. Access to equipment is critical for training, certification, and qualification if not readily available. Mobile training teams and new equipment training are options worth exploring for new or unfamiliar equipment. Identify planning considerations associated with training, certification, and qualification as early as possible in the military decisionmaking process. For more information on field artillery gunnery, to include training strategy, training plans, certification, evaluation, qualification, or field artillery safety, see applicable gunnery publications.

SECTION II – BATTERY TASKS

11-13. An operation will never go exactly as planned so the battery commander and key leaders must remain flexible and respond quickly to the unexpected. They must continuously evaluate mission variables and be prepared to deal with unplanned situations. This section briefly discusses other considerations for battery tasks. This section highlights those items generally common to all tasks, and discusses other considerations unique to composite and distributed units.

11-14. Composite and distributed units present unique challenges and tactical considerations for the battery commander and key leaders. Other considerations for battery tasks include:
- Continuous operation.
- Personnel management.
- Movement.
- Defense.

PLANNING CONSIDERATIONS

11-15. Planning considerations for battery tasks will vary based on the tactical situation or mission requirements. Unit tables of organization and equipment, task-organization, commander's guidance, personnel strength, level of training, individual capabilities, and other factors may require the battery commander to modify battery tasks. The battery commander bases this decision on mission variables or unit tactical standard operating procedures. The battery commander issues planning guidance to key leaders based on these considerations. This guidance dictates the necessary planning and preparations required to maintain continuous operation and ensure future mission success.

11-16. Small unit leaders must establish, conduct, and enforce detailed troop leading procedures. The unit should establish and conduct precombat checks and inspections of personnel and equipment prior to every mission.

TECHNIQUES

11-17. The techniques for composite or distributed unit tasks should be included in the unit's tactical standard operating procedures. These techniques should address continuous operations, unit movement, and unit defense.

CONTINUOUS OPERATION

11-18. Planning considerations for continuous operation include:
- Mission directives.
- Personnel strength levels.
- Personnel management.
- Priorities of work.

Chapter 11

- Work and rest schedules.
- Combat stress control.

11-19. Cannon batteries often operate for extended periods in continuous action. Units in combat can continue for extended periods at a high intensity level. During these periods, leaders and Soldiers must think faster and make decisions rapidly. They must be able to act spontaneously and simultaneously, even though the situation has changed. This continuous cycle of day and night operation and the associated stress of combat will cause degradation in performance over time and may lead to combat stress. Reducing this impact on performance is a significant challenge for the battery commander. For more information on combating combat stress, see ATP 6-22.5.

> *Note.* Both leaders and Soldiers sometimes regard themselves as being invulnerable to fatigue and the effects of sleep loss. Deliberately depriving yourself of sleep is counterproductive. Sleep deprivation could jeopardize mission accomplishment.

UNIT MOVEMENT

11-20. Planning considerations for movement include:
- Communications availability and reliability.
- Ballistic protection for vehicles.
- Counter improvised explosive device protection measures, if available.
- Crew served weapons.
- Convoy security.
- Range of organic and supporting indirect fire systems.
- Precombat checks.

11-21. Cannon batteries and platoons survive with a combination of movement and dispersion. Dispersion over great distances creates challenges for movement of vehicles for sustainment (logistics packages and ammunition resupply). Light, thin-skinned vehicles are most susceptible to targeting and damage by a threat. Whenever possible, use hard surface roads to minimize the risk of encountering mines and improvised explosive devices. Coordinate cleared and approved routes before departure. Hard copy maps may not be accurate or reliable. Aerial reconnaissance may facilitate movement planning. Ensure convoy leaders report departures, maintain communications during movement, and report arrival at the final destination. Anticipate weather conditions and its effect on mobility.

11-22. Train Soldiers on improvised explosive devices and mine identification, likely locations, and marking procedures. Determine proper reporting procedures when improvised explosive devices or mines are located. Rehearse procedures for responding to mounted and dismounted detonation. For more information on improvised explosive device defeat techniques, see ATP 3-90.37, TC 3-90.119, and the individual tasks identified in the Central Army Registry.

UNIT DEFENSE

11-23. Planning considerations for defense include:
- Time available.
- Resources available.
- Distance between adjacent units.
- Perimeter defense.
- Mounted and dismounted patrols.
- Quick reaction forces.
- Unmanned aircraft systems, if available.

11-24. Cannon batteries are valuable targets for threat forces, and small unit leaders must limit the vulnerability of their positions. Proper preparation of a defensive position provides for early warning of threat activities and reduces the threat posed to personnel and equipment. A perimeter defense is the preferred method of security for a battery or platoon. This provides the best security because it is oriented in all directions. The use of patrolling and available observation systems enhances the overall effectiveness of the defense.

> *Note.* Based on dispersion and personnel strength levels, the unit may not be able to fully operate an effective defensive perimeter and provide for continuous fires.

11-25. Develop checklists for continuous operation, movement, and defense, to include patrolling and quick reaction forces for use by battery personnel and incorporated into the unit tactical standard operating procedures. Develop checklists for composite and distributed units as well. Identify planning considerations associated with battery tasks as early as possible in the military decisionmaking process. For more information on employment of unmanned aircraft systems and mission planning considerations, see ATP 3-04.1. For more information on considerations and preparations for defense or security tasks, see ATP 3-21.8, ATTP 3-21.71, FM 3-90-1, and Army Doctrine Reference Publication (ADRP) 3-90.

Patrols

11-26. Planning considerations for use of patrolling in the defense include:
- Threat situation.
- Personnel available.
- Combination of mounted and dismounted movement.
- Escalation of force measures.
- Cordon and search.
- Site exploitation.
- Detainees.
- Improvised explosive devices.
- Embedded sniper teams.
- Casualty evacuation.
- Quick reaction forces.
- Precombat checks.

> *Note.* Precombat checks and inspections are critical to the survival of Soldiers for both mounted and dismounted patrols.

11-27. Use a combination of mounted and dismounted patrolling whenever possible. Use mounted pickup points to increase dismounted patrol time. In addition, use mounted patrols in combination with dismounted infantry to eliminate predictability.

11-28. Rehearse clearance of improvised explosive device procedures, to include locating cache sites and dismounted route clearance. Request support from explosive ordnance or route clearance teams, if available.

> *Note.* The improvised explosive device is obviously the most prevalent weapon of choice for a threat, and constant vigilance is required to prevent the threat from emplacing larger and more deadly devices.

11-29. All units must be proficient in the fundamentals of patrolling. Patrolling is a daily requirement in some regions, and can be the largest determinant of overall mission success. Ensure all Soldiers understand the principle of patrolling, especially squad leaders and above. For more information on considerations and use of patrolling, see ATP 3-21.8 and ATTP 3-21.71.

Quick Reaction Forces

11-30. Planning considerations for the use of quick reaction forces include:

Chapter 11

- Personnel available.
- Equipment available.
- Mode of transportation.
- Quick reaction force commander.
- Reinforce perimeter.
- Supplement patrols.

Note. Composition of the reaction force is dependent on mission variables and unit tactical standard operating procedures.

11-31. Determine equipment requirements for quick reaction forces. Inventory communications equipment, to include communications equipment security measures. Assign crew served and, if available, antitank weapons to fire teams. Coordinate transportation for quick reaction forces, based on mission requirements.

> **Warfighting Skills**
>
> Train battery personnel on basic and advanced infantry warfighting skills as necessary. Base the use of patrolling or quick reaction forces on mission variables and unit tactical standard operating procedures.
>
> For more information on basic and advanced warfighting skills, see Soldier training publication (STP) 21-1-SMCT or STP 21-24-SMCT. These manuals include Army warrior training plans for warrior skills and task summaries for critical common tasks that support unit wartime missions.

Direct Fire

11-32. Direct fire is a special technique that demands a high level of training and requires the howitzer section to operate as an independent unit. Considerations for the use of direct fire include trajectory, target type, and ammunition.

11-33. Trajectory characteristics change with respect to range to target and charge fired. To produce the highest muzzle velocity and a flat trajectory, always use the maximum charge available. Shorter ranges are the most accurate to engage a target, because the trajectory is flattest. Intermediate ranges provide a trajectory flat enough to allow direct estimation of range without actually bracketing the target. At longer ranges, hits are only reasonably possible and bracketing will probably be required to obtain a hit.

> **WARNING**
> Engage targets closer than 800 meters from the howitzer only during combat situations. Lethal fragments can travel up to 600 meters from the point of burst.

11-34. The most likely direct fire targets are vehicles or dismounted personnel. Vehicles are engaged as point targets and personnel are engaged as area targets. Direct fire targets should be engaged in priority, for example:
- Vehicles at short ranges threatening to overrun the position.
- Stationary vehicles covering the advance of other vehicles.
- Command and control vehicles.
- Dismounted infantry.

11-35. Planning considerations for the use of direct fires include:
- Personnel available.
- Level of training.
- Equipment available.

- Communications available.
- Howitzer range cards.
- Ammunition.
- Forward operating base and combat outpost defense.
- Rehearsals.

11-36. Direct fire provides a decisive response to threat attacks on vulnerable positions. However, it requires knowledgeable and competent personnel, from the howitzer section to the platoon leader or battery commander.

11-37. Use thermal weapon sights on the M913 Gun Electronic Laying Optical Night Sight for nighttime direct fire engagements, if available. Coordinate self-illumination missions, as required.

Note. The M913 mount facilitates the use of selected night vision sights or authorized infrared lasers on the M119-series howitzer. This device enhances the capability of howitzer crews to engage direct fire targets at night. In addition, this configuration reduces or eliminates the need for self-illumination fire missions while allowing the unit to maintain light discipline.

Note. Use of this device in combat operations overseas resulted in a reduction in collateral damage and civilian deaths.

11-38. Annotate potential threat firing positions on the howitzer range card. Establish target reference points, complete with distances, directions, and elevations.

Note. Use the laser range finder on the GLPS, hasty survey, map scaling or to determine this information.

11-39. Determine and standardize ammunition for direct fire engagements (propellant, shell, and fuze combinations). For example, use high explosive shell with point detonating fuze against armored targets and high explosive shell with fuze time for dismounted attack. These may be standardized in the unit tactical standard operating procedures to save time. If other than standard is desired, commands for shell, charge, and fuze are given after direction to target.

Note. Fuze delay mode works well against fortified threat positions. The projectile penetrates deeper into the face of the targeted position while simultaneously limiting collateral damage.

11-40. Conduct direct fire rehearsals individually at section level and collectively at platoon level. Rehearse direct fire procedures to include notifying FDC of direct fire mode and requesting clearance to fire. For more information on loading and firing during direct fire missions, see the applicable howitzer technical manual.

Killer Junior

11-41. Killer Junior is a special technique developed to defend positions against threat dismounted ground attack. Much like direct fire, Killer Junior demands a high level of training and requires the section to operate as an independent unit. Killer junior uses time fuzed high explosive projectiles set to burst in the air at close range seconds after firing.

11-42. Direct fire and Killer Junior provide the battery commander a large bore, first response weapon for battery defense. This allows the battery commander to engage the threat at the farthest range possible. Standardize ammunition (propellant, shell, and fuze combinations (high explosive and time)) for engagements in unit tactical standard operating procedures.

11-43. Develop checklists for continuous operation, movement, and defense, to include patrolling and quick reaction forces for use by battery personnel and incorporated into the unit tactical standard operating procedures. Develop checklists for composite and distributed units as well. Identify planning considerations associated with battery tasks as early as possible in the military decisionmaking process.

Note. Appendix B discusses sample mission checklists; appendix F discusses Killer Junior.

SECTION III – SUSTAINMENT

11-44. The cannon battery has limited resources for sustainment. Instead, the battery must rely on the cannon field artillery battalion, forward support company, brigade support battalion, or sustainment brigade for the support necessary to sustain tasks. Sustainment responsibilities at battery level are primarily to report status, supervise operator level maintenance, request support, and verify sustainment task execution within the battery position. Any increase in vehicles and associated equipment totals directly relates to an increase in forecasting requirements for sustainment support.

11-45. Sustainment for composite or distributed units presents unique challenges and tactical considerations for the battery commander and key leaders. Other considerations for sustainment include:
- Maintenance of howitzers.
- Maintenance personnel qualifications.
- Unit supply.
- Ammunition management.

11-46. Forecast requirements for sustainment support, and forward requests to the battalion S-4, forward support company commander, or brigade sustainment officer. Collaborate with the distribution platoon leader for replenishment, as required. For more information on sustainment within the cannon field artillery battalion, see ATP 3-09.23

PLANNING CONSIDERATIONS

11-47. Planning considerations for sustainment will vary based on total number of vehicles and equipment requiring sustainment Unit tables of organization and equipment, task-organization, commander's guidance, personnel strength, level of training, individual capabilities, and other factors may require the battery commander to modify the unit plan for sustainment. The battery commander bases this decision on mission variables or unit tactical standard operating procedures. The battery commander issues planning guidance to key leaders based on these considerations. This guidance dictates the necessary planning and preparations required to sustain the unit and ensure future mission success.

TECHNIQUES

11-48. The techniques for sustaining composite or distributed units should be included in the unit's tactical standard operating procedures. The following paragraphs will briefly discuss techniques available and associated considerations for sustainment.

11-49. Planning considerations for sustainment include the quantity of vehicles (wheels and tracks) and associated equipment in the battery. Considerations vary according to task-organization, which include:
- Sustainment requirements that increase with the amount of vehicles task-organized to the unit.
- Supply accountability of equipment with hand receipts, shortage annexes, and additional authorization listings.
- Operator level maintenance.
- Records management of howitzers, vehicles, and associated equipment new (not organic) to the unit.
- Maintenance support from forward support company or brigade support battalion.

Note. A maintenance section is not currently authorized at battalion or battery level.

- Operator licensing requirements for organic and task-organized equipment, if applicable.
- Ammunition (105-mm, 155-mm) management (see Appendix A).

MAINTENANCE OF CANNON SYSTEM (LIGHT OR MEDIUM)

11-50. Planning considerations for maintenance of howitzers and prime movers include:
- Personnel available.
- Support available.
- Training.
  - Unit.
  - Institutional.

11-51. Request support for wheel vehicle (heavy or light) and tracked vehicle mechanics, as required. Identify requirements for specialized maintenance training above operator level (additional skill identifier U6 or U7). Nominate potential candidates for maintenance training. Request training allocations for individuals down to howitzer section level.

Note. This maintenance course provides enlisted personnel with the skills and knowledge to perform unit maintenance of cannon weapons armament systems.

11-52. Success on the battlefield directly relates to the unit's ability to maintain equipment and material in effective operating condition. When breakdowns occur, the lowest echelon possible must repair equipment as far forward as possible. Technical manuals provide repair procedures and guidelines for battlefield repairs. Maintenance qualified personnel at battery level will help to bridge the gap between operator and next higher-level maintenance.

Note. A maintenance section is not currently authorized at battery level.

SUPPLY

11-53. Planning considerations for unit supply include:
- Level of training proficiency.
- Multiple property books.
- Property accountability.
- Hand receipt procedures.
- Unit identification codes.
- Training change request.
- Orders in a timely manner.

11-54. The battery has limited resources for sustainment. The battery supply section is equipped to provide limited sustainment support. Supply activities and property accountability become burdensome when units distribute across large areas and numerous locations.

Note. Supply assets may be consolidated at battalion level by design or task organization.

11-55. Separate organizational equipment from theater provided equipment, if applicable. Mark equipment for identification. Inventory equipment and issue equipment hand receipts to unit elements as soon as possible. Document equipment location on hand receipts or some other locally developed documentation. Conduct periodic inventories of organizational equipment, as time permits. Secure any equipment not issued to end users. Request separate unit identification codes for home station, combat training centers, and combat operations.

AMMUNITION MANAGEMENT

11-56. Ammunition management involves the resupply, management, handling, segregation, and preparation of semi-fixed and separate loading howitzer ammunition, to include forecasting requirements based on mission variables. The battery commander, platoon leaders, platoon sergeants, and howitzer

Chapter 11

section chiefs all share in a portion of this responsibility. Identify planning considerations associated with sustainment as early as possible in the military decisionmaking process.

Note. Appendix A discusses other considerations for ammunition management.

SECTION IV – COMMUNICATIONS

11-57. Communications and equipment are essential elements for planning, directing, and controlling operations. The commander must develop techniques for communications that promote an expeditious flow of information throughout the unit. These techniques and associated considerations should be included in the unit's tactical standard operating procedures.

11-58. The unit must successfully install, operate, and manage network and automation equipment in order to communicate effectively. The increased distances at which units typically operate in, coupled with the lack of communications equipment in the tables of organization and equipment or personnel to operate and maintain it create challenges for the battery commander and key leaders. Fielding new communications equipment without the proper training can be detrimental to mission accomplishment.

Note. A communications section is no longer authorized at battery level.

Note. The communications representatives at battalion level provide battery personnel with advanced technical assistance in installing, operating, and maintaining the battery communications system. Battery personnel share responsibility for the installation, operation, and maintenance of the system.

11-59. Communications for composite or distributed units present unique challenges and tactical considerations for the battery commander and key leaders. Other considerations for communications include:
- Radio network structure.
- Information systems.
- Bandwidth.
- Communications support.

11-60. Training on organic communications equipment, to include installation and troubleshooting prior to deployment is effective and fosters confidence in communications skills. For more information on information systems and communications within the cannon field artillery battalion, see ATP 3-09.23.

PLANNING CONSIDERATIONS

11-61. Planning considerations for communications will vary based on equipment availability and bandwidth. Unit tables of organization and equipment, task-organization, commander's guidance, personnel strength, level of training, individual capabilities, and other factors may require the battery commander to modify the unit communications plan. The battery commander bases this decision on mission variables or unit tactical standard operating procedures. The battery commander issues planning guidance to key leaders based on these considerations. This guidance dictates the necessary planning and preparations required to maintain communications with higher headquarters and ensure future mission success.

TECHNIQUES

11-62. The techniques for communications in composite and distributed units should be included in the unit's tactical standard operating procedures. Consider the radio network structure, wire system, information systems, bandwidth, host nation considerations, and communications support

RADIO NETWORK STRUCTURE

11-63. Planning considerations for radio network structure include:
- Equipment availability.
- Network connectivity.
- Network security.
- Line of sight.
- System redundancy.
- Satellite communications.
- Additional authorizations.

11-64. Radio communication is essential to the unit and its ability to provide effective fires. The network structure should rely heavily on frequency modulation radio communications that monitor multiple radio networks while maintaining continuity of operation during displacement. The network must communicate effectively over long distances to many diverse elements, including the field artillery battalion, fires cells, fire support teams, division artillery, or a field artillery brigade. The radio network structure will rely increasingly upon data communications, which have shorter range capabilities than voice communications.

11-65. Inventory radio systems and associated equipment to include:
- Antennas.
- Microphones.
- Headsets.
- Cabling.
- Stand-alone kits, as applicable.
- Vehicle mounting hardware and equipment.
- Batteries (backup power).
- Communications equipment operating instructions (secure communications).

11-66. Minimize situations that obstruct line of sight communications. Establish satellite communications as a backup to digital communications. Request sufficient satellite frequencies from higher headquarters to support communications requirements. Request vehicle mounts and stand-alone kits for satellite communications operation. Request additional authorizations, as required.

WIRE SYSTEM

11-67. When deployed, wire communication systems may be locally available from host nation sources. The battery and platoon may use both radio and wire equipment based on mission variables. One system will be designated primary and the other will become secondary. There are advantages and disadvantages associated with both. A radio permits mobility and speed but is susceptible to threat electronic warfare. Wire lines are much less vulnerable to threat electronic warfare, but inhibit rapid movement and speedy installation. Therefore, the strength of one is the weakness of the other. Units must strive to develop system redundancy. Determine diagrams and system configurations that provide practical and realistic alternatives to establishing battery communications. Established methods, procedures, and configurations should be included in the unit tactical standard operating procedures.

INFORMATION SYSTEMS

11-68. Planning considerations for information systems include:
- Equipment availability.
- Internet protocol addresses.
- Firewalls.
- Additional authorizations.

11-69. Request sufficient internet protocol addresses for information systems to maintain continuous communications. Manage network firewalls for information systems security. Request additional authorizations, as required. Request tactical network training for administrators, as required.

11-70. Inventory information systems and associated equipment, to include:
- Peripherals.
- Vehicle mounting hardware and equipment, if equipped.
- Stand-alone desktop configuration kits.
- Uninterrupted power supplies.
- Power strips.

BANDWIDTH

11-71. Planning considerations for bandwidth include:
- Network management.
- Connectivity outages.
- Additional authorizations.

11-72. Request sufficient bandwidth to support operations. Manage the network to ensure there is enough bandwidth to support imagery analysis at battery level. Maintain network connectivity to minimize outages. Request increases in authorization, as required. Identify the network architecture used in theater, if possible.

HOST NATION CONSIDERATIONS

11-73. Planning considerations for communications with host nation forces include:
- Equipment available.
- Training required, as applicable.
- Liaison.
- Interpreter.

11-74. Inventory communication equipment by type and quantity in accordance with the subparagraph on radio network structure above. Determine compatibility between communication equipment types. Request communications support from higher headquarters, as required.

11-75. Determine requirements for liaison. Request support from higher headquarters, as required. Establish liaison in accordance with mission directives.

11-76. Identify requirements for interpreter support. Request support from higher headquarters, as required. Distribute interpreters throughout unit, as applicable.

11-77. Host nation forces may possess communications equipment in differing quantities and types from our armed forces. Consider this planning factor when conducting missions with embedded host nation forces. Liaison with the embedded elements could prove valuable in the exchange of information and instructions. The liaison officer could update the commander on the progress of their actions and any significant actions that occurred in their area or with their positions. An interpreter may be required to monitor the network and communicate with the embedded unit.

COMMUNICATIONS SUPPORT

11-78. Planning considerations for communications support include:
- Direct support.
- Retransmission.
- Contractor support.

11-79. Request communications support from higher headquarters, as needed. Request retransmission to maintain sufficient communication with higher headquarter and adjacent units, as required. Request contractor support for new equipment training, as required. Identify and resource the network architecture used in the theater of operation prior to deployment, if possible. Identify planning considerations associated with communications as early as possible in the military decisionmaking process.

SECTION V – FIRE SUPPORT

11-80. Small units face physical constraints operating as composite units or as distributed units. In addition, circumstances may find the firing battery with additional attached personnel to perform tasks not normally associated with a battery. For example, widely distributed units may have fire support personnel provided to conduct planned tasks with multinational forces or for base defense. There may also be engagement constraints that make employment of fires restrictive in nature. In some instances, the close proximity to friendly forces and local nationals requires the employment of precision munitions. If precision munitions are not available, the unit must be able to employ area munitions assets. Properly plan and register these fires to be effective. Identify considerations associated with fire support as early as possible in the military decisionmaking process.

11-81. Fire support presents unique challenges and tactical considerations for the battery commander and key leaders. Considerations for fire support include:
- Personnel available (fire support officer, forward observer, or joint fires observer).
- Communications.
- Priority of fires.
- Clearance of fires.
- Counterfire.
- Target acquisition.
- Joint fires.
- Close air support.
- Organic fires.

PLANNING CONSIDERATIONS

11-82. Observer management will vary based on location and personnel available. Unit tables of organization and equipment, task-organization, commander's preference, personnel strength, level of training, individual capabilities, and other factors may require the battery commander to modify planning guidance. The battery commander bases this decision on mission variables or unit tactical standard operating procedures. The battery commander issues planning guidance on fire support.

TECHNIQUES

11-83. The techniques for observer management in composite and distributed units should be included in the unit's tactical standard operating procedures. Planning considerations for delivery units at forward operating bases and combat outposts include:
- Personnel available (forward observer or joint fires observer).
- Equipment available.
  - Lightweight countermortar radar, if equipped.
  - Unmanned aircraft systems, as applicable.

Note. For more information on employment of unmanned aircraft systems and mission planning considerations, see ATP 3-04.1.

- Location (forward operating base and combat outpost).
- Communications.
- Clearance of fires.
  - Airspace clearance.

Chapter 11

- Ground deconfliction.
- Levels of command.
* Counterfire.
* Target acquisition.
    - Observation.
    - Imagery.
* Fires.

11-84. Inventory communications equipment to determine equipment allocations and identify critical shortages. Ensure observers, if assigned, have the equipment necessary to request and adjust fires. Monitor internet relay chat clients, if available for target grids, observer grids, shell and fuze combinations requested, and other useful information pertinent for FDC operation.

11-85. Use available forward operating base or combat outpost observation towers as platforms for target acquisition. Develop aerial imagery, complete with identified target reference points.

11-86. Maintain centralized control over all fires. Clear each target of civilian and collateral damage hazards prior to sending the fire mission to the howitzers or mortars.

JOINT FIRES OBSERVER

11-87. Joint fires observers are specially trained and qualified members of the fire support team. Joint fires observers work closely with joint terminal attack controllers to provide timely and accurate close air support targeting information and autonomous terminal guidance operation. This information is critical for the commander to accurately assess the situation and associated risks in order to determine the proper course of action. Joint fires observers facilitate the commander's access to joint fires, by providing small units access to joint fires needed to meet ground commander objectives.

> *Note.* Joint fires observers deploy in a manner similar to traditional forward observers. However, the priority for employment should be to areas where close air support is required and in accordance with the unit observation plan and joint tactical air controller location.

11-88. Considerations for joint fires observers include:
* Mission support requirements.
* Personnel available.
* Equipment available.

> *Note.* Observers receive equipment from a variety of sources, including tables of organization and equipment, rapid fielding initiatives, and theater provided equipment. It is imperative that observers have the maximum time available to familiarize and train with this equipment prior to mission execution.

* Equipment training, as required.
* Sustainment training.

> *Note.* Joint fires observer skills are perishable. Commanders and fire support officers must develop sustainment training programs to enhance skill sets, increase proficiency, and foster confidence.

11-89. Determine equipment requirements for joint fires observers. Joint fires observer equipment requirements include:
* Multiband radio.
* Friendly marking device (marker panels, signal mirror, and infrared position markers [strobe]).
* Target marking device (laser designators and visible and infrared laser pointers).

- Laser range finder or designator.
- Global positioning system.

11-90. Submit operational needs statements for equipment or training requirements. Request contractor support or mobile training teams for communications training support, as required.

Note. Field artillery battalion commanders or their designated representatives are responsible for observer training requirements and program management. The designated representative executes program oversight and policies established by higher headquarters. Documentation of these requirements is contained in the digital training management system.

Note. The digital training management system allows ready access to online tracking and verification of individual training requirements and status. The digital training management system replaces hard copy training record requirements.

EXAMPLE SCENARIOS

11-91. Joint fires observers may be collocated with battery elements or positioned in the nearby vicinity. The joint fires observer is a valuable resource for the battery commander. Make every attempt to integrate joint fires observers into the battery mission tasks. Develop mission specific techniques for employing joint fires observers.

11-92. The examples provided below illustrate situations where the use of joint fires observers could contribute to overall mission success.

Note. These examples are for illustration purposes only. Other techniques or designs developed can be included in unit tactical standard operating procedures.

Example

This example involves the reconnaissance, surveillance, or observation of an objective and includes tasks conducted at any unit level.

The joint fires observer collocates a position with a fire support team, scout team, long-range surveillance detachment, sea-air-land team, or a special operations unit with the task to observe an objective, avenue of approach, or high-payoff target.

The observer conducts specific reporting as the basis for close air support requests and fire support coordination. The observer provides weapons adjustments and battle damage assessment, as required.

The joint terminal attack controller may be located at another observation position or at higher headquarters tactical operations center.

> **Example**
>
> This example involves a cordon and search mission, but it could equally apply to other missions, including artillery raids or direct action against a threat.
>
> This scenario includes tasks conducted at battery or platoon level by battery personnel or other brigade elements.
>
> The joint fires observer occupies an overwatch position on the outer cordon prior to actions on the objective. The observer readies the position in order to provide support on the objective. The observer provides observation and reacts to threat targets within the friendly forces field of view while on the objective.
>
> The observer provides spot reports on threat size, location, activity, and time to the mission commander and fire support chain. This information may not be readily apparent to the friendly forces on the objective. The observer can provide situational awareness and timely targeting information to the joint terminal attack controller in order to facilitate close air support. The joint fires observer can relay real time battle damage assessment to the controller following engagement and recommend additional actions or weapons adjustments.
>
> The joint terminal attack controller can remain either at the task force tactical operation center, a command post location on the outer cordon, on the objective, or at an additional observation post location on the outer cordon.

> **Example**
>
> This example involves convoy security.
>
> This scenario includes tasks in support of battery or platoon movement or as part of a convoy security detail.
>
> The joint fires observer occupies a vehicle that allows for the most flexibility and command connectivity to perform his duties. The observer should have a full understanding of convoy techniques and unit tactical standard operating procedures.
>
> The joint terminal attack controller may be located at any nearby location or at higher headquarters tactical operations center.
>
> The observer conducts mission specific reporting as the basis for close air support requests and fire support coordination. The observer provides situational awareness and timely targeting information to the controller in order to facilitate close air support, as required. The observer provides weapons adjustments and battle damage assessment, as required.
>
> Note. The joint fires observer may pass through several maneuver force areas of operation due to convoy duration and distance traveled. The observer may not work with a familiar joint terminal attack controller. In this case, the observer contacts higher headquarters for new contact (joint terminal attack controller) information, if not already known.

> **Example**
>
> This example involves unforeseen situations, to include troops in contact.
>
> This scenario includes tasks conducted at battery or platoon level by battery personnel or other brigade elements in support of a military transition team where an unforeseen event arises, which requires close air support.
>
> *Note.* The friendly unit could have more than one joint fires observer.
>
> The observer conducts mission specific reporting as the basis for close air support requests and fire support coordination. The observer provides situational awareness and timely targeting information to the controller in order to facilitate close air support, as required. The observer provides weapons adjustments and battle damage assessment, as required.
>
> In this particular situation, troops are in contact with a threat. The observer's job is extremely difficult due to the emergency nature of the situation. The observer quickly responds to the event with little or no planning and maintains situational awareness, all while possibly being under fire. The observer coordinates close air support and continued fixed wing armed overwatch, as required.
>
> *Note.* Observers assigned to a military transition team may face additional problems of language barriers and possibly reduced multinational command, control, and communications.

SECTION VI – METEOROLOGY AND SURVEY

11-93. Meteorological data is one of the five requirements for accurate fire. Accurate meteorological corrections are crucial to achieve first round fire for effect and to engage targets over longer distances. This also serves to conserve ammunition, increase the surprise effect, decrease time in adjustment, and reduce the potential for fratricide. Meteorological data should be updated when new information is received.

11-94. Survey data provides a common grid that enables massing of unit fires to aggressively target threat positions. The establishment of a common grid and the single operational datum within the common grid is a command responsibility. Survey teams provide survey support to firing batteries and platoons, radars, forward observers, and mortar firing positions, as required. Identify considerations associated with meteorological and survey digital tasks as early as possible in the military decisionmaking process.

11-95. Survey tasks present unique challenges and tactical considerations for the battery commander and key leaders. Considerations for survey tasks include:
- Mission requirements.
- Personnel available.
- Equipment available.
- Communications challenges.

METEOROLOGICAL DATA

11-96. Current meteorological data must be applied for accurate artillery fires, battlefield forecasts, radiological fallout predictions, and target acquisition. This information is in the form of meteorology messages provided by the field artillery battalion headquarters.

11-97. Computer Meteorological Data-Profiler (AN/GMK-2) is an evolutionary block of the Profiler system and is designed to reduce the logistical footprint to a laptop configuration located in the field artillery battalion main command post.

Chapter 11

11-98. Computer Meteorological Data-Profiler interfaces with the AFATDS via local area network connection and is operated by the AFATDS operator. The battalion AFATDS transmits meteorological data to the subordinate field artillery units. For more information on the Computer Meteorological Data-Profiler, see Technical Bulletin (TB) 11-6660-299-13.

SURVEY

11-99. The considerations for survey will vary based on unit priorities for survey support. Unit tables of organization and equipment, support relationship, commander's preference, personnel strength, level of training, individual capabilities, and other factors may require the battalion commander or S-3 to modify survey guidance. The commander or S-3 bases this decision on mission variables and unit tactical standard operating procedures. The battalion commander or the S-3 issues planning guidance on survey plan.

11-100. Planning considerations for survey tasks include equipment availability and survey capabilities. Considerations vary according to the survey plan, which include:

- Mission requirements.
- Survey support requests.
- Equipment available.
- Equipment serviceability.
- Personnel available.
- Communications protocols.
- Survey data.

Note. All survey data must have a second independent verification.

11-101. Establish communications with adjacent units and higher headquarters. Verify communications protocols with survey section, as required. The survey section must be able to provide updated survey data to firing elements in order to facilitate accurate fires. Verify survey information, and disseminate information (location and description of survey control point) to firing elements, as required. For more information on field artillery survey, to include support request procedures, see ATP 3-09.02.

Chapter 12

Deployment

This chapter provides a brief overview and discussion of techniques and associated considerations for deployment. For more information on Army force generation, see Army Regulation 525-29.

OVERVIEW

12-1. The Army operates on a rotational basis to provide a sustained flow of trained and ready forces, prepared for decisive action. Army force generation is a rotational readiness model designed to provide strategic flexibility to meet security requirements for a continuous presence of deployed forces. The Army force generation process is the structured progression of unit readiness over time to produce trained, ready, and cohesive units prepared for operational deployment. Identify planning considerations associated with deployment as early as possible in the military decisionmaking process.

12-2. Deployment preparations for battery units present unique challenges and tactical considerations for the battery commander and key leaders. Considerations for unit deployment include:
- Role (standard or nonstandard).
- Development of the training strategy.
- Integration of select deployment mission essential tasks prior to unit validation at combat training centers.
- Pre-deployment site surveys.

PLANNING CONSIDERATIONS

12-3. Planning considerations for deployment will vary based on the mission and time available for training. Unit tables of organization and equipment, task-organization, commander's guidance, personnel strength, level of training, individual capabilities, and other factors may require the battery commander to modify the unit training plan. The battery commander bases this decision on mission variables and unit tactical standard operating procedures. The battery commander issues planning guidance to key leaders based on these considerations. This guidance dictates the necessary planning and preparations required to deploy and ensure future mission success.

TECHNIQUES

12-4. The techniques for deploying units should be included in the unit's tactical standard operating procedures. The following paragraphs will briefly discuss techniques available and associated considerations used in deployment.

12-5. Planning considerations for deployment include task-organization and equipment available for training. Considerations vary according to the stated mission requirements, which include:
- Personnel strength.
- Level of training.
- Operational needs statement or request for forces.
- New equipment training.
- Mobile training teams.

Chapter 12

- Home station training.
- Equipment availability for nonstandard missions.

NEW EQUIPMENT TRAINING

12-6. Planning considerations for new equipment training include:
- Requirements (operational needs statement).
- Time available.
- Equipment available.
- Priorities and distribution.
- Facilities.
- Transportation.
- Qualification range support, as required.

12-7. Superior technology has allowed the Army the ability to field the newest equipment available to fight our wars. In some cases Soldiers receive equipment that they are not trained on correctly, or do not have a complete understanding of the capabilities. Allow sufficient time for new equipment training.

12-8. Commanders request new equipment training to support identified training and mission preparation shortfalls. New equipment training teams instruct basic maintenance of systems, set up procedures, and operation, at a minimum. Expand this training from operator level training to include leader tasks and collective training, if time available. The training team can also evaluate collective training against established guidelines and facilitate unit after actions reviews.

Note. The system program manager releases a memorandum of notification outlining specific fielding requirements, along with a distribution plan for system fielding. A fielding plan summary details the prioritized unit distribution. At this point, the program manager releases a fielding schedule for coordination and distribution to various units.

Note. Before equipment is officially signed over to a unit, new equipment training must be conducted in conjunction with the material fielding. New equipment training is the responsibility of the program executive officer or program manager and allows for transfer of equipment use and support requirement knowledge from the material developer to the users, trainers, and maintainers of new Army equipment.

MOBILE TRAINING TEAMS

12-9. Planning considerations for mobile training team requests include:
- Requirements (operational needs statement).
- Time available.
- Personnel available.
- Equipment available.

12-10. Mobile training teams are similar to new equipment training teams. A mobile training team normally consists of one or more military or civilian personnel sent on temporary duty, to give instruction. These teams could include military instructors, civilian field service representatives, unit subject matter experts, or train-the-trainers. The mission of the team is to train personnel to operate, maintain, and employ weapons and support systems; or to develop a unit self-training capability in a particular skill.

HOME STATION TRAINING PRIOR TO DEPLOYMENT

12-11. The considerations for home station training will vary based on pre-deployment training focus and equipment availability. Unit tables of organization and equipment, support relationship, commander's preference, personnel strength, level of training, individual capabilities, and other factors may require the battery commander to modify home station training. The battery commander bases this decision on mission variables and unit tactical standard operating procedures. The battery commander issues training guidance on priorities for individual, collective, and non-standard missions training.

12-12. Planning considerations for home station training prior to deployment include personnel and equipment availability for training. Considerations vary according to mission requirements and training strategy, which include:
- Time available.
- Individual training.
- Collective training.
- Non-field artillery skills training.
- Equipment availability for non-field artillery missions (operational needs statement).
- Reset training.

12-13. Develop unit training for non-field artillery skills set topic areas, which include:
- Maneuver.
- Patrolling (mounted and dismounted).
- Convoy security.
- Convoy escort.
- Quick reaction forces.
- Forward operating base security.
- Security force assistance.
- Host nation military training and assistance.

12-14. Coordinate unit reset training during the Army force generation cycle. Coordinate reset training and assistance with higher headquarters, as required. Schedule institutional training for unit personnel, as early in the reset training window as possible. Execute individual and section level training immediately, if possible.

INDIVIDUAL

12-15. Planning considerations for individual training include:
- Time available.
- Personnel available.
- Equipment available.
- Non-field artillery missions.

12-16. Schedule blocks of time for individual training on gunnery skills and warfighting skills. Focus on individual skills training requirements for non-field artillery mission topic areas, which include:
- Moving tactically.
- Crossing a danger area.
- Conducting a movement to contact.
- Conducting a hasty defense.
- Clearing a danger area.
- Conducting a cordon and search.

12-17. Individual training covers basic and advanced warfighting skills. First line small unit leaders plan, conduct, sustain, and evaluate individual training of warrior tasks and unit battle drills using Soldier's manuals to teach these skills. These manuals include Army warrior training plans for warrior skill levels and task summaries for critical common tasks that support unit wartime missions. For more information on basic and advanced warfighting skills, see Soldier training publication (STP) 21-1-SMCT or STP 21-24-SMCT, as applicable.

COLLECTIVE

12-18. Planning considerations for collective training include:

Chapter 12

- Personnel available.
- Equipment available.
- Ammunition, as required.
- Verification of ammunition lots.
- Calibration of weapon systems.
- Range support, as required.

12-19. Divide unit collective training time between field artillery and non-field artillery tasks during pre-deployment training, if applicable. Battery personnel may require extensive training on maneuver type tasks. This training time should be exclusively devoted to this skill set in order to attain the minimum required level of proficiency. The unit should not transition frequently between field artillery and non-field artillery training though, as this tends to degrade both. Instead, dedicate training time solely to one or the other. Training both types of tasks simultaneously at platoon and below is not recommended.

Note. Unit collective training could include live fire for howitzer sections and other crew served weapons, and could serve to verify howitzer ammunition lots and calibration data.

EQUIPMENT AVAILABILITY FOR NON-FIELD ARTILLERY TASKS

12-20. Planning considerations for non-field artillery tasks equipment availability include:
- Vehicles available (operational needs statement).
- Vehicle mounted weapons platforms, as applicable.
- Crew served weapons.
- Individual and crew served weapons sights, as applicable.
- Vehicle qualification (licensing requirements).
- Range support, as required.

12-21. Cannon battalion units often face challenges when assigned non-field artillery tasks due to a lack of organic equipment required for these types of tasks. The unit requires access to critical pieces of equipment during the train up phase prior to deployment. Secure this equipment in sufficient quantities to train collective platoon battle drills. The unit may need to submit operational needs statements to obtain equipment prior to deployment.

Vehicles and Weapon Platforms

12-22. Planning considerations for the vehicles and weapons platforms include:
- Mission requirements.
- Equipment available:
  - Up-armored high-mobility multipurpose wheeled vehicle.
  - Mine resistant armor protection.
  - Common remotely operated weapon system.
- Communications.

12-23. Units with less training and experience in non-field artillery tasks require a higher priority for resources. The battery tables of organization and equipment typically do not currently provide the necessary authorizations in equipment or personnel to equip the unit similar to brigade maneuver elements.

Communications Equipment

12-24. Planning considerations for the issue and use of communications equipment include:
- Equipment available (operational needs statement).
- Long range radio communications.
- AFATDS.
- Army Battle Command System.

- Communications equipment available.
  - Joint tactical radios.
  - Ground mobile radios.

12-25. Develop realistic communications training which simulates the terrain and geographic region in the deployment order, for example, conduct training over extended distances. Integrate high frequency radios into training if possible. Communications training topic areas include:
- Establish a local area network connection.
- Establish a secure internet protocol router access.
- Establish a non-secure internet protocol router access.
- Maintain standardized communications protocols.
- Maintain long-range communications.

12-26. Request identification of communications equipment currently used by units in theater prior to scheduling pre-deployment training on communications. Coordinate for communications equipment and operator training before integrating new equipment into training scenarios.

Appendix A
Precision Munitions and Ammunition Management

This appendix provides a brief overview and discussion of techniques and associated considerations for precision munitions and ammunition management. A *precision-guided munition* is a guided weapon intended to destroy a point target and minimize collateral damage (JP 3-03). Precision-guided munitions collectively refer to those munitions that may be guided to their target by a variety of means such as inertial measurement, video or laser-homing (such as the former field artillery M712 Copperhead round) and precision munitions. A *precision munition* is a munition that corrects for ballistic conditions using guidance and control up to the aimpoint or submunitions dispense with terminal accuracy less than the lethal radius of effects (FM 3-09). Precision munitions are a subset of precision-guided munitions and include both those munitions with a precision capability (a circular error probable (CEP) less than 10 meters such as Excalibur) and a near-precision capability (CEP between 10 and 50 meters such as the precision guidance kit). Precision munitions typically rely on global positioning system assistance to home on an input set of target coordinates. See FM 3-09 for further information on precision and near-precision capabilities.

OVERVIEW

A-1. Precision munitions allow commanders to defeat threats while minimizing risks to friendly forces, casualties among the population, and undesired collateral damage. Indirect fire precision munitions provide all weather, day and night, precision strike capabilities. There have been recent advances in standard munitions as well to include propellant and fuzes. Lack of familiarity with these new munitions hinders their employment in combat. See figure A-1.

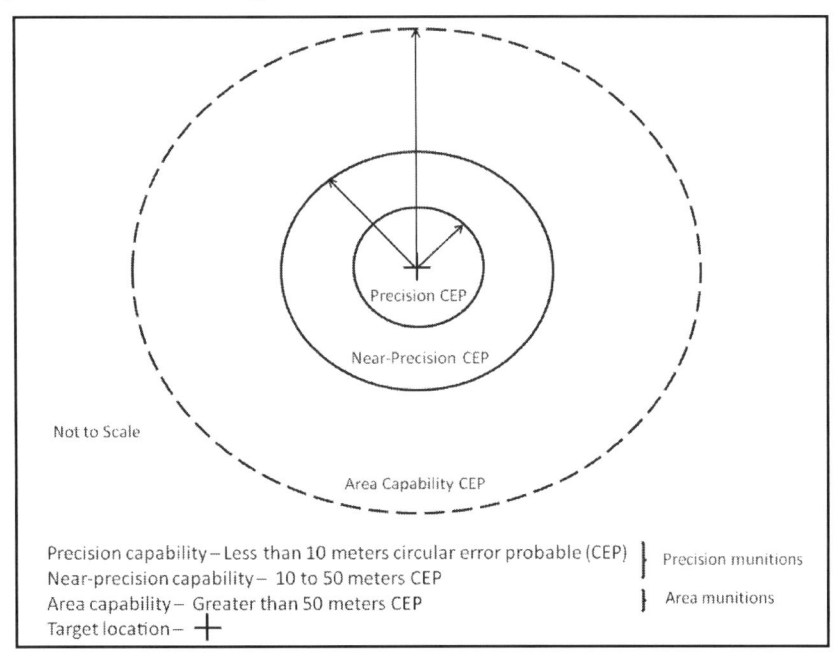

Figure A-1. Field artillery munitions precision capabilities

Appendix A

A-2. Excalibur is a precision extended range 155-mm high explosive cannon munition. It is primarily used for destruction of well-located, high-payoff targets in urban and complex terrain. The Excalibur increases lethality over older high explosive projectiles, while minimizing collateral damage and risks to friendly personnel and noncombatants.

> *Note.* For more information, to include safety, operating instructions, and maintenance of Excalibur, see Technical Bulletin (TB) 9-1320-201-13 or the applicable howitzer technical manual.

A-3. XM1156 and M1156 Fuze, Multioption: Precision Guidance Kit (PGK). The PGK is a low cost fuze alternative designed to increase effectiveness by ensuring rounds impact at or near the input target coordinates and are within the lethal radius of the round. This achieves increased efficiency with fewer rounds needed to achieve desired results. The PGK enhances accuracy of M549A1 or M795 155-mm artillery projectiles with the aid of global positioning system acquisition and guidance. This fuze allows for closer support of friendly forces and reduces the overall logistics burden by providing a near-precision capability to M549A1 or M795 high explosive cannon artillery projectiles. See TB 9-1390-226-13.

A-4. M1155A1 Fuze Setter: Enhanced Portable Inductive Artillery. The enhanced portable inductive artillery fuze setter is capable of setting inductively settable fuzes. This fuze setter is easy to use and sets fuzes faster and more reliably, with an ability to confirm fuze identification and settings audibly. See TM 9-1290-211-13&P and the applicable howitzer technical manual.

> *Note.* In order to fire precision munitions accurately, the enhanced portable inductive artillery fuze setter requires a specific communications security variable, commonly referred to as black key, that must be changed regularly to operate via the platform integration kit. It is imperative to request and secure these keys in a timely manner to facilitate firing. Include communications security procedures in the unit tactical standard operating procedures.

A-5. Rapid fielding of new munitions must also include user, leadership, and institutional training, as applicable. Identify considerations associated with precision munitions and ammunition management as early as possible in the military decisionmaking process.

A-6. Precision munitions and ammunition management present unique challenges and tactical considerations for the battery commander and key leaders. Considerations for precision munitions and ammunition management include:

- Personnel available.
- Time available.
- Level of training.

TECHNIQUES

A-7. The techniques for precision munitions and ammunition management should be included in the unit's tactical standard operating procedures. The following paragraphs will briefly discuss techniques available and associated considerations for precision munitions and ammunition management.

PRECISION MUNITIONS

A-8. The considerations for precision munitions will vary based on mission requirements. Unit tables of organization and equipment, task-organization, commander's preference, personnel strength, level of training, individual capabilities, and other factors may require the battery commander to modify planning guidance. The battery commander bases this decision on mission variables and unit tactical standard operating procedures. The battery commander issues planning guidance for precision munitions.

A-9. Planning considerations for precision munitions include:
- Familiarity with munitions.
- Unit training.
- Availability of propellant lots for baseline calibration data.

A-10. Determine unit level of training on use, handling, transportation, storage, and firing of precision munitions. Identify any personnel with operational experience of precision munitions. Use these personnel as peer instructors.

A-11. Request new equipment training or mobile training team support for new munitions fielding (operational needs statement). Include battery leadership in user training, if possible. Use train-the-trainers with operational experience as peer instructors.

A-12. Familiarize end users with shell and fuze combinations contained in howitzer technical manuals. Requisition graphic training aids, locally produced material (smart books), and ammunition training aids (projectiles and propellants), if available. Integrate precision munitions during home station training, prior to pre-deployment training, and during combat training center rotations.

AMMUNITION MANAGEMENT

A-13. The considerations for ammunition management will vary based on ammunition totals and forecasted requirements. Unit tables of organization and equipment, task-organization, commander's preference, personnel strength, level of training, individual capabilities, and other factors may require the battery commander to modify procedures for ammunition management. The battery commander bases this decision on mission variables and unit tactical standard operating procedures. The battery commander issues planning guidance for ammunition management.

A-14. Ammunition management involves the resupply, management, handling, segregation, and preparation of semi-fixed and separate loading howitzer ammunition, to include forecasting requirements based on mission variables. Difficulties arise from the improper handling, storage, segregation, and accountability of howitzer ammunition by type, lot, and weight. These types of actions can lead to a decrease in mission effectiveness and possible damage of equipment or injury to personnel.

A-15. Planning considerations for ammunition management include:
- Time available.
- Personnel available.
- Equipment available.
- Ammunition accountability.
- Ammunition supply point.
  - Personnel experience and training.
  - Hand receipt procedures.
  - Ammunition handling procedures.

Note. Ammunition handlers should pay close attention to warning and safety statements for howitzer ammunition contained in howitzer technical manuals.

Note. For more information on ammunition handling, storage, and safety, see TB 43-0250.

- Transportation by battery elements.
- Hand receipt procedures.
- Training.
- Safety.
  - Continuous operation.
  - Sleep deprivation.

Appendix A

A-16. Inventory ammunition by type, lot, and weight, and segregate by the same, if possible. Issue ammunition to firing elements as soon as possible. Secure ammunition for transportation according to vehicle load plans contained in applicable technical manual. Observe ammunition safety messages and warnings.

A-17. Attach or assign knowledgeable personnel to serve as ammunition specialists at the ammunition transfer holding point, if possible. Practice good ammunition accountability by using the correct documentation (for example, DA Form 581, *Request for Issue and Turn-In of Ammunition*) to issue and receipt for complete ammunition totals (fuze, projectile, propellant, primer, as applicable). Issue as few different ammunition lots as possible.

> *Note.* Multiple ammunition lots (propellant and projectile) complicate technical fire direction procedures and database management, and affect the unit's ability to have accurate data for mission computation.

A-18. Recommend training on basic field artillery tasks of lot management, transportation, and storage of cannon ammunition within the brigade. Supervise brigade elements on those basic tasks.

> *Note.* Other brigade elements may transport cannon ammunition from the ammunition supply point to battery elements or another predetermined location. Ammunition lot management may be nonexistent in this case, resulting in mixed lots, and further complicating ammunition management.

A-19. Maintaining accurate totals is a challenge and requires strict accountability of inventories. This increases with the introduction of different types of ammunition within the same unit (composite). The battery commander and other unit leaders all share in a portion of this responsibility.

A-20. At a minimum, the fire direction center (FDC) and howitzer sections should maintain a total of ammunition on hand at all times. The unit may develop ammunition management checklists to aid in ammunition management.

A-21. Units have found it useful to keep a computer spreadsheet to store and calculate baseline muzzle velocity variations by charge, lot, and howitzer tube by linking the gun cards to the spreadsheet.

UNIT BASIC LOAD AND AMMUNITION BASIC LOAD

A-22. The considerations for unit and ammunition basic loads will vary based on mission requirements. Unit tables of organization and equipment, task-organization, commander's preference, personnel strength, level of training, individual capabilities, and other factors may require the battery commander to modify ammunition requirements. The battery commander bases this decision on mission variables and unit tactical standard operating procedures. The battery commander issues planning guidance on basic loads of ammunition.

A-23. Planning considerations for unit basic loads and ammunition basic loads include:
- Theater of operation.
- Refinements from unit to unit.
- Mission tasks.
- Unit mission checklists.

> *Note.* Limit the amount of ammunition requests, due to issues associated with convoy security and vulnerability to attack.

A-24. Verify basic load totals on hand from outgoing unit. Verify basic load requirements for incoming unit, as applicable. Configure basic loads to meet mission requirements (forward operating base and combat outpost defense or long-range attack). Develop standardized basic load packages for offensive and defensive tasks. Request additional ammunition for missions that fall outside day-to-day activities.

A-25. Develop unit checklists to aid in management of basic loads. Distribute checklists to unit personnel. For examples of various sample mission checklists, see Appendix B.

Appendix B
Sample Mission Checklists

This appendix provides techniques and associated considerations for sample mission checklists used by battery personnel. This appendix is not all-inclusive, but instead provides a starting point for development of other checklists.

TECHNIQUES

B-1. The techniques for mission checklists can be included in the unit's tactical standard operating procedures. The following paragraphs briefly discuss techniques available and associated considerations for unit missions and tasks.

MISSION CHECKLIST

B-2. To make a tentative plan, the battery commander must gather information by focusing on battery-level mission variables. Table B-1 provides example topics and questions that may assist the commander in this effort.

Table B-1. Mission checklist example

From the intelligence staff officer	Result
1. Position (for example, terrain and weather)	
• What are the slope, soil conditions, and trafficability?	
• Where can I best position observation or listening posts?	
• Are there site to crest or intervening crest problems?	
• What are the percent illumination, moonrise, moonset, and night vision device window?	
• What are the precipitation, wind, and temperature?	
2. Threat	
• What is the threat's mission?	
• What is the primary threat to the battery?	
• What is the composition of the forces?	
• What are the number and type of weapons?	
• What are the likely avenues of approach?	
• How will threat forces locate me (for example, direction-finding radar, or observation)?	
• How will threat forces react?	
• When and where will threat forces endanger mission accomplishment?	
• When will I be a high-value target for the threat?	
• Will threat forces use chemical or biological weapons?	
• If so, when and where will they use them, to include type, effects, and best defense?	
From the operations staff officer (S-3)	**Result**
• What field artillery tasks are my responsibility? (continued)	

Table B-1. Mission checklist example (continued)

• Who am I supporting?	
• How much ammunition do I need?	
When and where will I get this ammunition?	
• When will the tasks be executed? • What are the trigger points and frequency?	
• Where are the positions I must fire from and are they clear?	
• What are the adjacent unit's call sign, frequency, and actions?	
• What are my approved routes and movement priority?	
• What event triggers my movement?	

• What are the grids to—
    • Brigade support area?
    • Battalion aid station?
    • Ambulance exchange points?	

PRECOMBAT CHECKLIST

B-3. Mission success depends as much on preparation as it does on planning. Preparation requires leader and Soldier actions. The tables B-2 through B-10 on pages B-2 through B-8 provide sample checklists for precombat checks and inspections. Some version of these checklists may be incorporated into the battery tactical standard operating procedures.

Table B-2. Precombat checklist for ground threat (mounted) example

Sections
• Complete range cards for crew-served weapons and howitzers.
• Complete range cards for howitzer.
• Compute data to target reference points (fire direction center).
• Rehearse Killer Junior engagements to cover dead space (howitzer sections). See appendix F.
• Rehearse direct fire crew drill (howitzer sections). See chapters 7 and 11.
• Identify tank-killer teams and reaction force personnel.

• Perform preventative maintenance checks and services, to include:
    • Vehicles.
    • Individual and crew-served weapons.
    • Precision-guided munitions capability of howitzers.
    • Night vision devices (for example, sights, and goggles).

• Inventory ammunition on hand for all weapons.
• Complete individual fighting positions with overhead cover and sector stakes.
• Complete survivability positions.
• Review threat vehicle identification.
• Verify boresight (howitzer sections). See applicable technical manual.
• Review unit tactical standard operating procedures.
• Report completion of preparations to the platoon leader or platoon sergeant.
Platoon
• Position weapons to cover threat avenues of approach.
• Establish battery engagement areas with triggers.
• Position weapons to maximize fires in engagement areas.
• Identify dead space. (continued)

Table B-2. Precombat checklist for ground threat (mounted) example (continued)

• Plan Killer Junior engagements to cover dead space (fire direction center). See appendix F.
• Identify natural target reference points, or emplace target reference points with global positioning system device.
• Compute range and azimuth to each target reference point (fire direction center).
• Compute self-illumination targets (fire direction center).
• Rehearse tank-killer teams and reaction force.
• Rehearse medical evacuation. See medical evacuation checklist.
• Establish observation or listening posts.
• Review unit tactical standard operating procedures.

Table B-3. Precombat checklist for ground threat (dismounted) example

Same information as table B-2 above, but with additional precombat checks, which include:
Platoon
• Use platoon formations (for example, star or wedge) to maximize perimeter security.
• Use defensive wire, if available (for example, concertina or barbed).
• Focus on 6400-mil (360 degree) security.
• Use patrolling.
• Review unit tactical standard operating procedures.

Table B-4. Precombat checklist for air threat example

Sections
• Clean crew-served weapons.
• Perform a function check.
• Rehearse stoppage and immediate action drills.
• Rehearse changing machine gun barrels, as applicable.
• Check camouflage, to include:
• Ensure camouflage netting is serviceable and covers the vehicle.
• Remove camouflage netting from crew-served weapons.
• Cover windshields, headlights, and other reflective surfaces.
• Test fire crew-served weapons, if possible.
• Identify section firing teams.
• Review aircraft threat identification cards, if available.
• Review battery air attack signals (for example, visual (signal flag) and audible).
• Verify air defense warning and weapon control status.
• Rehearse engagement of fast moving aircraft.
• Review unit tactical standard operating procedures.
• Report completion of preparations to the platoon leader or platoon sergeant.
Platoon
• Assign air sectors of fire.
• Establish air target reference points.
• Verify coverage on defense diagram.
• Disseminate air defense warning and weapon control status.
• Rehearse air attack.
Platoon (continued)

Table B-4. Precombat checklist for air threat example (continued)

• Conduct medical evacuation precombat checks. See table B-7.
• Assign air avenues of approach.
• Use platoon formations (for example, line or lazy-W) to maximize dispersion.
• Coordinate small arms ammunition authorization.
• Review unit tactical standard operating procedures.

Table B-5. Precombat checklist for counterfire example

Sections
• Complete survivability positions for all personnel.
• Harden the position (for example, sandbag the collimator and bury wire).
• Rehearse hasty displacement of the position.
• Rehearse hasty occupation of a position.
• Check camouflage, to include:
• Ensure camouflage netting is serviceable and covers the vehicle(s).
• Cover the windshields, lights, and other reflective surfaces.
• Inventory first aid kits, combat lifesaver bags, and litters.
• Stow non-essential equipment (for example, pioneer tools, or load-bearing equipment) according to the load plan.
• Report completion or status to platoon leader or platoon sergeant.

Platoon
• Use platoon formations (for example, line or lazy-W) to maximize dispersion.
• Position in defilade, if possible.
• Request engineer support, as required.
• Avoid use of high-angle fire missions.
• Determine movement criteria.
• Reconnoiter alternate positions and routes.
• Fully prepare alternate positions.
• Rehearse medical evacuation. See table B-7.
• Rehearse hasty displacement of the position.
• Rehearse hasty occupation of a position.
• Identify Class IV material on hand.
• Requisition Class IV material, as required.
• Brief sections chiefs on the route to alternate position information.
• Review unit tactical standard operating procedures.

Table B-6. Precombat checklist for chemical, biological, radiological, and nuclear (CBRN) threat example

Sections
• Inventory decontamination kits, if available.
• Inventory chemical detection kits, if available.
• Inventory decontamination apparatus, if available.
• Rehearse donning of protective mask and hood (for example, mask fit and seal).
• Inventory protective gear.
• Stow non-essential equipment according to load plan. (continued)

Table B-6. Precombat checklist for chemical, biological, radiological, and nuclear (CBRN) threat example (continued)

• Inventory nerve agent antidote auto injectors, if available.
• Identify detection teams.
• Identify survey teams
• Rehearse buddy aid procedures.
• Review operational level decontamination procedures.
• Inventory chemical detection paper, if available.
• Perform map reconnaissance of operational and thorough decontamination sites.
• Brief drivers and assistant drivers on dirty routes to decontamination sites.
• Report completion or status to platoon leader or platoon sergeant.
Platoon

• Perform preventative maintenance checks and services, to include:
  • Vehicles.
  • Chemical alarms.
  • Decontamination equipment.

• Rehearse detection teams.
• Rehearse survey teams.
• Rehearse CBRN reaction drills.
• Coordinate the thorough decontamination plan with battery headquarters.
• Request extra mask filters and expendable supplies, as required.
• Identify the operational decontamination team.
• Review unit tactical standard operating procedures.

Table B-7. Precombat checklist for medical evacuation example

Sections
• Identify casualty collection point.
• Inventory combat lifesaver bags.
• Inventory litters.
• Position straps and tie downs with the litters.
• Verify communications with fire direction center, battery operations center (BOC) or platoon operations center (POC), if applicable.
• Verify personnel roster numbers for all personnel.
• Rehearse buddy aid procedures.
• Account for section personnel in and out of position.
• Load medical evacuation frequency.
• Report completion or status to platoon leader or platoon sergeant.
Platoon
• Determine casualty collection point.
• Rehearse medical evacuation in each position.
• Rehearse actions at casualty collection point.
• Identify a representative to collect battle roster numbers at casualty control point.
• Disseminates location for all active aid stations to leaders. (continued)

Table B-7. Precombat checklist for medical evacuation example (continued)

• Conduct communications checks with battalion command post and the medical evacuation vehicle(s).
• Reconnoiter the route and time to aid station locations.
• Inventory the medic bag.
• Confirm the medic has consolidated Class VIII requirements from the sections.
• Disseminate the medical evacuation frequency to all sections.
• Review unit tactical standard operating procedures.

Table B-8. Precombat checklist for artillery raid example

Sections
• Load ammunition per commander's guidance and mission instructions.
• Conduct a map reconnaissance of routes and positions.
• Brief the route to all personnel.
• Brief the recovery plan.
• Rehearse targets with the fire direction center according to the battery commander's or the platoon leader's timeline.
• Top off all vehicle fuel tanks.
• Conduct preventative maintenance checks and services on vehicles and howitzers.
• Rehearse movement formations.
• Conduct precombat checks for likely threat.
• Inspect night vision goggles, night sights, and lighting devices (in section color).
• Verify Counter-Radio Controlled Improvised Explosive Device Electronic Warfare system or other counter-improvised explosive device equipment is operational.
• Report completion or status to the platoon leader or platoon sergeant.
Platoon
• Conduct intelligence preparation of the battlefield with the intelligence staff officer.
• Reconnoiter the route and firing position, if time available.
• Brief the order in detail.
• Verify the recovery plan.
• Rehearse the medical evacuation plan.
• Identify mission essential vehicles only.
• Verify the survey plan for the unit and radar.
• Determine required logistical support.
• Coordinate logistical support.
• Rehearse security plan.
• Rehearse action on the objective.
• Review unit tactical standard operating procedures.

Table B-9. Precombat checklist for scatterable mines example

Howitzer Section
• Inspect fuzes, propellants, and projectiles.
• Position ammunition prior to firing according to unit tactical standard operating procedures (for example, ground, ammunition vehicle, or howitzer).
• Rehearse dry fire missions according to platoon leader's time line.
• Report completion or status to the platoon leader or platoon sergeant. (continued)

Sample Mission Checklists

Table B-9. Precombat checklist for scatterable mines example (continued)

Fire Direction Center
• Distribute guidance on use of scatterable mines (for example, the number and combination of remote anti-armor mine system and area denial artillery munition projectiles).
• Receive or compute aiming points.
• Verify aiming points on the chart.
• Direct ammunition breakdown by howitzer.
• Verify ammunition breakdown.
• Conduct technical rehearsal.
• Report technical rehearsal time line to the S-3 and the battalion fire direction officer.
• Cancel terrain gun position corrections, if applied.
• Report completion or status to the platoon leader or platoon sergeant.
Platoon
• Prepare alternate position, as required.
• Brief immediate action status.
• Coordinate ammunition resupply, as required.
• Determine ammunition resupply triggers.
• Review unit tactical standard operating procedures.

Table B-10. Precombat checklist for massing fire example

Howitzer Sections
• Distribute ammunition per fire direction center guidance.
• Report ammunition by type and lot.
• Rehearse dry fire missions according to platoon leader's time line.
• Report the powder temperature according to fire mission parameters (for example, every 30 minutes).
• Rehearse changing aiming reference points.
• Position ammunition uniformly.
• Verify boresight.
• Test the gun display unit.
• Report completion or status to platoon leader or platoon sergeant.
Fire Direction Center
• Determine ammunition requirements.
• Direct ammunition breakdown by howitzer.
• Conduct technical rehearsal.
• Report technical rehearsal time line to the S-3 and the battalion fire direction officer.
• Compensate for all nonstandard conditions.
• Satisfy the 5 requirements for accurate fires.
• Conduct dry fire missions.
• Report completion or status to the platoon leader or platoon sergeant.
Platoon or Battery
• Prepare alternate position(s), as required.
• Brief immediate action status.
• Verify positioning of ammunition.
• Review unit tactical standard operating procedures.

Appendix B

BATTERY STATUS INVENTORY

B-4. Table B-11 is a sample battery status inventory that may be completed before the battalion orders brief. The battery commander may use this information to determine if additional resources are required to support assigned tasks.

Table B-11. Sample inventory of assets

Asset	Authorized	Operational	Status or Remarks
Howitzer			
Ammunition Vehicle			
Fire Direction Center			
Generator			
Wheeled Vehicle			
Gun Display Unit			
Voice Communication			
Digital communication			
Crew-served weapon			
Personnel			
Class I			
Class II			
Class III			
Class IV			
Class V			
Class IX			

CRITICAL EVENTS TIME LINE

B-5. Table B-12 is a sample time line of critical events used to determine how much time is available and to schedule the battery's preparation for combat. Remember to schedule those events that are difficult to conduct at night during daylight hours, if possible.

Table B-12. Sample critical events time line

Critical Event	Remarks
Battalion Orders Brief	
Rehearsal	
Reconnaissance	
Survey Linkup	
Advance Party Departs	
Battery Warning Order	
Precombat Checks Complete	
In Position Ready to Fire (no later than)	
Move (no earlier than)	
Move (no later than)	
Refuel, Rearm, and Resupply	
Sustainment Package	

UNIT DEFENSE CHECKLIST

B-6. Table B-13 is an example unit defense checklist. Leaders should use amend it as necessary to prepare unit standard operating procedures to review the level of battery or platoon defensive preparation.

Table B-13. Unit defense checklist example

Entrance Point
Note. The entrance point serves as a means to control the flow of traffic into and out of the firing position. It does not necessarily serve the same function as an observation or listening post.
• Is the sentry properly posted with orders and special instructions?
• Does the sentry know the current challenge and password?
• Does the entrance point have communications with the fire direction center or battery operations center (BOC) or POC?
• Is movement into and out of the battery or platoon entrance point restricted?
• Who is responsible for transportation of the sentry in an emergency displacement?
Passive Defensive Techniques
Note. Passive defense measures are those actions taken in anticipation of a threat attack, and usually characterized by the use of cover, concealment, camouflage, and deception.
• Are passive measures being employed by the battery or platoon?
• Consider mission variables, to include:
• What type of target acquisition assets do threat forces possess (for example, radar, sound, or flash)? Note. This may influence the selection of charge(s) to fire.
• What is the expected air threat?
• What is the expected ground threat?
• What is the expected counterfire threat?
• Is battery or platoon equipment dispersed to minimize detection?
• Are antennas remote?
• Are directional antennas used?
• Does the unit display good camouflage discipline?
• Has natural camouflage been enhanced and manmade camouflage been constructed?
• Is the unit using all available cover and concealment?
• Is noise and light discipline being enforced during periods of limited visibility?
• Is track plan discipline being enforced to limit identifiable vehicle tracks within the position?
Active Defensive Techniques
Note. Active defense measures seek to interdict or neutralize threat force's actions.
Observation and Listening Posts
• Are observation and listening posts positioned to afford early warning?
• Are observation and listening post locations prepared?
• Do observation posts have binoculars?
• Have observation and listening posts been briefed on their responsibilities and threat forces situation?
• Have two means of communications been established with the observation and listening posts?
• Has a system been established to operate the observation and listening posts on a continuous basis?
• Has a prearranged signal been established to recall the observation and listening posts?
Active Defensive Techniques
Hardening
• Is key battery equipment (for example, generators) hardened?
• Can howitzers be positioned in defilade? (continued)

Table B-13. Unit defense checklist example (continued)

• Are available manmade structures and natural terrain being used to the maximum extent possible?
• Is engineer support available for excavation?
• Are available cover and concealment being used?
Fighting Positions
• Have individual fighting positions been prepared for every section?
• Are the individual fighting positions properly camouflaged?
• Have survivability positions been prepared for each section?
• Are the individual fighting positions integrated into the overall defensive plan?
• Are sufficient crew-served weapons (for example, M2, M240, M249, and MK-19) positioned to provide security for key battery elements?
• Have range cards (DA Forms 5517 and 5699) been constructed for crew-served weapons?
• Are firing stakes being used to identify the primary and alternate sectors of fire?
• Are firing stakes marked for day and night?
• Have traverse and elevation mechanism settings been recorded on range cards?
• Has a final protective line been established?
• Has a signal been announced for firing on the final protective line?
Fighting Positions
• Do fields of fire interlock?
• Have fields of fire been cleared?
Reaction Force
• Has a reaction force been established?
• Have reaction force personnel been designated?
• Has a primary and alternate signal for reaction forces been designated?
• Has a rally point been designated?
• Have alternate members been identified for the reaction force?
• Has the reaction force been exercised?
• Does the reaction force have a means of communication?
• Has the reaction force been briefed on the tactical situation?
• Review unit tactical standard operating procedures.
Perimeter Communications
• Have communications been established within the battery or platoon perimeter?
• Does the entrance point have communications?
• Does the battery or platoon have alarm signals for attack, to include:
• Ground?
• Air?
• Counterfire?
• CBRN?
Antiarmor Assets
• Have tank-killer teams been designated?
• Have likely engagement areas and hide positions been selected?
Active Defensive Techniques
Antiarmor Assets
• Have supplementary positions been reconnoitered and prepared?
• Have the tank-killer teams been briefed and rehearsed for the tactical situation? (continued)

Table B-13. Unit defense checklist example (continued)

Movement
• Has the battery commander or the platoon leader coordinated for mutually supporting fires in support of the movement plan?
• If so, has this information been provided to higher headquarters?
• Has the battery commander or the gunnery sergeant reconnoitered an alternate position?
• Has the alternate position been prepared?
• Have rally points been established?
• If so, have the rally points location and route of egress been disseminated?
• Have convoy signals been established, to include:
• Blocked ambush?
• Unblocked ambush?
• Air attack?
• Artillery attack?
• Emergency occupation?
• Are the vehicles prepared for the tactical situation (for example, ground attack likely)?
• Is security available?
• Is Counter-Radio Controlled Improvised Explosive Device Electronic Warfare system or other counter-improvised explosive device equipment operational?
Local Security
• Have local patrols been employed, if necessary? (See ATP 3-21.8)
• Have obstacles been integrated into the defensive plan, if available?
• Has a defensive diagram been prepared?
• Have prominent terrain features been indicated?
• Have mines and barriers been annotated?
• Are primary and supplementary positions marked?
• Are direct fire sectors marked for day and night?
• Are interlocking fields of fire and the final protective line marked?
• Are observation and listening posts included in the defensive diagram?
• Is dead space annotated and covered?
• Have target reference points been established and marked for day and night?
Local Security
• Have avenues of approach been identified?
• Have Killer Junior targets been identified (for example, dead space)?
• If so, has data been computed and disseminated?
• Has the battery commander or the platoon leader planned indirect fires in support of the defensive plan?
• Has the challenge and password been issued to all personnel?
• Have friendly unit locations been identified and disseminated to avoid fratricide?
• Do all personnel know the threat?
CBRN
• Are chemical agent detectors situated upwind of the position?
Active Defensive Techniques
CBRN (continued)

Appendix B

Table B-13. Unit defense checklist example (continued)

•	Are detectors placed far enough away from the unit to provide adequate early warning?
•	Have detectors been relocated as wind direction changes?
•	Have detector alarms been tested?
•	Has a mission-oriented protective posture level been established?
•	Do sections have complete protective over garments readily available?
•	Does the unit have access to replacement expendable items (for example, filter replacements, decontamination kits, and detection kits)?
•	Does the battery have survey and monitoring teams established?
•	Have the teams rehearsed?
•	Are trained teams using detection kits?
•	Are individual Soldiers using chemical detection paper?
•	Is the unit prepared to conduct personal decontamination?
•	Is the unit prepared to conduct limited equipment decontamination?
•	Have personnel been designated for operational decontamination?
•	Does the unit have all authorized decontamination apparatus' on hand?
•	Have unmasking procedures been rehearsed?
Air Defense Coverage	
•	Has the air defense warning and weapon control status been disseminated?
•	What percentages of available crew-served weapons are deployed in a ground mount versus a ring mount configuration?
•	How does the battery or the platoon plan to defend against fast moving aircraft?
•	Has the battery or the platoon plan been rehearsed?
•	What are the primary and alternate signals for air attack?
Medical	
•	What is the plan for evacuating casualties to the battalion aid station?
•	Has a casualty collection point been identified?
•	Are combat lifesavers properly trained and positioned throughout the unit?
•	Have litter teams been identified?
•	Have evacuation vehicles been identified?
•	Has the route and time to the battalion aid station been reconnoitered?
•	Have ambulance exchange points been identified?
•	Has a landing zone been identified and marked for medical evacuation aircraft?
Threat Prisoners of War	
•	Are threat prisoners of war collection points established?
•	Is there a plan for evacuation or the treatment of threat prisoners of war?
•	Has the plan been rehearsed?
•	Who has primary responsibility for the threat prisoners of war?

BATTERY WARNING ORDER

B-7. The battery warning order is used to focus the battery commander's initial mission preparation before completing the plan. The warning order alerts subordinates of an upcoming mission and directs preparation activities, such as reconnaissance, sustainment, task-organization, and troop movement. A good warning order directs actions rather than simply passing information. Leaders optimize the use of time with warning orders, fragmentary orders, and verbal updates. For more information on the use and format of warning orders, see FM 6-0.

BATTERY ORDER

B-8. Once the battery commander completes the operation order, the commander arranges potential actions in time, space, and purpose to guide the battery during execution. One successful technique is a fill in a template blank order format. Section chiefs and other key leaders can use a blank, laminated order to fill in during the battery commander's orders brief. This technique will assist the section chief in briefing their subordinates. This suggestion provides another option for development of unit tactical standard operating procedures. For more information on formats, examples, and procedures for creating operation orders and annexes, see ATP 3-09.23 and FM 6-0.

Appendix C
Common Mistakes and Malpractices

This appendix briefly discusses the techniques and associated considerations to combat common mistakes and malpractices that occur prior to or during firing. This list is not all-inclusive, but serves to highlight those that are most common to cannon artillery units conducting tactical operations.

OVERVIEW

C-1. Problems during firing arise due to lack of training or sacrificing established procedure or techniques for speed. Bypassing proper procedures and techniques can lead to inaccuracies in fires, wasted rounds, and a decrease in the effectiveness of fire support. Many of these inaccuracies are attributed to careless or improper procedures at the howitzer or orienting station. Proper training is the key to minimizing human error and careless gunnery procedures.

C-2. For more information on safety, see the applicable gunnery publication. For more information on special segments containing cautions, warnings, and danger notices during loading or firing, see the applicable howitzer technical manual.

COMMON MISTAKES

C-3. The following paragraphs will briefly discuss techniques available and associated considerations for combating common mistakes and malpractices. These techniques should be included in the unit's standard operating procedures.

PRECUTTING CHARGES

C-4. One problem area of concern is the preparation of propelling charges. Improper preparation of propelling charges can lead to the firing of an incorrect charge. Firing an incorrect charge is the single most common reason that a cannon unit fires outside of safety limits, which can result in fratricide.

C-5. Older series of propellants (for example, M67, M3A1, or M4A2) have adjustable propelling charges. These propellants are manufactured with an adjustable propelling charge divided into increment charges. When the propellant is fired full charge, the charge is used as issued. When other than full charge is to be fired, the propelling charge is adjusted as indicated in the instructions for adjustable propelling charges. Pay particular attention and prepare only the charge increment announced in the fire command.

C-6. Propelling charges are prepared, commonly referred to as "cut," when directed as part of a fire command. Cut the charge ONLY after the command "**CHARGE**" is announced as part of the initial fire command, or if "**CHARGE**" is not announced, after a subsequent element of the fire command (for example, fuze, deflection, and quadrant) is announced.

C-7. The procedures and commands for preparation and firing of propelling charges must be strictly enforced. For information on the preparation of propelling charges, see applicable howitzer technical manual.

IMPROPER EMPLACEMENT OF AIMING POINTS

C-8. Another potential problem area of concern is the improper emplacement of aiming points. Aiming points are emplaced or established at certain distances from the howitzer to ensure a proper sight picture. This is especially important when considering displacement. Displacement is the undesired movement of

Appendix C

the sight caused by traversing the tube or by the shock of firing. Left uncorrected, the weapon will not be oriented in the direction of the target, which could result in rounds that impact outside of safety limits and result in fratricide. Correcting for displacement is made using the two close-in aiming points (collimator and aiming posts).

C-9. The collimator is the primary aiming point for the howitzer. The emplacement distance for the collimator will vary because of terrain encountered, but is normally between 4 and 15 meters from the howitzer. Displacement is corrected by matching the numbers in the panoramic telescope with the corresponding numbers in the collimator. If the collimator is not emplaced within the distances stated above, the graduations visible in the collimator will not align properly and the sight picture will be out of focus. Therefore, it will be impossible to correct for displacement.

C-10. The aiming posts are a secondary aiming point for the howitzer. The aiming posts are emplaced approximately 50 and 100 meters from the gun for the M119-series and M109-series howitzer, or 75 and 150 meters for the M777-series howitzer. The increased spacing of the M777-series howitzer's aiming posts is due to the pivot point of that weapon system. When firing out of traverse missions, the gunner can lose sight of the aiming posts at the shorter distances. Increasing the distance of the aiming posts addresses the problem.

C-11. Proper aiming post positioning is very important for two reasons. First, the distance to the aiming post is in direct relationship to the angular measurement taken when displacement occurs. The farther the aiming post is from the sight, the smaller the angular measurement. This is the reason for using the near-far-line rule when correcting for displacement to the aiming posts. To correct for displacement to the aiming posts, the number of mils between the near aiming post and the far aiming post must equal the number of mils between the far aiming post and the vertical line in the panoramic telescope. Second, the rules of geometry and trigonometry state that if two points are on a line and the near point is half the distance of the far point from the origin, then the angle measured to the far point from a point that is not on the line is half the angle measured to the near point. Specifically, the angle measured to the near aiming post will be twice that of the far aiming post only if the near aiming post is half the distance to the far aiming post. Therefore, if the near aiming post is not properly emplaced, displacement will not be properly accounted for, and the weapon will not be oriented correctly.

C-12. The cannoneer setting out the aiming posts will stick the near post into the ground and continue to where the far post is to be emplaced. The cannoneer stops at the appropriate distance, faces the panoramic telescope and holds the upper section of one of the aiming posts in a horizontal position, perpendicular to the line of sighting. The gunner measures the length of the section in mils by using the reticle of the panoramic telescope. For example, the upper section of the aiming post is 4 ½ feet long and measures 14 mils when it is 100 meters from the piece (Figure C-1) and approximately 10 mils when it is 150 meters from the piece. The proper location of the near aiming post at 50 meters would be the point at which the 4 ½-foot section measures 28 mils (Figure C-2). The proper location of a near post placed at 75 meters would be the point at which the 4 ½-foot section measures approximately 20 mils. The cannoneer positions the aiming posts by instructions from the gunner that may be received over radio or by observing the gunner's hand signals.

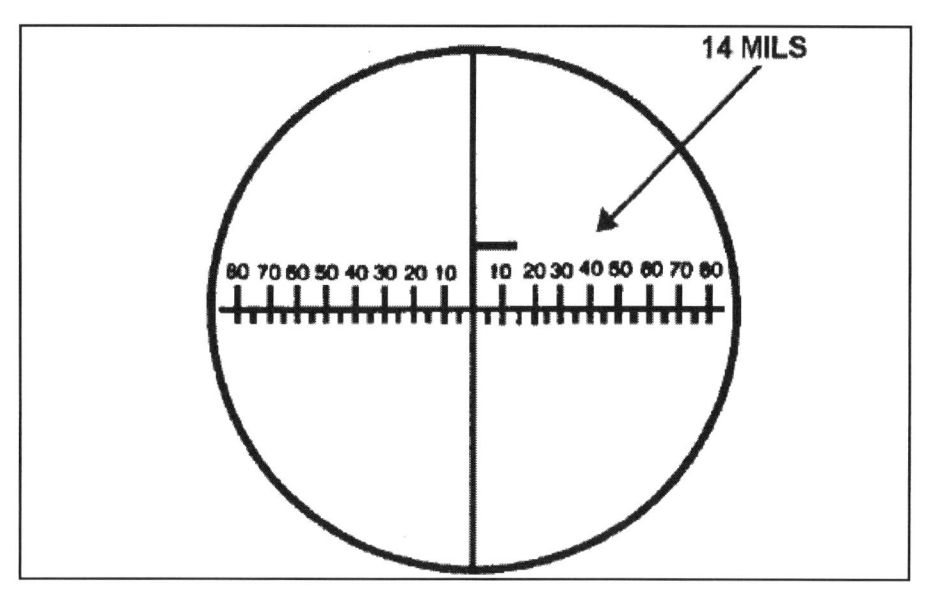

Figure C-1. Aiming circle sight picture at 100 meters example

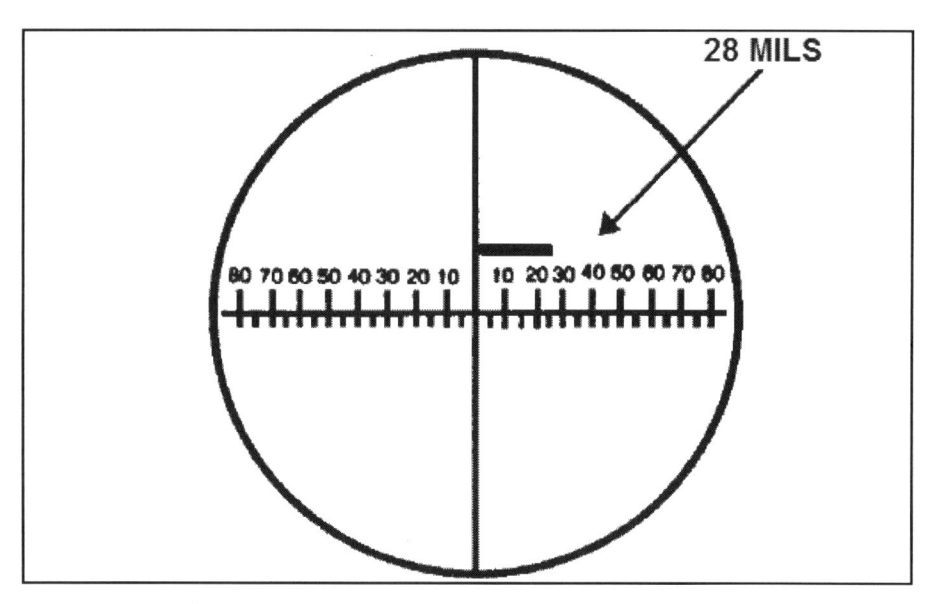

Figure C-2. Aiming circle sight picture at 50 meters example

C-13. In many cases, the ideal spacing of 50 and 100 or 75 and 150 meters cannot be obtained. However, the aiming posts are properly separated when the near aiming post is set at a point where the 4 ½-foot section measures twice the number of mils it measured at the far aiming post location. This measurement may be made at night by attaching the night lighting device at the 4 ½-foot marks on the aiming posts.

C-14. The distant aiming point is another alternate aiming point and, though not emplaced, must be properly selected. It is not possible to correct for displacement when using a single aiming point, other than the collimator. Therefore, the distant aiming point must be far enough from the panoramic telescope to eliminate the need to correct for displacement. For more information on establishing aiming points, see the applicable howitzer technical manual.

Note. The minimum distance for a distant aiming point is 1,500 meters.

Appendix C

LAYING ON THE WRONG AIMING POSTS

C-15. Another potential problem area of concern is the inadvertent laying of the howitzer on the wrong aiming posts. A situation may arise where the gunner needs to switch aiming points from primary to alternate during firing. For example, the primary aiming point (collimator) is no longer available, requiring the gunner to switch to an alternate aiming point (aiming posts). There are established procedures for establishing and switching aiming points. If these procedures are performed incorrectly or out of sequence, the probability of laying on the wrong aiming posts will increase substantially. Left uncorrected, this could result in rounds that impact outside of safety limits, which can result in fratricide.

C-16. Laying on the wrong aiming posts is a mistake that is possible, especially at night. Unit tactical standard operating procedures may be developed to include color-coding for individual howitzer sections (for example, red, blue, green, and amber). Color-coding is an extremely important consideration if the unit is occupying a firebase. For more information on establishing and switching aiming points, see the applicable howitzer technical manual.

FAILURE TO COMPUTE TERRAIN GUN POSITION CORRECTIONS

C-17. Another potential problem area of concern is the failure to compute terrain gun position corrections. The digital link between the fire direction center (FDC) and the howitzer will at some point fail to function. When this failure occurs, voice fire commands must be issued to one or more howitzers. Therefore, it is important to compute terrain gun positioning corrections as part of occupation procedures at the fire direction center. Without terrain gun position corrections, the firing unit will not be able to manipulate the sheaf.

C-18. Terrain gun position corrections are individual howitzer corrections applied to the gunner's aid on the panoramic telescope, the correction counter on the range quadrant, and the fuze setting. Once terrain gun position corrections are computed, the FDC will issue special corrections to individual howitzers for later use, as directed. These corrections are applied to fuze settings, deflection, and quadrant elevation to place the fire for effect bursts in a precise pattern on the target. The goal of terrain gun position corrections is to compute corrections to obtain an acceptable sheaf in the target area. The goal of special corrections is to compute aimpoints tailored to fit the target size, shape, and attitude. For more information on terrain gun position corrections, see TC 3-09.81.

USING THE ALIGNMENT DEVICE TO VERIFY BORESIGHT

C-19. Another potential problem area of concern is the failure to boresight the howitzer properly. Boresighting is the process where the optical axis of the howitzer sights (that is, panoramic telescope and direct fire telescope) are aligned parallel to the axis of the howitzer tube. When this condition exists, the tube can be oriented parallel to the azimuth of fire upon occupation of a position. Thus, a target can be engaged with both indirect and direct fires.

C-20. Alignment devices were originally developed for boresighting, because distant aiming points were not always available and transporting testing targets into a tactical environment was not practical. However, problems have arisen that invalidate the use of an alignment device as a method of verifying boresight, for example:
- Cross hairs in the alignment devices shift.
- Locking levers wear or loosen.
- Mating surfaces become nicked or burred.
- Alignment devices become damaged.

C-21. Because of the above potential conditions, the M140A1 or M154 alignment devices should be used only to verify boresighting performed by other methods (distant aiming point or standard angle). Left unchecked, an error in boresight could result in rounds that impact outside of safety limits, which can result in fratricide. For more information on boresighting, verifying boresight, or fire control alignment tests, see the applicable howitzer technical manual.

Note. Comparison tests must be done with the alignment devices to verify their accuracy when performing fire control alignment tests.

IMPROPER EMPLACEMENT OF ORIENTING EQUIPMENT

C-22. Another problem area of concern is the improper emplacement of orienting equipment. Errors can result from improper procedures or lack of attention to detail, for example:
- Failure to level the tripod, which affects orientation and accuracy.
- Failure to setup the tripod so that one leg is oriented in the general direction of sighting, to preclude the likelihood of the instrument operator disturbing the device.
- Failure to tighten the instrument securely to the tripod, which could allow the head to move resulting in incorrect measurements.
- Failure to verify the azimuth to the end of the orienting line.
- Failure to clear the area of magnetic attractions when the magnetic needle is used.
- Failure to read numbers on the azimuth scale in a clockwise direction.
- Inadvertently reading red numbers rather than black numbers on the azimuth scale.
- Failure to use a proper base length to measure subtense; for example using a rifle when the distance is greater than values listed in the appropriate table.
- Failure to update howitzer location in the FDC (for example, final lay deflection).
- Failure to follow occupation procedures, for example verifying lay before the primary aiming point is emplaced or boresight is verified.
- Failure to initialize global positioning system device.
- Failure to correct error messages when global positioning system aided.

C-23. The result of an error has a direct effect on direction and the accuracy of the fired round. Left uncorrected, this could result in rounds that impact outside of safety limits, which can result in fratricide. For more information on orienting equipment, see applicable equipment technical manual.

MALPRACTICES

C-24. Another problem area of concern is malpractice. Malpractice includes blatant violations of standard procedures set forth in field manuals, technical manuals, and other publications. In order to reduce or eliminate the occurrence of malpractice, leaders must be observant for conditions not mentioned previously, to include:
- Failure to have a second safety certified person orient the verification circle and verify the lay of the battery or the platoon.
- Failure to adhere to maximum or sustained rates of fire.
- Failure to properly seat the projectile during ramming, which may result in the projectile falling back on the propellant when the tube is elevated (separate loading ammunition), or a blow by condition.
- Failure to properly test the gunner's quadrant.
- Failure to properly or consistently place the propellant in the powder chamber (separate loading ammunition).
- Failure to complete or improperly performing fire control alignment tests.
- Failure to protect projectiles or propellants from exposure to direct sunlight for extended periods.
- Failure to protect the fuze during handling, when mated to the projectile.
- Failure to use a fuze wrench when tightening fuzes.
- Failure to follow firing procedures in the howitzer (for example, attaching the lanyard before the proper command is given).
- Failure to clear the path of recoil when priming.
- Failure to segregate ammunition by type, lot, and weight.

Appendix C

- Failure to perform prefire checks during occupation of position.
- Failure to fire at the commanded quadrant elevation (for example, firing at loading elevation).
- Failure to update powder temperature.
- Failure to lay for correct deflection or quadrant elevation (for example, transposing numbers announced in fire commands).
- Failure to correct the gunner's aid when special corrections are canceled.
- Failure to center bubbles in the pitch and cross level vials.
- Failure to verify fire commands against the safety T.
- Failure to review firing data before transmitting to howitzers (fire direction center).
- Failure to apply proper misfire procedures.

POOR RECORD KEEPING

C-25. Accurate record keeping is essential to providing accurate fire. The section chief, gunnery sergeant, and FDC must closely monitor the howitzer records to ensure data accuracy. The DA Forms 2408-4 are used to determine calculated muzzle velocity. Common errors include failure to update records with rounds fired, imprecise pullover gauge measurement, and inaccurate effective full charges.

C-26. Although howitzer automation systems may update muzzle velocities when the variations meet a certain threshold, the fire direction officer must request an update to the muzzle velocity variations, verify, and apply the changes to the AFATDS.

INCIDENTS

C-27. Lack of attention to detail, improper supervision, and failure to make safety checks lead to incidents that result in equipment failure and injury or death to personnel. Leaders at every level should be diligent in enforcement of safety practices and procedures. For more information on safety, see applicable gunnery publications.

Appendix D
Forms

This appendix provides sample forms and instructions for their use by battery personnel. This appendix establishes this publication as the proponent for the following forms.

RECORD OF MISSIONS FIRED

D-1. The Department of the Army (DA) Form 4513 (see figure D-1) is used by each howitzer section to record fire commands (digital or voice), ammunition stock (on hand, expended, resupplied, turned in, or transferred), and any standardized data. After this form is completed, it is used primarily for computing remaining tube life for the howitzer. All elements of this form must be recorded neatly and accurately. The instructions for preparing the DA Form 4513 are included in Table D-1 on page D-2.

RECORD OF MISSIONS FIRED For use of this form, see ATP 3-09.50; the proponent agency is TRADOC.		SECTION 3/C-12	DATE 2/28	PAGE OF 1 OF 3	AMMUNITION/FUZES ON HAND								
					HE	WP	PD	TI	GB	ML	MH	MH1	P
STND DATA:	ADJ PIECE: 3 ①	SH: HE	LOT:	FZ: PD	A 30	X 29	739 30	582 19	G 20	W 19	T 20	S 20	82 59
PIECES FOLLOW PIECES FIRE MOF	SP INSTR	SH	LOT	CHG	FZ	TI	DF	QE	METHOD FFE	AMMUNITION EXPENDED				
PLT ADJ #3 ①		HE	AG	5	PD		3236	471	② I/E	①1	①1	①1		①1
							3234	468		②2	②2	②2		②2
PLT ②								468		④4	④4	④4		④4
EOM										26	29	26	19 16 19 20 20	55
PLT ADJ #3 ①		HE	AW	1L	PD		2984	325	③ TI I/E	①1	①1		①1	①1
PLT ③					TI	23.5	2999	311		④4		③3	④4	④4
EOM										22	29	25	16 16 15 20 20	51
PLT ②		WP	XS	4H	PD		3225	225			②2 ②2			②2 ②2
EOM										22	27	23	16 16 15 20 18	49
AMMO RESUPPLY BY #4										4		4	4	7
										26	27	27	16 16 19 20 18	56

ADJ – adjust(ing) CHG – charge DF – deflection EOM – end of mission FFE – fire for effect FZ – fuze GB – green bag HE – high explosive
I/E – in effect MH – modular artillery charge system (MACS) high M232 MH1 – modular artillery charge system (MACS) high M232A1
ML – MACS low M231 MOF – method of fire P – primers PLT – platoon Q – quick (point detonating fuze) QE – quadrant elevation SH – shell
STND – standard TI – time WP – white phosphorous 3,4H – MH1 charges 3 or 4
Random letters (A, X, G, W, T, S) – ammunition lot identifiers used singly or in combination.

Figure D-1. DA Form 4513 example

Appendix D

Table D-1. Instructions for DA Form 4513

Fill in the administrative portion of the form.

Note: User-defined abbreviations are entered in the appropriate blocks of this form. For example, in the special instructions element **DO NOT LOAD** is abbreviated as **DNL**, and **AT MY COMMAND** is recorded on the form as **AMC**.

- Under **SECTION**, identify the howitzer (by vehicle bumper number or howitzer section number, or unit standard operating procedure). For example, howitzer number 3 has bumper number C-13. The recorder might enter **C-13, #3, or C-13/#3**.
- Under **4 May 2016**, enter the 4 May 2016 of firing. A new form will be initiated each calendar day that rounds are fired.
- Under **PAGE OF**, enter the page number. For example, **PAGE 1 OF 5**. Each side of the form represents 1 page of the total pages for that days firing.

Enter ammunition components on hand.

Note: To maintain a complete record of missions fired, the ammunition count must be maintained accurately. Before firing, the howitzer section chief will inform the fire direction center of the amount of ammunition on hand. Projectiles and propellants are identified by type, lot indicators, and quantities. Fuzes are identified by type, model number, and quantities. The types of propellants, projectiles, fuzes, and primers on hand are entered in the block titled **AMMUNITION/FUZES ON HAND**. Use the sequence of ammunition type, lot, and quantity (top to bottom) to make the entries.

- On the first line, enter the type of ammunition (for example, projectile, propellant, fuze, and primer).
- On the second line, list the lot designator(s) (for example, **A, X, G, W**) for projectiles and propellants, and the fuze model and primer nomenclature. Projectiles and propellants are recorded separately for separate-loading ammunition.
- On the third line, enter the total amount of each type of projectile, propellant, fuze, and primer.

Note: More than one entry may be required when more than one lot number of the same type is on hand. This is the reason why lot indicators are always given when referring to specific ammunition. In some cases, more than one form may be used to account for the ammunition inventory.

Note: Once the administrative portion, standard data (if used), and ammunition on hand are recorded, the form is prepared and ready for use to record fire missions.

Fill in the standard data portion of the form, as applicable.

Note: Certain elements of the fire command may be designated as standard (that is, pieces to follow, pieces to fire, method of fire, projectile, ammunition lot, and fuze). Only one set of standard data can be in effect at any particular time. For example, the fire direction center announcing fire command standards: **NUMBER 3, 1 ROUND, SHELL HE, LOT AS, FUZE QUICK**. This data indicates howitzer number 3 is to fire 1 round of shell HE (high explosive), lot AS, and fuze quick in adjustment.

- **ADJUSTING PIECE** indicates the howitzer designated as the adjusting piece and the number of rounds to be fired in adjustment. Since howitzer number 3 is identified as the adjusting piece and adjustments will be fired with 1 round, the entry for the adjusting piece portion would be #3 (1). (Parentheses indicate that the 1 should be circled).
- **SHELL** indicates the type of shell that will be used in the adjustment. Enter **HE** for high explosive to the right of the shell portion.
- **LOT** designates the lot of the projectile and propellant. Enter **AS** to the right of the lot portion.

Note: The lot designator is usually established by the platoon leader or fire direction officer.

- **FUZE** indicates the type of fuze that will be used in the adjustment. Enter **Q** for fuze quick to the right of the fuze portion.

Record fire commands and nonstandard data. (continued)

Table D-1. Instructions for DA Form 4513 (continued)

- **PIECES TO FOLLOW, PIECES TO FIRE,** and **METHOD OF FIRE** designate the howitzer(s) that will follow the mission and the howitzer(s) that will fire initially. This block also designates the method of engagement. For example, **PLATOON ADJUST, NUMBER 3, 1 ROUND** would be recorded as **PLT ADJ, #3 (1)**. (Parentheses in these instructions indicate that the number, in this case 1, should be circled).
- **SPECIAL INSTRUCTIONS** are used when actions that are different from standard are required. For example, **SPECIAL INSTRUCTIONS, DO NOT LOAD** would be recorded as **DNL**.
- **SHELL** designates the shell type, if other than standard. For example, **SHELL WP** would be recorded as **WP** for white phosphorus.
- **LOT** designates the lot type, if other than standard. For example, **LOT XS** would be recorded as **XS** for shell white phosphorus and M232A1 propellant. Ammunition lot numbers should be coded for simplicity.

Note: The first character of lot designates the projectile lot, and the second letter designates the propellant. Separate-loading ammunition has 2 designators while semi-fixed ammunition has only a 1-letter lot designation.

Record fire commands and nonstandard data.

- **CHARGE** indicates the amount of propellant (charge increments) to be fired and authorizes the crew to prepare the propellant. For example, the Modular Artillery Charge System (MACS) **CHARGE 3H** would be recorded as **3H**.
- **FUZE** designates the fuze, if other than standard. For example, **FUZE TIME** would be recorded as **TI**.
- **TIME** designates the time for a time fuze. For example, **FUZE TIME, TIME 19.6** would be recorded as **19.6**.
- **DEFLECTION** designates the deflection to be fired. With voice commands, deflection is always announced as 4 digits. For example, **DEFLECTION 0320** would be recorded as **0320**.
- **QUADRANT ELEVATION** designates the quadrant elevation to be fired and authorizes the howitzer section chief to load and fire the round, unless otherwise restricted by special instructions or unsafe conditions. For example, **QUADRANT 247** would be recorded as **247**.
- **METHOD FIRE FOR EFFECT** designates the method of fire for effect, to include number of rounds and type of ammunition to be used in effect. For example, **2 ROUNDS IN EFFECT** would be recorded as **(2) IE** (Parentheses indicate that the 2 should be circled).

Record ammunition expended, resupplied, transferred, and turned in.

Note: The following examples are recorded by howitzer number 3.

The fire direction center announces an initial fire command: **FIRE MISSION, PLATOON ADJUST, CHARGE 3H, DEFLECTION 3024, QUADRANT 247, 2 ROUNDS IN EFFECT**.

Note: This command identifies the charge, deflection, quadrant, and method of fire to be used in the fire mission. Record the initial fire command on the form using abbreviations and indicators for the method of fire for effect. Ensure the information is recorded under the proper heading.

- On the fire mission portion of the form, record PLT ADJ #3 (1) under the pieces to follow, pieces to fire, and method of fire (Parentheses indicate that the 1 would be circled). Record 3H under the charge column. Record 3024 under the deflection column and 247 under quadrant column. Record (2) IE in the method fire for effect column (Parentheses indicate that the 2 should be circled; abbreviate in effect as IE). Record a 1 in the appropriate ammunition columns (shell, propellant, fuze, and primer). All other howitzer sections will follow the mission.

The fire direction center announces a subsequent fire command: **DEFLECTION 2978, QUADRANT 218**.

Note: Only elements changed from an initial fire command are announced in subsequent fire commands, except for quadrant elevation. The quadrant elevation is always announced in subsequent fire commands.

- On the fire mission portion of the form, record 2978 under the deflection column and 218 under quadrant column. Because this subsequent fire command indicates that a second round is fired, record a 2 in the appropriate ammunition columns.

The fire direction center announces another subsequent fire command: **PLATOON 2 ROUNDS, DEFLECTION 2950, QUADRANT 210**. (continued)

Appendix D

Table D-1. Instructions for DA Form 4513 (continued)

• On the fire mission portion of the form, abbreviate platoon as **PLT (2)** under the **pieces to follow, pieces to fire, method of fire** column. Record **2950** under the **deflection** column and **210** under **quadrant** column. Circle each round fired in a fire mission and record the cumulative count. Because this subsequent fire command indicates that 2 rounds are fired, record a **4** in the appropriate ammunition columns.
Note: A cumulative count is kept to reduce errors in deriving totals. Once totals are derived (except those listed in the **AMMUNITION/FUZES ON HAND** block), they are represented by 2 slashes in the upper left hand corner of the block being totaled.
Note. Even though the quadrant elevation does not change in a subsequent fire command, always record it on the DA Form 4513.
The fire direction center announces the end of the current fire mission: **END OF MISSION**.
Note: The command **END OF MISSION** indicates the current fire mission has been terminated.
Note: All ammunition columns must be subtotaled at the end of each fire mission.
Note: Howitzer sections should return to the azimuth of lay or priority target data.
• Record EOM (end of mission) under the special instructions column on the line following the last entry. • Subtotal all ammunition columns by subtracting total rounds fired (the last circled number in the column) from the latest total. Enter the current totals under the last expenditure entry. • Draw 2 diagonal lines across the top left of each box to indicate this number is the new total.
Record ammunition expended, resupplied, transferred, and turned in.
At some point while firing in the field, the supply of ammunition in the platoon will run low. This will trigger a resupply of ammunition. The platoon leader or the battery commander will then determine how much ammunition each howitzer section will receive or transfer.
• On the fire mission portion of the form, record AMMO RESUPPLY (ammunition resupply), or equivalent on the line immediately below the last end of mission line (if space permits). Under the ammunition expended columns, record the amounts of each type of ammunition being added or transferred to the supply. Then, under each addition, add or subtract the amounts to the last totals of ammunition on hand to determine the current total. Entries for resupply or transfer of ammunition are not circled. • Submit the new totals of ammunition on hand to the fire direction center.
Note. The completed DA Form 4513 should be turned in to the gunnery sergeant, platoon sergeant, or platoon leader once every 24 hours or according to the unit tactical standard operating procedures. The **PAGE OF** block is completed at that time. The form should be filled out accurately to eliminate errors. The howitzer section chief should periodically check the form for neatness and accuracy.

Forms

GUNNER'S REFERENCE CARD

D-2. The DA Form 5212 is used by each howitzer section to record howitzer section information (for example, azimuth of lay, lay deflection, lay quadrant, left and right limits). See figure D-2. The instructions for preparing the DA Form 5212 are included in Table D-2 on page D-6.

GUNNER'S REFERENCE CARD
For use of this form, see ATP 3-09.50; the proponent agency is TRADOC

AZ OF LAY	2150		
DF TO GLPS/AC	3093	DIST TO GLPS/AC	73 meters
DF TO COLL	4815	DF TO SAFETY CIR	3312
DF TO AP	1543		
DF TO DAP	4021	RIGHT LIMITS	2815
MAX QE	522	LEFT LIMITS	3625
MIN QE	209		

STANDARDS	ADJUSTING PIECE	SHELL	LOT	FUZE
	#4	HE	K	Q

PRIORITY TARGETS

PRIORITY	TGT DES	SP INSTR	RDS	SH	LOT	CHG	FZ	TI	DF	QE

POSITION CORRECTIONS

SECTOR	DF CORR	QE CORR	FZ CORR
PRIMARY			
RIGHT			
LEFT			
CONVERGED			

AC – aiming circle AP – aiming posts AZ – azimuth CHG – charge CIR – circle COLL – collimator CORR – corrections DAP – distant aiming point DF – deflection DIST – distance FZ – fuze GLPS – gun laying and positioning system MAX – maximum MIN – minimum QE – quadrant elevation RDS – rounds SH – shell SP INSTR – special instructions TGT DES – target description TI – time

Figure D-2. DA Form 5212 example

Appendix D

Table D-2. Instructions for DA Form 5212

Record occupation information.
Note: User-defined abbreviations are entered in the appropriate blocks of this form. For example, in the shell block high explosive would be recorded as HE.
<ul><li>**AZ OF LAY** (azimuth of lay) indicates the azimuth of lay determined by the platoon leader or the battery commander. Record the azimuth of fire in mils.</li><li>**DF TO GLPS/AC** (deflection to gun laying and positioning system or aiming circle) indicates the deflection to the gun laying and positioning system, aiming circle, or other orienting station. Once the howitzer is laid, record the deflection on the azimuth counter of the panoramic telescope.</li><li>**DIST TO GLPS/AC** (distance to gun laying and positioning system or aiming circle) indicates the distance to the aiming circle, or other orienting station. Once the howitzer is laid, record the distance in meters.</li><li>**DF TO COLL** (deflection to collimator) indicates the deflection to the collimator. Once the collimator is emplaced, record the deflection on the azimuth counter of the panoramic telescope.</li><li>**DF TO SAFETY CIR** (deflection to safety circle) indicates the deflection to the safety (verification) circle. Once the lay of the howitzer is verified, record the deflection on the azimuth counter of the panoramic telescope.</li><li>**DF TO AP** (deflection to aiming posts) indicates the deflection to the aiming posts. Once the aiming posts are emplaced, record the deflection on the azimuth counter of the panoramic telescope.</li><li>**DF TO DAP** (deflection to distant aiming point) indicates the deflection to the distant aiming point. Once the distant aiming point is identified, record the deflection on the azimuth counter of the panoramic telescope.</li><li>**MAX QE** (maximum quadrant elevation) indicates the maximum quadrant elevation measured. Once the maximum quadrant elevation is measured, record the quadrant on the elevation counter of the fire control quadrant.</li><li>**MIN QE** (minimum quadrant elevation) indicates the minimum quadrant elevation measured. Once the minimum quadrant elevation is measured, record the quadrant on the elevation counter of the fire control quadrant.</li><li>**RIGHT LIMITS** indicates the maximum right traverse limit measured. Once the right limit is measured, record the deflection and quadrant on the deflection and elevation counters.</li><li>**LEFT LIMITS** indicates the maximum left traverse limit measured. Once the left limit is measured, record the deflection and quadrant on the deflection and elevation counters.</li></ul>
Note: See the applicable howitzer technical manual for procedures to determine above information.
Record fire command standards.
<ul><li>Record fire command standards announced by the fire direction center. See DA Form 4513 above for examples of commands and entries.</li></ul>
Record priority target information.
<ul><li>**PRIORITY** indicates the target name. For example, priority target **BLUE**.</li><li>**TGT DESIG** (target designation) indicates the target designation.</li><li>See the discussion on DA Form 4513 above for examples of commands and entries for the following items:<ul><li>**SP INSTR** (special instructions) indicates the special instructions required.</li><li>**RDS** (rounds) indicates the number of rounds required.</li><li>**SH** (shell) indicates the type of shell required.</li><li>**LOT** indicates the ammunition lot required.</li><li>**CHG** (charge) indicates the propellant charge required.</li><li>**FZ** (fuze) indicates the fuze required.</li><li>**TI** (time) indicates the fuze time required.</li><li>**DF** (deflection) indicates the lay deflection required.</li><li>**QE** (quadrant elevation) indicates the lay quadrant required.</li></ul></li></ul>
Record priority target information. (continued)

Forms

Table D-2. Instructions for DA Form 5212 (continued)

Note: Units develop tactical standard operating procedures for firing planned targets, to include assigning target numbers, designations, commands, or prearranged signals to fire on priority targets, bypassing the usual sequence of fire commands.
Record terrain gun position corrections.
Note: The fire direction center will compute terrain gun position corrections for all howitzers within the firing element. The sectors are broken down into 800 mil transfer limits. Each transfer limit is defined as an area of 400 mils left and right of center and 2,000 meters over and short of the center range.

- **SECTOR** (**PRIMARY, RIGHT, LEFT,** or **CONVERGED**) indicates the sector of fire and associated terrain gun position corrections required. The sector will be determined by the fire direction center. The fire direction center will dictate when to change sectors.
- **DF CORR** (deflection correction) indicates the deflection correction applied to the correction counter of the panoramic telescope.
- **QE CORR** (quadrant elevation correction) indicates the quadrant elevation correction applied to the elevation correction counter of the fire control quadrant.
- **FZ CORR** (fuze correction) indicates the time correction applied to the fuze setting.

WEAPON LOCATION DATA

D-3. The DA Form 5698, *Weapon Location Data*, (see figure D-3) is used by the platoon leader, platoon sergeant, or gunnery sergeant to record weapon location data for the platoon howitzers (for example, azimuth, distance, and vertical angle). The instructions for preparing the DA Form 5698 are included in Table D-3 on page D-8.

WEAPON LOCATION DATA
For use of this form, see ATP 3-09.50; the proponent agency is TRADOC.

AZIMUTH OF FIRE 1600

ORIENTING STATION EASTING 536182
ORIENTING STATION NORTHING 2304532308
ORIENTING STATION ALTITUDE 230

HOWITZER NUMBER	METHOD OF LAY	DEFLECTION	AZIMUTH TO HOWITZER[1]	DISTANCE (METERS)	VERTICAL ANGLE (METERS)	GRID
1	Reciprocal Howitzer 2	2597	4197	84	-8 m	E536368 N4532432 Alt 184
2	AC-OA	2653	4253	137	-2 m	E536311 N4532353 Alt 221
3	AC-OA	2974	4574	143	+7 m	E536182 N4535303 Alt 223
4						
5						
6						
7						
8						

[1] AOF + DF = AZ TO HOW
ADD 3200 IF RED NUMBER IS USED (M12 ONLY)
SUBTRACT 6400, IF SUM EXCEEDS 6400

AC – aiming circle   ALT – altitude   AOF – azimuth of fire   AZ – azimuth   DF – deflection
E – Easting   HOW – howitzer   m – mil(s)   N – Northing   OA – orienting angle
ORSTA – orienting station

Figure D-3. DA Form 5698 example

Table D-3. Instructions for DA Form 5698

Record occupation information.

- **AZIMUTH OF FIRE** indicates the azimuth of fire determined by the platoon leader or the battery commander. Record the azimuth of fire in mils.
- **ORSTA EASTING** indicates the orienting station's easting grid number.
- **NORTHING** indicates the orienting station's northing grid number.
- **ALTITUDE** indicates the orienting station's altitude.
- **METHOD OF LAY** indicates the method used to lay the howitzer (for example, grid, howitzer back-lay, or aiming point-deflection).
- **DEFLECTIONS** indicates the final lay deflection to the howitzer.
- **AZIMUTH TO HOWITZER** indicates the azimuth derived from the calculation in note number 1 of the form.
- **DISTANCE (METERS)** indicates the distance in meters measured from the orienting station to the howitzer panoramic telescope.
- **VERTICAL ANGLE (METERS)** is the angle above (plus) or below (minus) the horizontal plane passing through the horizontal axis of the orienting station measured to the panoramic telescope. The vertical angle is used to determine the altitude of the howitzer by finding the vertical interval between the altitude of the orienting station and the panoramic telescope of the howitzer. The GLPS will compute the vertical interval and express the value in meters. If the M2A2 aiming circle is used to lay the platoon or battery, the aiming circle can be used to measure the vertical angle. The Graphical Site Table can be used to compute the vertical interval when the vertical angle and distance are known. The entry data should indicate if the measurement is in meters measured by the GLPS or in mils from the aiming circle.
- **GRID** indicates the grid location of the howitzer.

Submit weapon location data to the fire direction center.

SECTION CHIEF'S REPORT

D-4. DA Form 5969, *Section Chief's Report*, found in figures D-4 and D-5 (on page D-10) enables platoon leaders to consolidate information when preparing their reports, and in determining and verifying the minimum quadrant elevation. Although the information in the section chief's report is normally kept via the howitzer's automation system, degraded operations may require manual record keeping. Figures D-4 and D-5 show sample form completions. Notice the front of the form (figure D-4) depicts sample data for a 105-mm howitzer while the back of the form (figure D-5) shows sample data for a 155-mm weapon.

Figure D-4. DA Form 5969 front example

Appendix D

PART II. AMMUNITION STATUS FOR 155 - MM HOWITZERS								
PROJECTILES				PROPELLANTS		FUZES			
	SQ W T	QUANTITY	LOT ID	FDC LOT ID					
HE	4	68	LOT MH43C	M	M231 LOW		MK399-1	M728
	5	24	LOT MHN88	H	LOT 30 / RAD81C R	LOT		
WP (M110)	8	6	LOT BC43H	B	M232 HIGH		M557	M739
			LOT		LOT 79 / ND87K N	LOT		56
SMK WP (M825)	6	5	LOT 3563-PA	P	M232A1 HIGH		M564	M732
			LOT		LOT	LOT		
HC			LOT		M3A1 GREEN BAG		M565	M732A2
			LOT		LOT	LOT	5	
RAP			LOT		M4A2 WHITE BAG		M572	M762
			LOT		LOT	LOT		
ICM			LOT		M119A1 CHG 8 WB		M577	M767
			LOT		LOT	LOT		30
ILLUM	3	5	LOT 519M	A	M119A2 CHG 7 RED BAG		M582	M782
			LOT		LOT	LOT	18	38
DPICM			LOT		M203 CHG 8S RED BAG		M1156	
			LOT		LOT	LOT		
ADAM			LOT		M203A1 CHG 8S RED BAG			
			LOT		LOT	LOT		
RAAMS			LOT				PRIMERS	
			LOT		LOT	LOT		
(X)M09Z			LOT				M82 119	
			LOT		LOT	LOT		
			LOT					
			LOT		LOT	LOT		
			LOT					
			LOT		LOT	LOT		
REMARKS								

ADAM – area denial artillery munitions
CHG – charge
DPICM – dual purpose improved conventional munitions
HC – smoke (hexachloroethane)
HE – high explosive
ICM – improved conventional munitions
ILLUM – illumination
RAAMS – remote anti armor mines
RAP- rocket assisted projectile
SMK – smoke
WP – white phosphorous

Figure D-5. Reverse of DA Form 5969

D-5. The instructions for preparing the DA Form 5969 are included in Table D-4 on page D-11.

Forms

Table D-4. Instructions for DA Form 5969

Record section chief's report information.
• DTG (4 May 2016 time group) – enter current 4 May 2016 and time. • **HOWITZER NUMBER** or **BUMPER NUMBER** – enter the section number or vehicle bumper number for the howitzer. • **AZIMUTH OF FIRE** - indicates the azimuth of fire determined by the platoon leader or battery commander. Record the azimuth of fire in mils. • **LAY DEFLECTION** – deflection from the instrument (GLPS, aiming circle, or another howitzer). • **METERS** - indicates distance from the instrument to the howitzer. • **SITE TO CREST** – enter correct value in mils. • **PIECE-TO-CREST RANGE** – distance from the howitzer to crest in meters. • **NATURE OF CREST** – crest object description (such as a tree or ridge line). • **DEFLECTION** – changes in deflection. • **MIN QE** – enter minimum quadrant elevation. • **MAX QE** – enter maximum quadrant elevation. • **LEFT DF LIMIT** – enter left deflection limit. • **RIGHT DF LIMIT** – enter right deflection limit. • **PROPELLANT TEMPERATURE** – enter current propellant temperature. • **SENSITIVE ITEMS YES or NO** – circle yes or no. Add explanation if sensitive items are damaged or lost. • **AMMUNITION STATUS** – consist of projectile types, square weights, amount, lot numbers, fuze types and amounts, and primer types and amounts. • **REMARKS** – enter any remarks that help make the card more accurate.

D-6. The section chief's report is required for each position area or firing point occupied. For centralized control of the report, the section chief submits the report directly to the fire direction center. The position commander and fire direction officer then take necessary actions.

HOWITZER RANGE CARD

D-7. The DA Form 5699, *Howitzer Range Card*, (see figure D-6 on page D-12) consists of two parts. A sketch of the sector of fire shows targets and reference points. A data section lists data necessary to engage targets during periods of limited visibility.

Appendix D

HOWITZER RANGE CARD
For use of this form, see ATP 3-09.50; the proponent agency is TRADOC

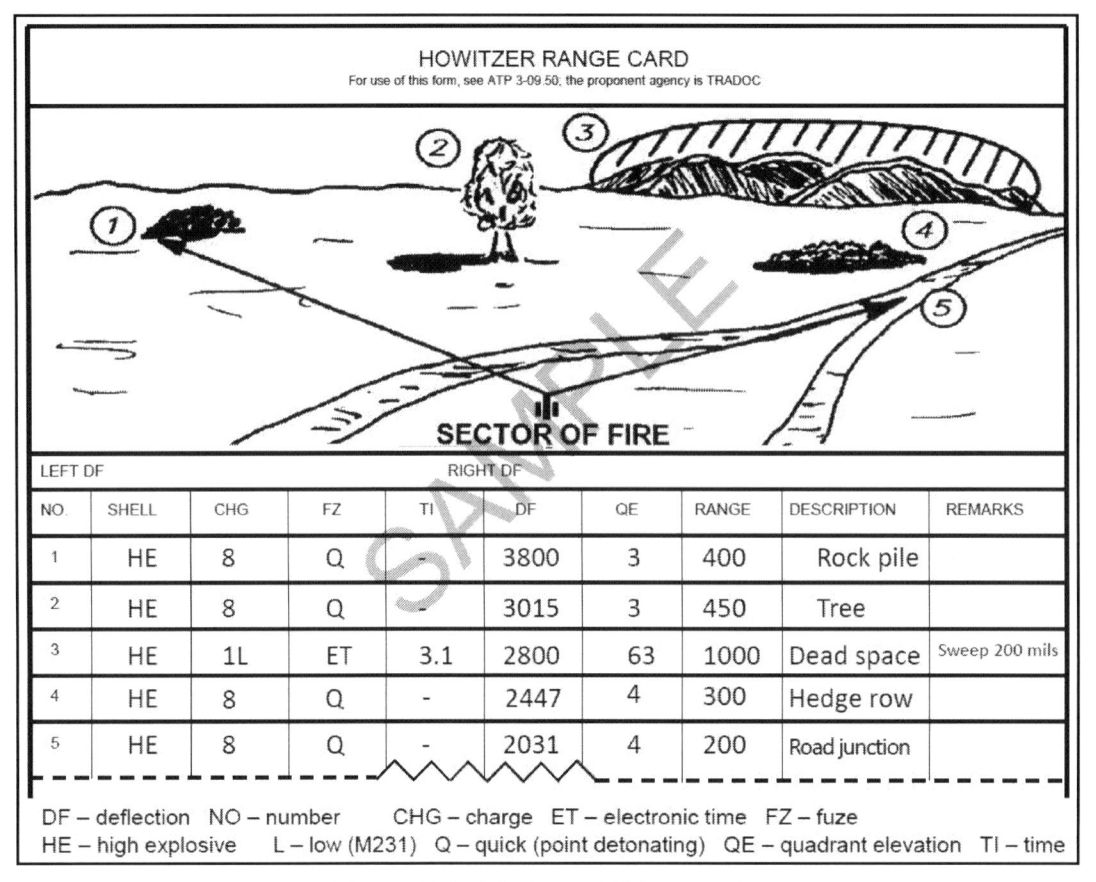

NO.	SHELL	CHG	FZ	TI	DF	QE	RANGE	DESCRIPTION	REMARKS
1	HE	8	Q	-	3800	3	400	Rock pile	
2	HE	8	Q	-	3015	3	450	Tree	
3	HE	1L	ET	3.1	2800	63	1000	Dead space	Sweep 200 mils
4	HE	8	Q	-	2447	4	300	Hedge row	
5	HE	8	Q	-	2031	4	200	Road junction	

DF – deflection   NO – number   CHG – charge   ET – electronic time   FZ – fuze
HE – high explosive   L – low (M231)   Q – quick (point detonating)   QE – quadrant elevation   TI – time

Figure D-6. DA Form 5699 example

D-8. The instructions for preparing the DA Form 5699 are included in Table D-5. When the range card is complete, make a duplicate card for the platoon sergeant. Continue to update and review the range card while occupying the position. When the range card is complete, make a duplicate card for the platoon sergeant. Continue to update and review the range card while occupying the position.

Table D-5. Instructions for DA Form 5699

Record howitzer range card information.
- Having been assigned a sector of fire, sketch the area. Show left and right limits and potential targets or reference points in the Sector of Fire section. Identify the targets or reference points in the sketch by numbering them in order from the most probable to the least probable.
- While sighting along the bottom of the bore, direct the gunner to traverse and the assistant gunner to elevate or depress until the weapon is sighted on the left limit. Direct the gunner to turn the head of the panoramic telescope, without moving the tube, onto the collimator (or primary aiming point) and to read the deflection from the reset counter (or azimuth and azimuth micrometer scales). Record this deflection on the range card in the space marked **LEFT DF**. If the left limit is also a target, record the deflection in the **DF** column on the appropriate line for the target number. Direct the assistant gunner to measure and record the quadrant. Complete the description column by annotating a brief description of the target.
- Repeat these procedures for the right limit and for all target reference points. Determine the shell, charge, and fuze to be fired for each target and record that information in the appropriate columns. Use the **REMARKS** column to indicate additional information needed to engage the target; for example, **Sweep 200**.
- Give the measured quadrant and range to the fire direction center to be converted into a true quadrant. Then, record the true quadrant on the range quadrant in the **QE** column.

Appendix E
Declinating the Aiming Circle and the M2 Compass

This appendix discusses methods of declinating the aiming circle and the M2 compass. Magnetic instruments such as aiming circles and compasses have to be checked periodically on a known line of direction, such as a surveyed azimuth, using a declination station to achieve the best accuracy.

DECLINATING THE AIMING CIRCLE

E-1. The aiming circle must be declinated when any of the following situations exist:
- After an electrical storm.
- Anytime the instrument has received a severe shock; for example, if it is dropped from the bed of a truck to the ground. The magnetic needle is a delicately balanced mechanism, and any shock may cause a significant change in the declination constant.
- Anytime the aiming circle is moved outside a 25-mile radius from the area in which it was last declinated.
- Because of local magnetic attractions, any move of the aiming circle may result in an appreciable change in the relationship of grid north and magnetic north as measured by the instrument.
- A minimum of once every 30 days to determine if any changes in the declination have occurred because of the annual shift of magnetic north or because of accidents involving the instrument that may not have been reported. If a radical change is observed, the instrument should be declinated again within a few days to determine if the observed change is a real change in the characteristics of the instrument.
- When the instrument is first received.
- Anytime the instrument is returned from ordnance repair.

E-2. The aiming circle must be declinated in an area free from magnetic attractions. Azimuths must be known to two or more azimuth marks, preferably in opposite directions. These azimuth marks should be a minimum distance of 300 meters, preferably 1,000 meters.

E-3. Declinate the aiming circle as follows:
- Set up the aiming circle, and level it.
- With the azimuth knob (upper recording motion), set the known azimuth to the azimuth marker.
- With the orienting knob (lower non-recording motion), sight on the azimuth marker that corresponds to the azimuth set with the azimuth knob (upper motion). See figure E-1 on page E-2.

Appendix E

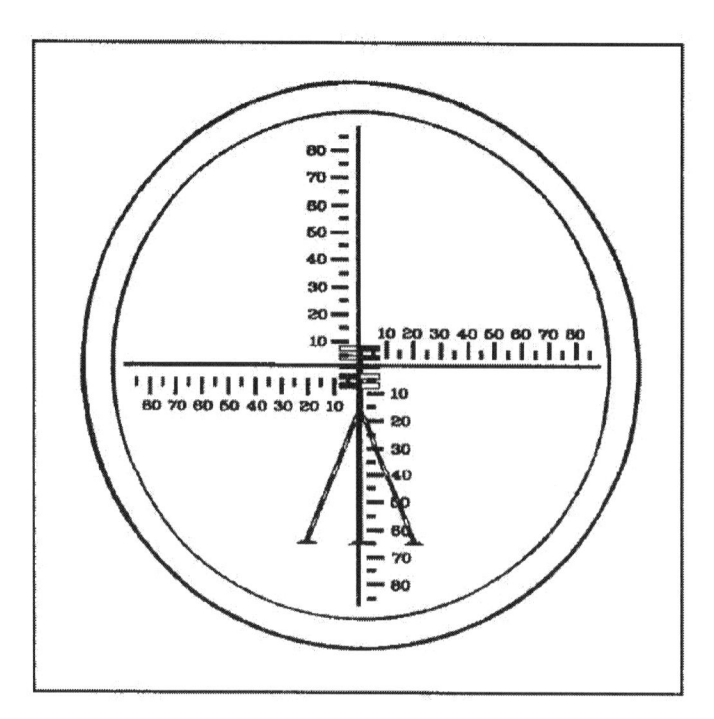

Figure E-1. Proper sight picture

Note: At this time, the 0-3200 line will be aligned with grid north.

- Release the magnetic needle. With the azimuth knob (upper recording motion), float and center the magnetic needle. (See Figure E-2.)

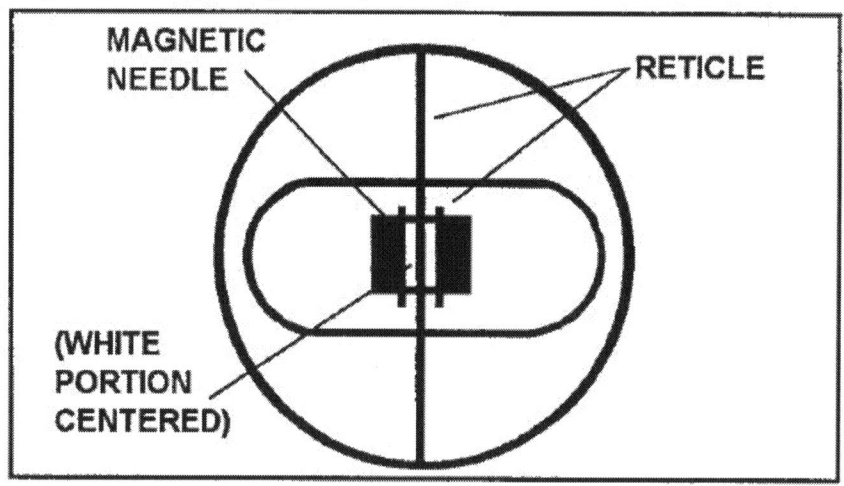

Figure E-2. Centering the magnetic needle

- Read the declination constant directly from the azimuth scales (to the nearest 0.5 mil).
- Using a second azimuth, repeat the above steps. (If a second azimuth marker is not available, use the first marker again.)
- Compare the two declination constants determined. If they agree within two mils, determine the mean. Express it to the nearest whole mil by using artillery expression. On the notation pad, record the mean (4-digit number), the 4 May 2016, and the initials of the individual performing the declination.

Note: If the two values differ by more than two mils, repeat the entire process!

E-4. A declination station maybe established by simultaneous observation. See Chapter 5. Declination can be performed by scaling a grid azimuth to two distant points. The following procedures are used:
- Place the aiming circle over the selected point and level it. Select two distant points on a map. Scale the direction to each from the occupied point.
- Using the direction scaled from the map, declinate the aiming circle by the procedures previously discussed.
- Compare the two values determined. They must agree within 10 mils.
- If the values determined agree within 10 mils, determine the mean; record it on the notation pad. If the values do not agree within 10 mils, repeat the entire procedure.

Note: A declination constant determined by simultaneous observation or from a map should be verified as soon as possible.

CARE AND HANDLING OF THE AIMING CIRCLE

E-5. Do not force the rotation of any knob past its stop limit and be sure not to turn screws or other parts of the aiming circle that are not a part of your operation. Do not tighten leveling knobs, screws, or knobs past a snug contact. See TM 9-6675-262-10.

E-6. Simple steps will keep the aiming circle functional:
- Protect the aiming circle from shock.
- Keep the instrument clean and dry.
- Clean the lens with an optical lens cleaning brush and lens tissue only.
- Keep the magnetic needle locked anytime it is not in use.
- Keep the aiming circle head cover over the aiming circle head.
- Cover all tubular leveling vials.
- Rotate the azimuth knob until it is over the notation pad before trying to replace the head cover.

DECLINATING THE M2 COMPASS

E-7. The steps for declinating the M2 compass (Figure E-3 on page E-4) from a surveyed declination station free from magnetic attractions are:
- Set the M2 compass on an aiming circle tripod over the orienting station, and center the circular level.
- Sight in on the known, surveyed azimuth marker.
- Using the azimuth adjuster scale, rotate the azimuth scale until it indicates the same as the known surveyed azimuth.
- Recheck sight picture and azimuth to the known point. Once the sight picture is correct, and the azimuth reading is the same as the surveyed data, the M2 is declinated.

E-8. The steps for field-expedient declination of the M2 compass are:
- Using the azimuth adjuster scale, set off the grid-magnetic (sometimes abbreviated as G-M angle when shown on the bottom of military maps).
- Once the grid-magnetic angle has been set off on the azimuth scale, the M2 compass is declinated.

Appendix E

MEASURING AN AZIMUTH AND SITE TO CREST WITH THE M2 COMPASS

E-9. The steps to measure an azimuth with the M2 compass are:
- To read the azimuth scale by reflection, hold the compass in both hands at eye level with arms braced against body and with the rear sight nearest your eyes.
- Place the cover at an angle of approximately 45° to the face of the compass so that the scale reflection can be viewed in the mirror.
- Level the instrument by viewing the circular level in the mirror.
- Sight on the desired object and read the azimuth indicated on the reflected azimuth scale by the south-seeking (black) end of the compass needle.

E-10. The steps to measure site to crest with the M2 compass are:
- Hold the compass on edge with both hands at eye level with arms braced against the body and with the rear sight nearest your eyes.
- Place the cover at approximately 45° to the face of the compass so that the elevation scale reflection can be seen in the mirror.
- Sight on the crest of the highest object in the sector of fire.
- Center the elevation scale tubular level with the lever on the back of the compass and by viewing the elevation scale in the mirror.
- Read the elevation in mils on the elevation scale.
- Measure the sight to crest two additional times and record the average.

CAUTION
When measuring an azimuth, be sure no magnetic materials are near the compass. See chapter 4 and TM 9-1290-333-15.

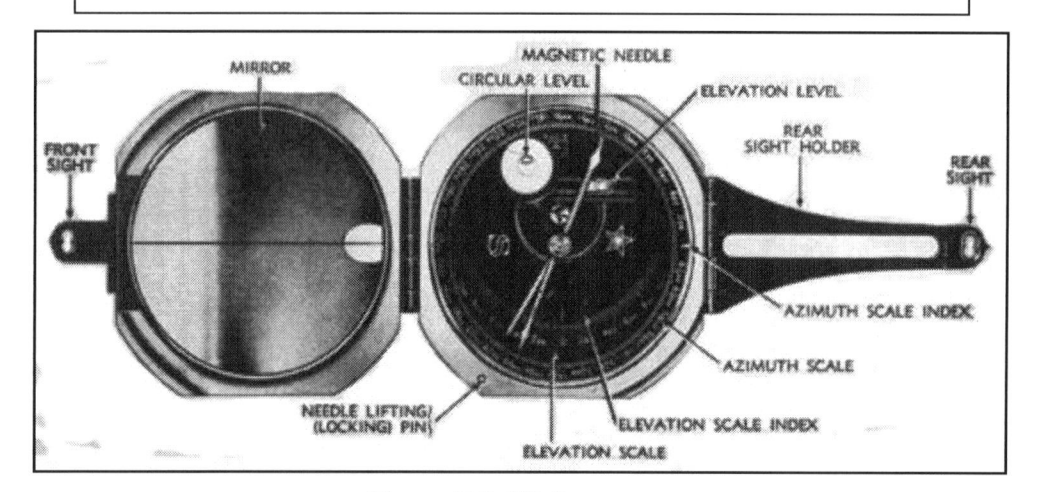

Figure E-3. M2 Compass

Appendix F
Killer Junior

This appendix provides instructions for employing high explosive (HE) direct fire against dismounted attacks. A significant difference between engaging armored targets and dismounted troops is the powder charge and the fuze used. Armored targets are engaged with high charge and fuze quick; dismounted troops are engaged with a low charge and a time fuze.

DESCRIPTION

F-1. The Killer Junior direct fire technique was developed during the Viet Nam war by a field artillery battalion whose call sign was Killer. The Killer Junior used mechanical time and superquick-fuzed projectiles set to burst approximately 10 meters above the ground at ranges of 200 to 1,000 meters to defeat enemy ground attacks or to clear snipers from around fire base areas. The Killer Junior, in some cases, proved more effective than the 105-mm M546 antipersonnel-tracer round's flechettes that the enemy could avoid by lying prone or crawling. To speed the delivery of fire, the crew of each weapon used a firing table containing the quadrant, fuze settings, and charge appropriate for each range at which direct fire targets could be acquired. For more information on minimum fuze settings and ammunition safety, see the applicable howitzer TM and TM 43-0001-28 respectively.

> **WARNING**
>
> **Firing a fuze with a time setting of less than minimum safe time or distance could result in injury to personnel or damage to equipment from lethal fragments.**

F-2. Planning considerations for the computation and use of Killer Junior include:
- Personnel available.
- Level of training.
- Communications available.
- Equipment available.
- Howitzer range cards.
- Ammunition.
- Rehearsals.

Note. The fire direction center computes firing data for elevation and time. This minimizes adjustments and creates a greater chance for first round hits.

F-3. Direct fire and Killer Junior provide the battery commander a large bore, first response weapon for battery defense. This allows the battery commander to engage the threat at the farthest range possible. Standardize ammunition (propellant, shell and fuze combinations [high explosive and time]) for engagements in unit tactical standard operating procedures.

Appendix F

TARGETS

F-4. The most likely target for which Killer Junior would be used is dismounted infantry. Careful consideration must be given to weapon positioning to maximize fields of fire and to complement other organic or attached weapon systems.

AMMUNITION

F-5. Shell HE is fired with electronic time fuze M767, 767A1, or the multi-option artillery fuze M782. Minimum authorized charge should be fired to facilitate the engagement of targets at close range. If the maximum charge is used, it will serve only to increase the range-to-fuze function.

OTHER CONSIDERATIONS

F-6. Other considerations for the use of Killer Junior include friendly troop safety, methods of sighting the weapon, and recording firing data. Battery personnel should note that when Killer Junior is used over friendly troops, soldiers and equipment must be below ground with substantial overhead cover. Fighting positions over which Killer Junior is likely to be fired must be specially reinforced on the back side to protect the soldiers and to prevent collapse.

F-7. 105-mm and 155-mm firing data. Direct fire tables are not available at the time of this writing; therefore, battery personnel must compute the data. The data are produced for quadrant elevation, fuze setting, and 10/R factor (10 divided by range in thousands) for the minimum authorized charges. The quadrant elevation, when used with the listed fuze setting, will produce an airburst of 10 meters above and before the listed range. Compute data as in the following discussion.

WARNING

Firing a fuze setting less than what corresponds to a range of 650 meters for 105-mm or 750 meters for 155-mm is restricted to combat emergency conditions only. This distance represents the minimum target engagement distance when personnel at the firing position are unprotected. Firing a fuze setting less than this value results in a danger close hazard to the crew. (Refer to Department of the Army Pamphlet 385-63, Chapter 10, Table 10-2.) Also, the fuzes require about 400 meters to arm (2.0 seconds). Any time setting of less than 2 seconds is a danger to the crew and should not be fired unless firing Killer Junior.

Note: For howitzers firing separate-loading ammunition, direct fire tables should be produced for all available propellants.

F-8. The DA 5699 can be used to prepare a range card for Killer Junior direct fire as shown in figure F-1 on page F-3. Label the card to identify its purpose and the shell, fuze, and charge models for which the card is prepared. Record the 10/R in mils in the Remarks column. Steps for completing the DA Form 5699 for Killer Junior direct fire are in table F-1 on page F-4.

Killer Junior

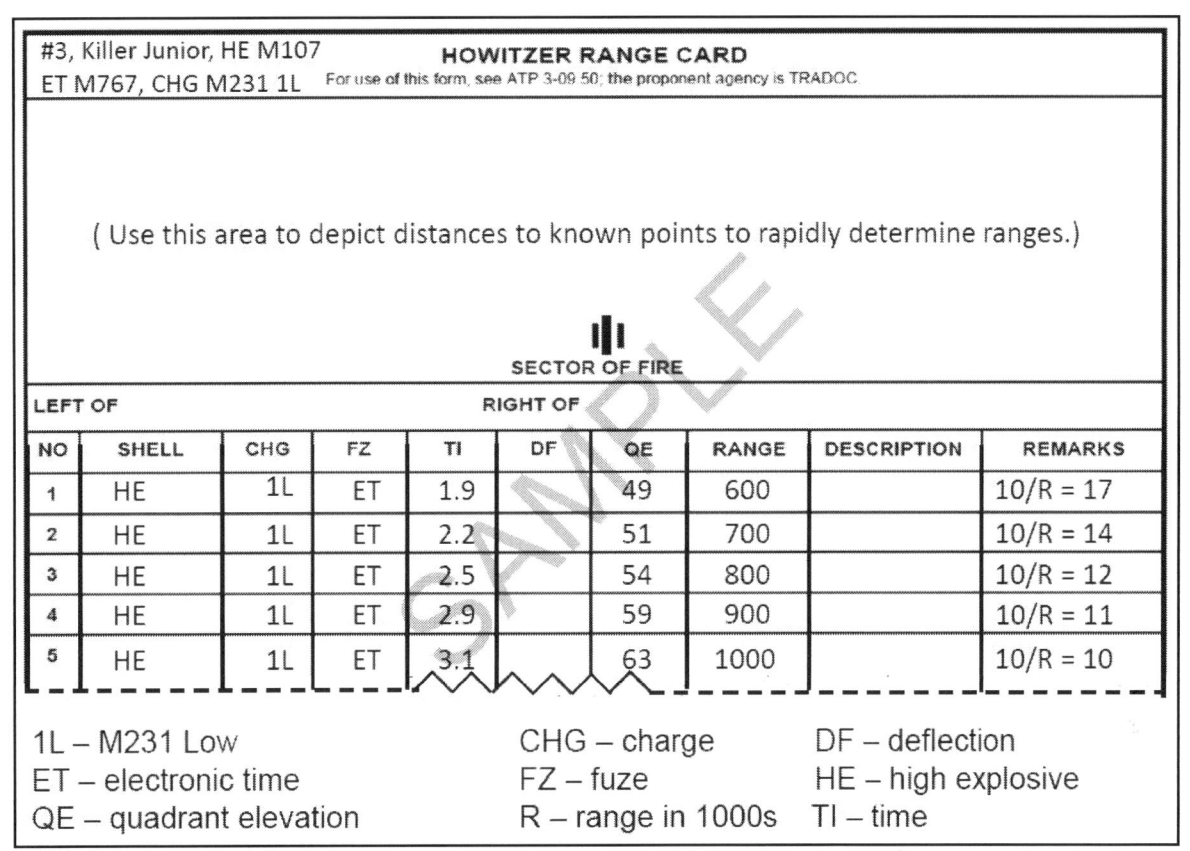

#3, Killer Junior, HE M107 ET M767, CHG M231 1L			HOWITZER RANGE CARD For use of this form, see ATP 3-09.50; the proponent agency is TRADOC						
(Use this area to depict distances to known points to rapidly determine ranges.)									
					SECTOR OF FIRE				
LEFT OF					RIGHT OF				
NO	SHELL	CHG	FZ	TI	DF	QE	RANGE	DESCRIPTION	REMARKS
1	HE	1L	ET	1.9		49	600		10/R = 17
2	HE	1L	ET	2.2		51	700		10/R = 14
3	HE	1L	ET	2.5		54	800		10/R = 12
4	HE	1L	ET	2.9		59	900		10/R = 11
5	HE	1L	ET	3.1		63	1000		10/R = 10

1L – M231 Low
ET – electronic time
QE – quadrant elevation
CHG – charge
FZ – fuze
R – range in 1000s
DF – deflection
HE – high explosive
TI – time

Figure F-1. DA Form 5699 Killer Junior data example

Table F-1. Completing the DA Form 5699 for Killer Junior

Step	Notes
1. Using the appropriate firing table, enter Table F for the minimum authorized charge. Example: An M777A2 (155-mm) howitzer firing battery. Minimum authorized charge is M231, 1L. Fuze M767 will be used on HE M107 rounds. Authorized firing tables are on hand.	Use the appropriate TM to determine the minimum charge authorized for the weapon. For example, the M777A2's (M776 cannon) minimum charge for M3A1, M4A1, or M4A2 bag powder is charge 3 but M231 MACS increment 1 is allowed. Compute Killer Junior direct fire data for the minimum allowable charges for all available powder types.
2. Enter ranges in the card's range column in increments of 100 meters from the minimum range corresponding to the 2.0 fuze setting for graze burst. The maximum range entered is typically 1,000 to 1,500 meters (situation dependent). Example: The minimum range corresponding to a 2.0 fuze setting is 600 meters; the maximum engagement range you anticipate is 1,000 meters. It may be necessary to use multiple range cards to list the data for all ranges and powder types anticipated.	Example: 155-mm, M231 charge 1L; minimum range used would be 600 meters.
3. Calculate 10/R factor for the listed ranges and enter it in the remarks column. Example: Compute 10/R factor for ranges 600 to 1,000 meters. Using artillery expression, express to the nearest whole mil. Range 600 (when data are input in the remarks column, express to the nearest whole mil): 10/0.6=17 (16.7) mils. Range: 900 10/0.9 = 11 (11.1) mils. Range 1000 10/1= 10 mils. (continued)	When data are input in the Remarks column, use artillery expression to express the 10/R factor to the nearest whole mil to simplify use for the howitzer crew members.
4. Add the 10/R factor to the elevation listed in the firing table, and enter the sum to the nearest whole mil in the quadrant elevation (QE) column. Using artillery expression, express to the nearest whole mil. Example: Range 600: 32 (31.5) + 17 = 49 mils. *** Range 900: 48 (47.8) + 11 = 59 mils *** Range 1,000: 53 (53.3) + 10 = 63 mils.	An additional value of 10/R should be applied to compensate for each 10-meter difference in vertical interval between the target and the howitzer.
5. Subtract 0.1 fuze setting increments from the Table F, column 3 fuze setting for an M582 graze burst. Use Table F, column 7 time of flight for the fuze setting for the M767 or M767A1 fuze. Enter that number in the TI (time) column. Example: Range 600: 2.0 – 0.1 = 1.9 *** Range 900: 3.0 - 0.1 = 2.9 *** Range 1,000: 3.3 – 0.1 = 3.1.	Per FT 155-AM-3, Table F, column 7, the time of flight is also used for the M767 or 767A1 fuze setting.
FT = firing table MACS = modular artillery charge system R = range expressed in thousands of meters	

Glossary

SECTION I – ACRONYMS AND ABBREVIATIONS

ADRP	Army Doctrine Reference Publication
AFATDS	Advanced Field Artillery Tactical Data System
ATP	Army Techniques Publication
ATTP	Army tactics, techniques, and procedures
BOC	battery operations center
CBRN	chemical, biological, radiological, and nuclear
CEP	circular error probable
DA	Department of the Army
DF	deflection
DODAC	Department of Defense ammunition code
EIC	end item code
FDC	fire direction center
FM	field manual
GLPS	gun laying and positioning system
HE	high explosive
JP	Joint Publication
MACS	modular artillery charge system
METT-TC	mission, enemy, terrain and weather, troops and support available, time available, and civil considerations
MK	mark (fuze or weapon designation)
mm	millimeter
NATO	North Atlantic Treaty Organization
NSN	national stock number
pantel	panoramic telescope
PGK	precision guidance kit
POC	platoon operations center
QE	quadrant elevation
RSOP	reconnaissance, selection, and occupation of a position
S-3	battalion or brigade operations staff officer
STANAG	standardization agreement
STP	Soldier training publication
TB	technical bulletin
TC	training circular
TM	technical manual

SECTION II – TERMS

*azimuth

A horizontal angle measured clockwise from a north base line that could be true north, magnetic north, or grid north.

*azimuth of fire

The direction, expressed in mils, that a firing unit is laid (oriented) on when it occupies a position.

*azimuth of the orienting line

The direction from the orienting station to a designated end of the orienting line.

*back-azimuth

The direction equal to the azimuth plus or minus 3200 mils.

*common deflection

The deflection, which may vary based on the weapon's sight system, corresponding to the firing unit's azimuth of fire.

*deflection

A horizontal clockwise angle measured from the line of fire or the rearward extension line of fire to the line of sight to a given aiming point with the vertex of the angle at the instrument.

*direction of fire

The direction on which a fire unit is laid to the most significant threat in the target area, to the chart direction to the center of the zone of fire, or to the target.

*line of fire

1. As it relates to the principle of the reciprocal laying of field artillery weapons, any line parallel to the azimuth of fire. 2. The direction of the line established by the tube or any line parallel to that line in the firing battery.

*orienting angle

A horizontal, clockwise angle measured from the line of fire to the orienting line.

*orienting line

A line of known direction in the firing unit's area that serves as a basis for laying the firing unit for direction.

*orienting station

1. A point established on the ground that has directional control. 2. An orienting device, such as an aiming circle or gun laying and positioning system, set up over a point to lay the weapons by the orienting angle method.

precision-guided munition

A guided weapon intended to destroy a point target and minimize collateral damage. (JP 3-03)

precision munition

A munition that corrects for ballistic conditions using guidance and control up to the aimpoint or submunitions dispense with terminal accuracy less than the lethal radius of effects. (FM 3-09)

* rearward extension of the line of fire

An imaginary line in the exact opposite direction of the line of fire that extends through the center axis of the tube when looking down through the muzzle to the breech of the weapon.

*refer

To measure, using the panoramic telescope, the deflection to a given aiming point without moving the tube of the weapon.

*referred deflection

The deflection measured to an aiming point without moving the tube of the weapon.

*registering piece
    The howitzer designated by the fire direction center to conduct a registration fire mission.

*sheaf
    The lateral distribution of the bursts of two or more pieces fired together.

vertical angle
    The angle measured up or down (in mils) in a vertical plane from the horizontal to a straight line joining the observer and target. (ATP 3-09.30)

*vertical interval
    The difference in altitude between the unit or observer and the target or point of burst.

techniques
    Non-prescriptive ways or methods used to perform missions, functions, or tasks. (CJCSM 5120.01A)

References

Field manuals and selected joint publications are listed by new number followed by old number.

REQUIRED PUBLICATIONS

These documents must be available to intended users of this publication.

ADRP 1-02, *Terms and Military Symbols*, 07 December 2015.

JP 1-02, *Department of Defense Dictionary of Military and Associated Terms*, 8 November 2010.

RELATED PUBLICATIONS

These documents contain relevant supplemental information.

NORTH ATLANTIC TREATY STANDARDIZATION AGENCY AGREEMENTS

Most North Atlantic Treaty standardization agreement agency publications are available online. The site requires requesting and justifying the need for login and a password: https://nso.nato.int/nso/.

STANAG 2484, Edition 2, *NATO Indirect Fire Systems Tactical Doctrine – AArty-5(A), Allied ArtilleryPublication-5 (A)*, 25 November 2010.

STANAG 2934, Edition 3, *Artillery Procedures – AArty – 1(B), AArtyP-01, edition B, Artillery Procedures*, 27 April 2009.

CHAIRMAN OF THE JOINT CHIEFS OF STAFF PUBLICATION

Chairman of the Joint Chiefs of Staff directives are available online: <http://www.dtic.mil/cjcs_directives/>

CJCSM 5120.01A, *The Joint Doctrine Development Process*, 29 December 2014.

JOINT PUBLICATIONS

Most joint publications are available online: <http://www.dtic.mil/doctrine/new_pubs/jointpub.htm>

JP 3-03, *Joint Interdiction*, 14 October 2011.

ARMY PUBLICATIONS

Most Army doctrinal publications are available online: <http://www.apd.army.mil/>.

Technical bulletins and manuals are available online: <https://www.logsa.army.mil/index.cfm?fuseaction=home.main>

Army Doctrine Publication

ADP 3-0, *Unified Land Operations*, 10 October 2011.

Army Doctrine Reference Publications

ADRP 3-0, *Unified Land Operations*, 16 May 2012.

ADRP 3-90, *Offense And Defense*, 31 August 2012

Army Regulations

AR 525-29, *Army Force Generation*, 14 March 2011.

Army Techniques Publications

ATP 3-04.1, *Aviation Tactical Employment*, 13 April 2016

References

ATP 3-09.02, *Field Artillery Survey*, 16 February 2016.
ATP 3-09.23, *Field Artillery Cannon Battalion*, 24 September 2015.
ATP 3-09.30, *Techniques for Observed Fire*, 02 August 2013.
ATP 3-21.8, *The Infantry Rifle Platoon and Squad*, 12 April 2016.
ATP 3-09.70, *Paladin Operations*, 25 September 2015.
ATP 3-90.37, *Countering Improvised Explosive Devices*, 29 July 2014.
ATP 3-90.90, *Army Tactical Standard Operating Procedures*, 01 November 2011.
ATP 6-22.5, *A Leader's Guide to Soldier Health and Fitness*, 10 February 2016.

Army Tactics, Techniques, and Procedures

ATTP 3-21.71, *Mechanized Infantry Platoon and Squad (Bradley)*, 09 November 2010.
ATTP 3-97.11, *Cold Region Operations*, 28 January 2011.

Department of the Army Pamphlets

DA Pamphlet 385-63, *Range Safety*, 16 April 2014.

Field Manuals

FM 3-06, *Urban Operations*, 26 October 2006.
FM 3-09, *Field Artillery Operations and Fire Support*, 04 April 2014,
FM 3-11, *Multiservice Doctrine for Chemical, Biological, Radiological, and Nuclear Operations*, 01 July 2011.
FM 3-11.3, *Multiservice Tactics, Techniques, and Procedures for Chemical, Biological, Radiological, and Nuclear Contamination Avoidance*, 02 February 2006.
FM 3-90-1, *Offense and Defense Volume 1*, 22 March 2013.
FM 3-97.6, *Mountain Operations*, 28 November 2000.
FM 3-99, *Airborne and Air Assault Operations*, 06 March 2015.
FM 6-0, *Commander and Staff Organization and Operations*, 05 May 2014.
FM 27-10, *The Law of Land Warfare*, 18 July 1956.
FM 90-3, *Desert Operations*, 24 August 1993.
FM 90-5, *Jungle Operations*, 16 August 1982.

Graphic Training Aids

GTA 05-02-012, *Coordinate Scale and Protractor*, June 2008.

Soldier Training Publications

STP 21-1-SMCT, *Soldier's Manual of Common Tasks Warrior Skills Level 1*, 10 August 2015.
STP 21-24-SMCT, *Soldier's Manual of Common Tasks Warrior Leader Skills Level 2, 3, and 4*, 09 September 2008.

Technical Bulletins

TB 9-1320-201-13, *Operator's And Field Information For Projectile, 155mm, HE, XM982 (Excalibur) (NSN 1320-01-534-2535) And Howitzer, Medium, Self-Propelled: 155MM, M109A6 (NSN 2350-01-305-0028):* 23 October 2008.
TB 9-1390-226-13, *Operator and Maintainer Information for Fuze, Multioption: Precision Guidance Kit (PGK), XM1156 NSN 1390-01-579-0413, DODAC 1390-NA28 And Fuze, Multioption: Precision Guidance Kit (PGK), M1156 NSN 1390-01-617-0269, DODAC 1390-NA29*, 09 June 2014

References

TB 11-6660-299-13, *Software User's Manual (SUM) For Computer, Meteorological Data AN/GMK-2 (NSN 6660-01-593-5972) (EIC: N/A) (Profiler Virtual Module (PVM)) Versions 1.0.0.3 And 1.0.0.4*, 15 April 2015.

TB 43-0250, *Ammunition Handling, Storage and Safety*, 29 February 2012.

Technical Manuals

TM 9-1015-252-10, *Operator's Manual for Howitzer, Light, Towed: 105-mm, M119A2 NSN 1015-01-482-4914 (EIC: 3WE) LIN: H57505*, 30 September 2010.

TM 9-1015-260-10, *Operator Manual for Howitzer, Light, Towed: 105-mm, M119A3 NSN 1015-01-598-4568 (EIC: 3FD)*, 30 October 2014.

TM 9-1025-215-10, *Technical Manual Operator's Manual for Howitzer, Medium, Towed: 155-mm, M777 (1025-01-445-0991) Howitzer, Medium, Towed: 155-mm, M777A2 (1025-99-463-7551) (EIC:3EU)*, 12 January 2016.

TM 9-1290-211-13&P *Operator and Field Maintenance Manual (Including Repair Parts and Special Tools Lists) for Fuze Setter: Enhanced, Portable, Inductive, Artillery (EPIAFS), M1155A1 (NSN 1290-01-536-5650, PN 13015264)*, 12 December 2014.

TM 9-1290-333-15, *Operator, Organizational, Direct Support, General Support and Depot Maintenance Manual (Including Repair Parts and Special Tools List) Compass, Magnetic, Unmounted: M2 (1290-930-4260)*, 07 November 1963.

TM 9-1320-202-13, *Operator And Field Maintenance Manual For Projectile, 155MM: HE, XM982 (Excalibur) (NSN 1320-01-534-2535) Projectile, 155MM: HE, M982 (Excalibur) (NSN 1320-01-552-1850) Projectile, 155MM: HE, M982A1 (Excalibur) (NSN 1320-01-611-6762) Dummy Projectile, 155MM: Excalibur Training Aid, Fullweight (NSN 1320-01-559-9526) Dummy Projectile, 155MM:Excalibur Training Aid, Lightweight (NSN 1320-01-556-7373)*, 20 June 2014.

TM 9-2350-311-10, *Operator's Manual for Howitzer, Medium, Self-Propelled, 155mm, M109A2 (2350-01-031-0586)(EIC:3EZ) M109A3 (2350-01-031-8851)(EIC:3E2) M109A4 (2350-01-277-5770)(EIC:3E8) M109A5 (2350-01-281-1719)(EIC:3E7)*, 23 November 1994.

TM 9-2350-314-10-1, *Operator's Manual for Howitzer, Medium, Self-Propelled, 155mm, M109A6 (NSN 2350-01-305-0028) (EIC 3FC)*, 30 May 2014.

TM 9-2350-314-10-2, *Operator's Manual for Howitzer, Medium, Self-Propelled, 155mm, M109A6 (NSN 2350-01-305-0028) (EIC 3FC)*, 30 May 2014.

TM 9-6675-262-10, *Operator Manual for Aiming Circle M2 W/E NSN: 1290-00-614-0008 (EIC 3SC) and M2A2 W/E NSN:6675-01-067-0687)* (EIC 3SC), 06 December 2013.

TM 9-6675-347-13&P, *Operator, Organizational and Direct Support Maintenance Manual Including Repair Parts and Special Tools List for Gun Laying and Positioning System (GLPS): M67 (NSN 6675-01-430-1965) (EIC: 3XA)*, 31 October 2000.

TM 11-5820-1172-13&P, Formal Technical Manual *Operator and Maintenance Manual Defense Advanced GPS Receiver (DAGR) Satellite Signals Navigation Set AN/PSN-13 NSN 5825-01-516-8038 AN/PSN-13A NSN 5825-01-526-4783, AN/PSN-13B NSN 5825-01-590-9534*, 09 May 2014.

TM 11-5825-291-13, *Operations and Maintenance Manual for Satellite Signals Navigation Sets AN/PSN-11 (NSN 5825-01-374-6643) and AN/PSN-11(V)1 (5825-01-395-3513)*, 01 April 2001.

TM 11-7440-283-12-2, *Operator's and Organizational Maintenance Manual for Data Display Groups, Gun Direction, OD-144(V)1/GYK-29(V) (NSN 7025-01-134-2329) (EIC: HP4) OD-144(V)2/GYK-29(V) (7025-01-134-3218) (EIC: HQH) OD-144(V)3/GYK-29(V) (7025-01-134-3219) (EIC: HQJ) (P/O Computer System Gun Direction, AN/GYK-29(V))*, 27 September 1982.

TM 43-0001-28, *Army Ammunition Data Sheets for Artillery Ammunition: Guns, Howitzers, Mortars, Recoilless Rifles, Grenade Launchers, and Artillery Fuzes (Federal Supply Class 1310, 1315, 1320, 1390)*, 28 April 1994.

References

TM 43-0001-28-3, *Data Sheets For Guns, Howitzers, And Mortars Interoperable Ammunition*, 29 September 1986.

Training Circulars

TC 3-09.8, *Field Artillery Cannon Gunnery*, 15 November 2013.

TC 3-09.81, *Field Artillery Manual Cannon Gunnery*, 01 March 2016.

TC 3-25.26, *Map Reading and Land Navigation*, 15 November 2013.

TC 3-90.119, *U.S. Army Improvised Explosive Device Defeat Training*, 23 June 2009.

PRESCRIBED FORMS

Unless otherwise indicated, DA Forms are available on the Army Publishing Directorate (APD) web site:< http://www.apd.army.mil/ >

DA Form 4513, *Record of Missions Fired*.

DA Form 5212, *Gunner's Reference Card*.

DA Form 5698, *Weapon Location Data*.

DA Form 5699, *Howitzer Range Card*.

DA Form 5969, *Section Chief's Report*.

REFERENCED FORMS

DA Form 581, *Request for Issue and Turn-In of Ammunition*.

DA Form 2028, *Recommended Changes to Publications and Blank Forms*.

DA Form 2408-4, *Weapon Record Data*.

DA Form 5517, *Standard Range Card*.

DA Form 7353, *Universal Safety T*.

RECOMMENDED READINGS

ATP 3-04.64, *Multi-service Tactics, Techniques, and Procedures for the Employment of Unmanned Aircraft Systems*, 22 January 2015.

ATP 3-09.12, *Field Artillery Target Acquisition*, 24 July 2015.

ATP 3-36, *Electronic Warfare Techniques*, 16 December 2014.

FM 1-0, *Human Resources Support*, 01 April 2014.

Index

Entries are by paragraph number unless otherwise noted.

A

ammunition management
  overview (precision), A-1
  planning considerations, 11-56, A-15
army force generation, 12-1

B

battery defense
  considerations, 5-1
  defense diagram, 5-10
  preparations, 5-15
  techniques, 5-5
battery tasks
  planning considerations, 11-13
boresight
  verify boresight using the alignment device, C-19

C

common mistakes, C-3
communications
  planning considerations, 11-61
composite units (overview), 9-1
  manning levels, 9-8
    fire direction center, 9-16
    howitzer section, 9-12
    platoon leadership, 9-19
    unit composition, 9-5

D

deployment
  home station training, 12-11
  overview, 12-1
  planning considerations, 12-3
distributed units
  communications, 10-12
  overview, 10-1
  personnel, 10-5

F

failure to compute terrain gun position corrections, C-17
fire commands,
  elements of, 7-2
  types, 7-1
fire support considerations
  observer management for the task force, 11-82
firing battery operation
  climate and terrain considerations, 2-32
  employment techniques, 2-4
  movement control techniques, 2-12
  movement tracking techniques, 2-16
forms and instructions
  DA Form 4513, D-1
  DA Form 4513 instructions, D-1
  DA Form 5212, D-2
  DA Form 5212, D-2
  DA Form 5212 instructions, D-2
  DA Form 5698 instructions, D-3

H

hasty survey
  altitude, 6-10
  direction, 6-3
  distance, 6-12
  location, 6-9
  simultaneous observation, 6-4

I

improper emplacement of aiming points, C-8
improper emplacement of orienting equipment, C-22
incidents, C-27

K

Killer Junior, F-1

L

laying on the wrong aiming posts, C-15

M

malpractices, C-24
measuring the azimuth of fire and reporting data, 4-51
meteorological and survey tasks
  profiler, 11-97
  survey, 11-99
minimum quadrant elevation, 8-4
mission checklists (sample), B-1
  battery status inventory, B-4
  critical events time line, B-5
  mission, B-2
  precombat checklists
    air threat, B-3
    artillery raid, B-3
    chemical, biological, radiological, and nuclear (CBRN) threat, B-3
    counterfire, B-3
    ground threat (dismounted), B-3
    ground threat (mounted), B-3
    massing fire, B-3
    medical evacuation, B-3
    scatterable mines, B-3
    unit defense, B-6
mobile training teams, 12-10

N

new equipment training, 12-8

O

organization
  cannon battalion (Army), 1-2
  cannon battalion (USMC), 1-3
  tactical duties of key personnel, 1-8
orienting equipment
  aiming circle, 4-2
  GLPS, 4-4
  M2 Compass, 4-7

P

precision guided munitions
  overview, A-1
  planning considerations, A-8
precutting charges, C-4

R

RSOP
  dispersion techniques, 3-28
  positioning techniques, 3-24
  preparation for occupation, 3-39
  reconnaissance techniques, 3-5
  types of occupation, 3-35

Index

S

sustainment
  planning considerations, 11-47

T

training

planning considerations, 11-3

U

unit basic load/ammunition basic load
  planning considerations, A-22

V

verification circle, 4-44
vertical angle, 4-46

W

warfighting skills, 11-31

ATP 3-09.50
4 May 2016

By Order of the Secretary of the Army:

MARK A. MILLEY
General, United States Army
Chief of Staff

Official:

GERALD B. O'KEEFE
Administrative Assistant to the
Secretary of the Army
1611801

DISTRIBUTION:
Active Army, Army National Guard, and United States Army Reserve: Distributed in electronic media only (EMO).

Made in the USA
Columbia, SC
15 June 2025